THE
BIBLE SAYS...

THE
BIBLE SAYS...

YOUNG

PR▮MIX
PUBLISHING
THE WRITE CHOICE

Primix Publishing
11620 Wilshire Blvd
Suite 900, West Wilshire Center, Los Angeles, CA, 90025
www.primixpublishing.com
Phone: 1-800-538-5788

Published by Primix Publishing   03/28/2023

ISBN: 978-1-957676-57-9(sc)
ISBN: 978-1-957676-58-6(e)

Library of Congress Control Number: Pending

Contents

Preface

Most of us begins to read the bible trying to understand our creator God and find out the way to escape from this troublesome world while struggling to cope with this fast running modern society to survive. But, reading through the bible alone would take a year, and yet finding out what it says is still another story. So, many of us close the bible before flipping over several pages and come back to wandering again for the same reason of enormous amount of scriptures and the difficulty to understand.

Simply, we are trapped in this busy world and this world does not allow us to think about where we come from, where we go to and why we live in this world. That was stated in the bible as dead saying as **"And another of his disciples said unto him, Lord, suffer me first to go and bury my father. But Jesus said unto him, Follow me; and let the dead bury their dead. (Matthew8-22)"**

I had the same problem and one-day God gave me the pleasure to understand and let me find the secret hidden in the bible. Sharing that pleasure with other brothers and sisters in God is the reason I came to write. As the bible says, **"No one can come to Me, unless the Father who sent Me draws him: and I will raise him up on the last day. (John 6-44)"**, it is not my intention to draw people into belief but to guide God's people that are lost. It doesn't necessarily mean that my way is the best way. So, anybody who knows the way should follow own way. But I encourage those lost and do not know which way to go to follow this way. When the time comes, one's own way will show up just like God allowed me.

I hear many people say that the bible has duality so this scripture should be applied to this case this way and to that case that way. But, I am going to build my house on the foundation based upon the very simple common sense that the truth is only one and never changes.

As God said through the king Solomon, **"If you seek her as silver, and search for her as for hidden treasures; Then you will discern the fear of the Lord, And discover the knowledge of God." (The proverbs 2-4),** those seekers will find.

That the seekers would find is a very plain truth and a common sense.

God is asking his children to stay awoke and discern standing on this very plain truth, the God's word.

However, due to lack of understanding, most people are inclined to accept and follow the unreasonable idea that all mighty God knows everything and so he will give what we need even before we ask and that we have nothing to do but to obey and follow. These are those lost in the darkness and could be compared to a saying "a blind following a blind".

The devil of this fast running modern society keeps people in busy holding them away from the wisdom of God as deaf and blind and makes them just obey and follow not knowing what they obey and follow. They take pride in their belief and obedience toward God. But when asked to explain about what God says to obey, they do not know. As the scripture says "Let it be accomplished as one believes", should something that oneself does not know will be accomplished to those who believe one does not know.

Since God is only one, obeying something else is not obeying God.

People would say this could cause disobedience, disbelief and lots of trouble among believers. But we should understand belief is not for everybody as the bible says. We should watch ourselves if we are ever caught by a net against the belief toward God and are obeying blindly. Actually, the human history shows trouble after trouble about this but what kind of troubles could there be in understanding the words of our creator God.

All these troubles are the results that each individual's interests are involved.

God will allow each individual as much belief as needed and each individual shall have so much belief as given. Likewise, those who were given much understanding shall understand as much and those who were given less understanding shall understand less. Only God's will is to be accomplished. Each one's idea is right only for oneself for both who teach others not knowing it is wrong and who are wandering in the darkness not knowing it is right. Because God made each one as appropriate for each one according to God's need. It is in the hand of God who has the option.

And the words of God who has the option are written in the bible. Therefore, digging and studying the bible is the only way to stay awoke and watch.

As God allowed different amount of belief and different kind of talent to each individual as God needed, it is quite natural that each one describes the same truth differently. So, one should not insist that one's idea is the only right idea. Each one should build own belief within each one's given spiritual body with humble mind.

Then God's Will planted on it would grow accordingly to reach God's only truth and understand. But since we are passing this limited world, somebody's profit is going to create disadvantage to the other people just like the lion profits by eating the weak animals causing big troubles to them at the same time. As Jesus Christ taught the children of God, we have to be wise like a snake not to be involved in troubles and pure enough to stand firm on one's own belief and stay awoke to discern.

As the bible says:

> **(Matthew 7-13) "Enter the narrow gate: for the gate is wide, and the way is broad that leads to destruction, and many are those who enter by it. For the gate is small, and the way is narrow that leads to life, and few are those who find it."**

We should not follow somebody's way. Only we should try to find our own narrow gate like we try to find the hidden treasures and enter the gate to get what we found.

As I mentioned previously, the way is in the bible. But after experienced it is not easy to find, I wanted to help those who are lost like me. Sharing how I found my treasure could help them find their treasure and that is my intention writing this book. So, I encourage anybody who once came to believe found the way even before finished reading this book to return to the bible and make own treasure map as bold as possible and follow it. That treasure map will lead him to the heaven built in his belief. But we need to stay awoke to discern whether the map is really the map leading to the heaven in the bible. That's how we make the map bold and that's the way we grow in God and build our belief toward God.

As Jesus Christ let us know, **"The kingdom of heaven is like a treasure hidden in the field; which a man found and hid; and from joy over it he goes and sells all that he has, and buys that field."(Matthew13-44),** the fact alone that we have found the map to heaven does not take us to heaven. If somebody with treasure map does not go for it, how could he get the treasure? Likewise, as this man sold all of his possession to buy the treasure, we should invest all of ours to go all the way and get it. But we shouldn't invest blindly. We have to be careful just like when we buy the treasure.

Readers will come across a lot of bible scriptures while reading this book. Since my treasure was found in the light of those scriptures, and sharing how I found my treasure prompted me to write this book, reading and appreciating those scriptures would be sharing the pleasure I had. I hope every reader take time to enjoy those scriptures and deepen the bible understanding. Somebody would say, "Why wouldn't I read the bible itself and find out more detail, accurate and reliable one?" I agree with that absolutely. However, even though so many treasures are hidden on earth, it is not only so hard to find out but also very seldom found. This book is the kind written by a person who happened to find a treasure and tell the story to others how and what he found.

Since, I believe "Believe in God" is going the way, not just thinking the way, I strongly urge anybody who found the way to go the way with firm belief to get what one found.

And, I encourage those who think lost in the darkness to stay on this way until their own ways come up. Needless to say, once their ways come up, these people also should follow their own ways.

And the bible says Jesus Christ is the way.

Author: Dae Young Choe

1. Presenting the bible

Old Testament

The bible is made with 66 books in total and classified as Old Testament (39 books, 929 chapters) and New Testament (27 books, 260 chapters) by the time of before and after the coming of Jesus Christ. Written by as many as about 40 people through 1,500 years of long time we can see the same spirit of God is flowing all through these books having a thread of connection between each book helping each other. That's because the author is the same only God who has been self-existed from the beginning and inspired these people to write. We can see God introducing himself to Moses as clearly as he is the same only God of Abraham, God of Isaac and God of Jacob who were died already several hundred years ago.

According to the Thompson bible, these 66 books of bible were bound into one book and divided by the chapters by Stephen Langton in A.D. 1228. The Old Testament was divided by more detail verses again by R. Nathan in A.D. 1448 and the New Testament by Robert Stephanus in A.D. 1551. The first bible bound completely into one book divided into detail chapters and verses was published in Geneva in A.D. 1560, and which is what we call the bible now.

Beginning with the book of **Genesis,** the first five books of the Old Testament **Exodus, Leviticus, Numbers** and **Deuteronomy** are known as "Pentateuch" or "Torah" and written by Moses.

The first book of **Genesis** begins with God's creation of this world. After God finished the creation, the first man Adam happens to eat the fruit of the knowledge of good and evil disobeying God's command not to eat and therefore be sent out from the garden of Eden where the tree of life is. As the result, he could not eat the fruit of the life and be destined to die.

Adam had two sons of Cain and Abel. After Cain killed own brother Abel, he begat another son Seth. Through this son man was to succeed the generation. Even the men were destined to die, men were to flourish till the time of Noah as God said unto Adam to multiply and replenish the earth. But disobedient Adam's descendants were so wicked and corrupted seriously that God blotted them all out of the earth by great flood except Noah who built a big ark and prepared for the flood obeying God's command (in the year of 1656 after Adam). Through the only survival Noah, the 8th descendant of Seth, men began to flourish again and spread all over the earth by Noah's three sons of Shem, Japheth and Ham.

Until Adam's 14th descendant Peleg (1755 years after Adam), men spoke only one language. They tried to build a city and a high tower called Babel lest scattered over the whole earth. But God wanted to accomplish God's will instead of men's will and confounded their language so they may not understand each other and scattered to have them under the restraint of God.

Of these three sons, Noah blessed the first son Shem and God was to accomplish what God planned from the beginning of creation, having Shem's family line lead the major role. Abraham was Shem's 10th descendant and God chose this Abraham for his faith towards God and set up the covenant on him that Abraham will be the father of many nations.

Abraham was the 1st born son and lived with his father together with his brother Haran's son Lot, because Haran died early. At the age of 75 Abraham left his father obeying God's command to move to the land of Canaan, where God appeared to him and promised to give the land to Abraham's descendants. After a while, both the Abraham and Lot became rich and could not dwell on the same land together. So, Lot first chose and moved to the plain of Jordan and dwelt in Sodom city where men were so wicked, and Abraham stayed in the land of Canaan moving his tent to the plain of Mamre which is in Hebron and dwelt there. Later God rained brimstone and fire to two cities of Sodom and Gomorrah to destroy completely because of their extreme sin. They were exceedingly wicked. Lot and his two daughters escaped this disaster by obeying God but his wife became a pillar of salt for looking back when she came out of the city to escape.

The 2nd book **Exodus** is the accomplishment of God's plan on Abraham. God told Abraham that his descendants shall be strangers in a foreign land to serve them as slaves for four hundred years and afterward shall they come out with great substance.

Abraham got the 1st son Ishmael from his Egyptian handmaid Hagar. He got the 2nd son Isaac from his wife Sarai in his late days of age 100. God blessed this 2nd born son Isaac. Isaac had twin sons of Jacob and Esau the older. And when they were still in their mother's womb God said **"Two nations are in thy womb, and two manner of people shall be separated from thy bowels: and the one people shall be stronger than the other people: and the elder shall serve the younger." (Genesis 25-23)**

This prophecy begins to accomplish when Isaac got old. He was going to bless the 1st son Esau. But deceived by Jacob who pretended to be Easu, he was to bless the younger son Jacob. God blessed Jacob and renamed him as Israel. This Israel's families are to play the major role in the Bible and the Easu's families are to serve them as God said.

Israel had 12 sons and these 12 sons are to make 12 branches of Israel people according to their family as time goes. Of these 12 sons, the 11th son Joseph was sold to Ishmaelites by his brothers for twenty pieces of silver and was brought to Egypt.

Starting with this incident, God's prearranged history of making Abraham's descendants strangers in foreign land and serve them as slaves for four hundred years and come out with great substance begins to accomplish.

When Joseph was brought to Egypt, he was put in jail and happened to interpret the dream of the Egyptian king. By interpreting the dream, he prophesied 7 years terrible famine after 7 years good harvest. For this incident Joseph got good trust from the king and was seated in a very high position next to the king and became to rule the Egypt to prepare for the coming famine. The famine was so terrible through out all over the region. Canaan where his families were living was not the exception and his brothers had to come to Egypt to buy foods. His brothers did not recognize him but Joseph did and forgave them. Joseph brought all of his 70 families including his father Jacob and let them live in Egypt.

In recognition of his good work, these 70 people prospered to exceed the Egyptians in number after several hundred years. The Egyptians were afraid of this and began to persecute them. The king commanded to kill every Israel's newly born baby boys. In this situation Moses was born in the house of Levi. The mother hid him for 3 months and when she could not hide any longer, she put the baby in an ark of bulrushes and laid it in the flags by the river's brink. The king Pharaoh's daughter happened to see it and brought to raise him as a son. Moses's own mother nursed him but they did not know she was Moses's own mother. When Moses grew up, he saw an Egyptian smiting a Hebrew. He slew the Egyptian and hid him in the sand. In fear of being uncovered of this incident to the king Pharaoh, he fled from the face of Pharaoh and dwelt in the land of Midian. God used this Moses to deliver the Israel people from the hand of Egyptians and bring them back to Canaan where milk and honey were out flowing. This Canaan was the land God had given to Abraham, Isaac and Jacob before.

God delivered the Israelites and led to the land of Canaan performing lots of miracles and wonders. But they turned away from God. This provoked God and none of the grown-ups over the age of 20 except Joshua and Caleb were allowed to go into the land of Canaan. All of them had to wander in the wide plain for 40 years and die.

The story of Joseph's introduction of his 70 families into Egypt, 400 years of slavery, deliverance from Egypt, the ten commandments from God, and the long journey to the promised land Canaan were written in the book of **Exodus**.

God appointed the house of Levi, one of the 12 tribes descended from Jacob's (God gave him a new name of Israel) 12 sons, as priest and let them perform every kind of religious service to keep the people in God. This Levi tribe was not allowed to have their share of land when they got into the land of Canaan later. But instead, God let the other 11 tribes bring 1/10 of their produce to them for the service and their living. Moses wrote the detail religious service procedures in the book of **Leviticus**.

The story about what happened after the Israelites' deliverance from Egypt, and before they enter the land of Canaan was written in the book of **Numbers**.

When the Isralites were wandering in the wilderness for 40 years God taught Israelites of his being only God, how to stay in God, what to do when they get into the land of Canaan and what God wants. God commanded them to follow those rules and obey. Moses wrote all these in the book of **Deuteronomy** and commanded the Levites to keep it in the side of the ark of covenant for the witness in the latter days.

Next, the books of **Joshua, Judges, I Samuel, II Samuel, I Kings, II Kings, I Chronicles,** and **II Chronicles** follow in order.

These books are the history of Israel. After they got into the land of Canaan, they prospered and went whoring after the strange gods of the land breaking the covenant God had set up with them. These history books show how they utterly corrupted themselves and turned aside from the way God had commanded. Because of this, they were to split into two nations of Israel and Judah later. The 10 tribes of Israel had Samaria as their capital city and went to ruin by Assyria which was the Jacob's brother Esau's descendants. The Israel people were taken to Assyria as slaves and were scattered to disappear at last. The one tribe of Judah had Jerusalem as their capital city. They also were ruined by Babylon and went captivity. (Today's Jewish nation Israel is from this Judah and the actual Israel in the bible means all of the 12 tribes descended from 12 sons of Jacob the Israel.) All these were as God told Moses already as following before Moses died hundreds year ago.

Deuteronomy 31-16)

And the Lord said to Moses, "Behold, you are about to lie down with your fathers; and this people will arise and play the harlot with the strange gods of the land, into the midst of which they are going, and will forsake Me and break My covenant which I have made with them.

Then My anger will be kindled against them in that day, and I will forsake them and hide My face from them, and they shall be consumed, and many evils and troubles shall come upon them; so that they will say in that day, "Is it not because our God is not among us that these evils have come upon us?

But I will surely hide My face in that day because of all the evil which they will do, for they will turn to other gods.

Now therefore, write this song for yourselves, and teach it to the sons of Israel; put it on their lips, in order that this song may be a witness for Me against the sons of Israel.

For when I bring them into the land flowing with milk and honey, which I swore to their fathers, and they have eaten and are satisfied and become prosperous, then they will turn to other gods and serve them, and spurn Me and break My covenant." Then it shall come about, when many evils and troubles have come upon them, that this song will testify before them as a witness (for it shall not be forgotten from the lips of their descendants); for I know their intent which they are developing today, before I have brought them into the land which I swore.

The song was written in **Deuteronomy chapter 32**.

Joshua is the one who led Israel people into the land of Canaan after Moses died. The story how they fought with the people in Canaan to enter the land and how they divided and occupied the land among them were written in the book of **Joshua**.

Even after they entered Canaan, they still had to fight with the people who were already there to settle down. In those days Israel had no king and every man did that were right in their eyes. The judges ruled the people by the words of God through Levites. These things including the famous story about the judge Samson and the story of Gideon were written in the book of **Judges**. Gideon is the one who confirmed if the words of God he heard was really from God by checking whether only the fleece of wool was wet by dew while all the other soil around it was dry after the night. He so asked God.

One of those days, there was a mighty and wealthy man named Boaz in Bethlehem. One of his kinsmen Elimelech had two sons and all of these people died leaving no child. Following the custom, Boaz happened to buy all that were Elimelech's and his son's together with the son's wife Ruth to succeed the Elimelech family. Ruth got a son from Boaz and named him as Obed, who is the grandfather of David the 2nd king of Israel. All the details were written in the book of **Ruth.** About a thousand years later the Jesus Christ came to this world through this family line as 30th descendant of Boaz.

Israel people wanted a king who would rule over them like other strange countries instead a judge rules by God's word. This means they wanted to accomplish men's will instead of God's will. God did not like this. But as they wanted to be ruled by a king so seriously, God left them alone allowing Saul as the 1st king of Israel. Samuel was the prophet in those days.

There was a war broke out between Israel and Philistines and Israel was in a difficult situation. At that time David the youngest son of Jesse, a shepherd, came to fight and defeated the Philistine's commander Goliath with some stones and a sling. When the war was over and David came back, women of Israel admired David more than the king Saul. Because of this, King Saul condemned David and David had to runaway. The detail story of this was written in the book of **I Samuel**.

As the 1ˢᵗ king Saul died and David became the 2ⁿᵈ king of Israel, there rose a lot of troubles among David's families and also between two parties of David and Saul. This shows what kind of problem could happen just by having a king, pursuing a man's will.

David had to bleed a lot for this and God did not allow David to build the house for God. But David relied on God through his life. The detail story of this is written in the book of **II Samuel**.

As the king David got old, there were struggles among David's sons for the succession to the throne, which was also another problem that was caused by having a king.

Solomon succeeded the throne. God asked Solomon what he wanted. Solomon asked the wisdom to rule the people. God was pleased to read his mind and gave wisdom together with the wealth he didn't ask.

In his early years, lots of people came from all over the world to hear his wisdom and to see the houses he built for God and for himself. He is the king who made the famous judgment in finding out a real mother out of two women who fought for a baby's parental authority. He ordered to cut the baby in half and give to each woman. One of the women cried and asked not to cut while the other woman agreed. King Solomon said the woman who asked not to cut the baby is the real mother.

With the wisdom, he wrote the bible **Proverbs** and the **Ecclesiastes**.

In his latter days, he had 700 wives and 300 concubines. Many of them were from aliens and did not know God. These women turned Solomon's heart away from God. As Solomon did evil in the sight of God, God was angry and to rend his kingdom into two pieces and gave the big Israel of 10 tribes to Solomon's servant and the small Judah of one tribe to Solomon's son. Jesus Christ was to come to this world through this Judah tribe later. The details of these were written in the book of **I King**.

Solomon loved a commoner Shulamite woman and wrote about it as a song, and which is the book of **Song of Solomon**.

The next book **II king** describes how the kingdom of Solomon were split into two, how the Israelites got away from God, corrupted and finally be destroyed by Assyria and Babylon respectively and went into captivity.

According to Thompson bible, the Kingdom of Solomon was divided into two pieces on B.C. 931 and destroyed respectively later.

The Israel of 10 tribes went ruin first by Assyria being destroyed of their capital Samaria on B.C.722 and the people went into captivity. They were dispersed to no where and disappeared as the Babylon destroyed Assyria on B.C.539.

After 136 years later, the other one tribe of Judah went ruin by Babylon being destroyed of their capital Jerusalem on B.C.586. This people were also going captivity by Babylon. But unlike from Israel, this Judah was to come back after 70 years when the Persia conquered Babylon on B.C.539. The Persian king Cyrus allowed them to return to Jerusalem and rebuild the Jerusalem castle and the temple.

The next two books of **I Chronicles** and **II Chronicles** were written based upon the Court Record by Ezra who used to work as a Court secretary. These 2 books cover the happenings from Adam to Solomon showing many parts the same contents as written in the book of I Kings and II Kings. These books are said written to encourage the people who came back from the captivity to rebuild the Jerusalem.

They had lots of trouble to rebuild Jerusalem due to surrounding strangers and they had to fight with one hand and build with other hand without discrimination between men and women, young and old.

How they happened to return to Jerusalem and what they did to rebuild the Jerusalem, what happened during rebuilding the Jerusalem and their returning back to God were written in the books of **Ezra** and **Nehemiah,** which was written by **Ezra** and **Nehemiah** respectively.

Esther was a stepdaughter of a Jewish Mordecai who was taken to Babylon. She became the queen and was to save her Jewish people from the conspiracy of Haman who was the second to the king. Haman was laying a plot to destroy all of Jewish people throughout the kingdom. The detail story was written in the book of **Esther.**

All of the books up to this **Esther** from **Genesis** are the history of Israel in Old Testament. God said he had chosen Israel to show God's being only God to all human beings through the history of Israel by accomplishing what God planned and promised to Abraham, Isac and Jacob the Israel.

Following the book of **Esther**, the faith and the prophecies of major religious people who had lived the latter days of Old Testament period continue up until **Malachi** the last book of Old Testament.

God allowed Satan to put the righteous man Job to test by taking away all of his possessions and give troubles. The book **Job** describes the faith and attitude of a man towards God when confronted such a difficult situation. It makes one ask oneself the fundamental question of what God is and leads to answer itself. Must be the best book to check own faith and attitude towards God and stand on the right track to the right religion.

The next book **Psalms** is said to be written for a long period of time but mostly at the time of David and Solomon (around B.C.1000) by several people in the form of hymn, which were collected to be made into one book. The Israel people sang these songs to praise God and confessed their faith to God. These songs are also read partly at church services nowadays.

Written by Solomon, the **Proverbs** is just right a book for the youngsters as Solomon introduced it as:

> **Proverbs 1-2**
> **To know wisdom and instruction, to discern the sayings of understanding, To receive instruction in wise behavior, Righteousness, justice and equity; to give prudence to the naive, To the youth knowledge and discretion, A wise man will hear and increase in learning, And a man of understanding will acquire wise counsel, To understand a proverb and a figure, The words of the wise and their riddles. The fear**

of the Lord is the beginning of knowledge; Fools despise wisdom and instruction.

Solomon wrote another book of **Ecclesiastes.**

Beginning with the word **VANITY**, this book makes one think what the life is, why and to where. He says everything in this world including the wisdom, effort, material and position are to be ended with vanity when it is used for the purpose of own life, so live the life as God commands; that's what, why and to where the life is about.

This book ends as following.

> **Ecclesiastes 12**
> **Remember also your creator in the days of your youth, before the evil days come and the years draw near when you will say, "I have no delight in them"; before the sun, the light, the moon, and the stars are darkened, and clouds return after the rain; ....**
> **The conclusion, when all has been heard, is; fear God and keep His commandments, because this applies to every person. For God will bring every act to judgment, everything which is hidden, whether it is good or evil.**

In other words, it says doing whatever in this world for oneself is to be ended vanity, so don't be heavily loaded trying to accomplish own will. Be loaded lightly and live the joyful life keeping God's commandment and rest, then God accomplishes as God wants. Jesus Christ said it also as following.

> **Matthew 11-28**
> **Come to me, all who are weary and heavy-laden, and I will give you rest.**

Next, comes the Solomon's love story **Song of Solomon.**

All the books following the Song of Solomon, the **Isaiah, Jeremiah, Ezekiel, Daniel, Hosea, Joel, Amos, Obadiah, Jonah, Micah, Nahum, Habakkuk, Zephaniah, Haggai, Zechariah** and **Malachi** are the books of prophecy named each after the prophets who had lived after Solomon till 400 years before the Jesus Christ's coming.

As Solomon did evil things, God split the Israel into two pieces and each were to be destroyed by Assyria and Babylon respectively and went captivity. After 70 years, about 50,000 Jews came back to rebuild the Jerusalem. During this difficult period God had warned and prophesied to Israel people through above prophets about what God was going to do.

The Israel people were extremely away from God and corrupted at that time. They did not like the prophets warn them. They wouldn't listen to these prophets. They rather beat, persecuted and killed them.

These books of prophesy are dealing not only with soon coming Israel's destruction but also the Jesus Christ's coming, a little here and a little there but in detail. It also refers about the Jesus Christ's 2nd coming, great distress, resurrection and judgment that are about to happen in the future after more than 2500 years in our generation.

The Old Testament ends with the last book **Malachi** and the New Testament begins with **Matthew**.

There were no prophets specially known for the period of 400 years between Malichi and Jesus Christ

For about 200 years, Israel was under the influence of Persia. When Alexander the Great of Greece conquered Persia (B.C.331), Israel people were put under the control of Greece and learned Greek culture, the Hellenism. The civilized Greek Hellenism is said to affect the Israel people as much as the idolatry had affected them up until Babylon destroyed them. The Hellenic language was spoken at that time like the English language is spoken nowadays. 72 people, six people each from Israel's 12 tribes, translated the Hebrew bible into Hellenic. Israel became independent of Greece (B.C.166), but again went under the control of Rome (B.C.63).

In the middle of this powerful Hellenism, Israel people had to protect their national religion. They were divided by couple of groups according to their social position. The groups of Pharisees were so eager to the commandment of Old Testament and separated themselves from Hellenism. One other group of nobles who were called Sadducee did not believe the resurrection, spirit or angels. These two groups are said to have hostile attitude toward each other.

Thus far we have examined the out line of Old Testament to get the rough idea about the bible. There wouldn't be a big mistake if we take it as we saw the bible what it looks like. The historic data was taken from Thompson Bible.

Now let's move on to the New Testament and see what it looks like.

New Testament

As God said **"My spirit shall not strive with man forever, because he also is flesh; nevertheless his days shall be one hundred and twenty years." (Genesis 6-3),** until Jesus Christ came to this world, men did not know about the spirit, judgment, resurrection, salvation, kingdom of heaven and the eternal life.

They had God's commandment, so they did know that if one lives by God's commandment one shall have a longer blessed life and that if one does not live by God's commandment one shall have a shorter and troublesome life. They only tried to live on God's commandment to be blessed and live a quality life in this world. In a word, their concern of life was only about the physical flesh beings while they live in this world. In that respect, our religion of going to church to be blessed and live a quality life is just like the people in Old Testament.

But as Jesus Christ came and taught, men began to think about the spirit and realize the spirit is the eternal life. As we keep on reading the bible, we come to realize that most part of the Old Testament is about the physical body and most part of the New Testament is about the spirit. So, if one does not read the New Testament in the light of spirit one can not understand what it says and would put oneself into conflict.

To make the New Testament in short, it says:

> "Know that men have eternal life of spirit in the physical body. When the harvest time comes, this spirit is going to be resurrected in unimaginable form of body which is different from what we have in this world and be judged according to each one's deed in this world. Since everyone's deed is only evil, no one is going to be saved but only those who believed in Jesus Christ will be regarded as Sons of God and forgiven to be saved by being moved from judgment to life on Jesus Christ's 2nd coming. Jesus Christ will rule for 1,000 years with these Sons of God. All others who have ever lived will be resurrected to stand for the judgment according to each one's deed. Those who did good in this world to the eternal life in heaven and those who did evil into never extinguishable fire which was described as the 2nd death (Revelation 20-14) to suffer forever."

Remember the New Testament is for the spirit in our physical body and the bible let us know we have never dying eternal life of spirit. That spirit is going to be saved from the 2nd death or judged to put into the 2nd death. Many would say if the spirit is the never dying eternal life, then why does it need to be saved from the 2nd death. The bible let us know that the death of spirit is different from the death we normally have in mind. The bible describes the 2nd death as suffering in unquenchable fire. We will discuss about this later.

As the apostle Paul said:

Romans3-10
There is none righteous, not even one; There is none
who understands, There is none who seeks for God;
All have turned aside, together they have become
useless; There is none who does good, There is not
even one All men are destined to suffer in unquenchable
fire forever. Unless the Jesus Christ let men know, men
wouldn't even think about it. And all of us are just to go
into the fire after a luxurious quality life in this world,
not even knowing that we are headed to unquenchable
everlasting fire. We were only to find ourselves in the
fire not knowing why.

This could be just a fictional story for those who do not believe
in Jesus Christ, but it would be a very serious problem for those who
believe in Jesus Christ. Regardless each one's belief or disbelief, the truth
remains always the same only one and never changes. As I mentioned
at the front page, the truth will come up as God allowed to each one.
So, let's go and figure out which way we are headed respectively.

The New Testament were made with 27 books and written by nine
persons for the period of 50 years after AD50.

The first 4 books of **Matthew, Mark, Luke** and **John** are called
the "Good News". These books were written by 4 different people and
named after each person. Since each person wrote about the same Jesus
Christ, what they saw and heard, much of each book describes the same
thing and helps each other not conflicting. As those books are titled
as the "Good News", the main idea is anybody who believes in Jesus
Christ will save their spirit, the eternal life, from the 2nd death and live
in peace in the kingdom of God. Today what we call evangelize or
engaging in missionary work is delivering this good news to the end of
the world. Jesus Christ taught this and did so many miracles to make

people believe and said he was doing it to prove it. And now we are about to examine whether it is true or not in our generation. Because I believe we are actually living that period of time.

Following the 4 books of "Good News", Luke who wrote one of four books of "Good News" described in detail what the apostles did after the ascension of Jesus Christ. Which was titled as **"The Acts of the apostles"**.

Continuing **The Acts of the apostles**, 21 epistles of **Romans, I Corinthians, II Corinthians, Galathians, Ephesians, Philippians, Colossians, I Thessalonians, II Thessalonians, I Timothy, II Timothy, Titus, Philemon, Hebrews, James, I Peter, II Peter, I John, II John, III John, Jude** follow. These epistles named after each writer or the churches were written to teach and encourage the people who escaped the Roman persecution on Christian and formed seven churches in different places.

The last one is **Revelation** written by Apostle John. As the title says, it reveals what is destined to this world and to the people. It says; a great distress is prearranged and in the end of the distress the Jesus Christ is coming to rule the world. Anybody who has ever lived in this world will be resurrected and judged according to their deed but before that the Sons of God will be saved and enter the Kingdom of God.

According to the Thompson Bible, these 27 books of New Testament were not said authorized as bible right after they were written. 350 years of examination and verification period was needed for the final recognition as bible. It was approved as bible from the religious conference of Carthage in A.D.397. None of the originals are said to be available but 4,500 and some Hellenic copies and about 8,000 Latin copies are.

Now let's look into the Thompson Bible again to see who wrote them.

Matthew, a customs officer who wrote **Matthew,** was good in stenography and calculation on behalf of his job.

John Mark who wrote **Mark** was a Jew fluent in Aramic language. He was a son of Mary who had considerable wealth and position. Banabas who accompanied Paul on his first missionary journey was his uncle. John Mark is said that he had not met Jesus Christ himself. However, since he was a disciple of Apostle Peter and helped him by translating, he had good chances to hear from Peter and could write what he heard.

Luke who wrote **Luke** and **Acts** was a doctor. He accompanied Apostles Paul and Peter's missionary journey. He neither saw Jesus Christ himself. But 10 years of missionary journey he accompanied made him able to collect lots of testimony from many witnesses who saw what Jesus Christ did. As he clearly mentioned at the forefront of **Luke**, he summarized the testimony and that is what the bible **Luke** is about.

Apostle John who wrote **John** was not a man of much knowledge or learned. He was born in a wealthy family of Galilee. **I John, II John, III John** and **Revelation** were written by him also. His brother apostle Jacob is different person from Jacob, the one of Jesus Christ's brothers that wrote **James**.

Apostle Paul wrote 13 letters of **Romans, I Corinthians, II Corinthians, Galathians, Ephesians, Philippians, Colossians, I Thessalonians, II Thessalonians, I Timothy, II Timothy, Titus** and **Philemon** which are almost 2/3 of the 21 letters of New Testament. Some say he wrote **Hebrews** also. He was a Pharisee and his original name was Saul. He was the leader in Christian persecution at first. But when he was on the way to go to Damascus to bring the Christians bound to Jerusalem, Jesus Christ appeared to him and blinded him. After three days without sight neither eating nor drinking Jesus Christ gave his eye back through the disciple Ananias. Due to this mysterious incident Saul became an apostle and began to preach the gospel to foreigners and was to be executed at Rome later.

Jacob, one of the brothers of Jesus Christ wrote **James** and another younger brother Jude wrote **Jude**.

Peter, the most beloved disciple of Jesus Christ wrote **I Peter** and **II Peter.**

He was a fisherman on the Sea of Galilee. His original name was Simon and the Jesus Christ gave him new name of Peter.

So far, we have examined the frame of bible to see what it looks like. Now let's find out the key to open it with the following instruction.

> **John 5-39**
> **You search the Scriptures, because you think that in them you have eternal life; and it is these that bear witness of Me; and you are unwilling to come to Me, that you may have life."**

2. Jesus Christ, the Son of God

Jesus Christ in Old Testament and New Testament

Through the prophets, God always let his chosen people know about his future plan. It is just like a history book written in reverse chronological order.

In the same way, if we trace the step of Jesus Christ and compare it with the scriptures written in the Old Testament, we can easily find the Jesus Christ is the central figure of the bible, the Son of God.

In this chapter, I am going to do the job of confirming Jesus Christ's being Son of God. That's because I recall what God said about the people who were away from god as:

> **(Matthew 13:13) Therefore speak I to them in parables: because they seeing see not; and hearing they hear not, neither do they understand.**
>
> **And in them is fulfilled the prophecy of Esaias, which saith, By hearing ye shall hear, and shall not understand; and seeing ye shall see, and shall not perceive: For this people's heart is waxed gross, and their ears are dull of hearing, and have closed; lest at any time they should see with their eyes, and hear with their ears, and should understand with their heart, and their eyes they should be converted, and I should heal them.**

So, returning back to God holds the key to understanding the bible and confirming that Jesus Christ is the Son of God is what returning back to God is.

Every country has their own way of counting calendar year like as Danki of Koreans, Showa of Japanese…. Of those, the most common one throughout the world is BC (Before Christ) and AD (Anno Domini, In the Year of the Lord or After Christ) which counts starting from Jesus Christ's coming as the year 1. This means Jesus Christ's Coming was the epoch-making event and affected this world greatly.

Constantinus the Great of Rome was said to had the inspiration that he shall conquer the whole Europe if he fought with the sign of cross after he saw the burning cross in the sky in dream. With the inspiration, he fought with the sign of cross and conquered the whole Europe and delivered the Christians from Roman persecution. In AD 313 he became a Christian himself to be a model to the people. There were a lot of troubles between Christians and other idol worshipers. So, he made one unified Christian doctrine of mixed religion to resolve the troubles between the peoples of different religions and let the people follow that doctrine under the name of Catholic and punished those who do not follow it. This caused another type of persecution begin and later it happens that even the kings were to be expelled by the Popes. Sunday worship and Easter…are said to be one of the examples of mixed doctrine. Due to this problem, the Christian Doctrine was to be altered inevitably. In 538 AD the Emperor Justenian decreed that the Pope should be the head of all the Christian churches and after that the Pope ruled for 1260 years until 1798 when Napoleon's general Berthier captured the Pope and took him to France. These 1260 years are called the "Dark Age" because the priests forbade anyone to read or even have a Bible in fear of the doctrine alteration be exposed to the public. In 1920, Italian government recognized Vatican City as an independent state and the Pope returned back to his position of king again.

This doctrine alteration caused the 16th century's Religion Reformation and the Christians were also divided into several different groups of Presbyterian, Evangelical, Methodist and Baptist…, which are all called the Protestant discriminating from Catholic.

But the Word of God is never changing despite the doctrinal change by the social leaders for their conveniences. So, it is a must that we have to stay awoke to grow only in real Word of God to have the right religion and stand on the right track of faith because it is going to be hard to find the right Christianity. That might be one of the reasons why Jesus Christ said to go into the narrow gate. With this idea, let's examine Jesus Christ's being Son of God through the bible to understand the bible.

500 years before Christ, the prophet Zechariah had prophesied.

(Zechariah9-9)
Rejoice greatly, O daughter of Zion! Shout in triumph, O daughter of Jerusalem! Be hold, your king is coming to you; He is just and endowed with salvation. Humble, and mounted on a donkey, Even on a colt, the foal of a donkey.

This was actually happened 500 years later when Jesus Christ entered Jerusalem. The New Testament described it as following.

(Matthew 21-1)   And when they had approached Jerusalem and had come to Bethphage, to the Mount of Olives, then Jesus sent two disciples, saying to them,"Go into the village opposite you, and immediately you will find a donkey tied there and a colt with her; untie them, and bring them to Me. "And if anyone says something to you, you shall say,"The Lord has need of them," and immediately he will send them." Now this took place that what was spoken through the prophet might be fulfilled, saying, "Say to the daughter of Zion, 'Behold your King is coming to you, Gentle, and mounted on a donkey, Even on a Colt, the foal of a beast of burden.' "And the disciples went and did just as Jesus had directed them, and brought the donkey and the colt, and laid on them their garments, on which He sat. And most of the multitude spread their garments

in the road, and others were cutting branches from the trees, and spreading them in the road. And the multitudes going before Him, and those who followed after were crying out, saying, "Hosanna to the Son of David; Blessed is He who comes in the name of the Lord; Hosanna in the highest!

Zechariah was a prophet of Judah that was destroyed by Babylon in BC 586. He prophesied for 3 years (BC 520-BC 518) when they were in captivity. He prophesied that the Babylon will be conquered by Persia, the Judah will return to Jerusalem after 70 years of captivity, Jesus Christ's coming and so on.

Following is one of those that described how Jesus Christ sold by his disciple Judas.

(Zechariah11-9)   Then said I, I will not pasture you: What is to die, let it die, and what is to be annihilated, let it be annihilated; and let those who are left eat one another's flesh." And I took my staff, Favor, and cut it in pieces, to break my covenant which I had made with all the peoples. So it was broken on that day, and thus the afflicted of the flock who were watching me realized that it was the word of the Lord. And I said to them, "If it is good in your sight, give me my wages; but if not, never mind!" So they weighed out thirty shekels of silver as my wages. Then the Lord said to me, "Throw it to the potter, that magnificent price at which I was valued by them, "So I took the thirty shekels of silver and threw them to the potter in the house of the Lord.

Let's look through New Testament what actually had happened about this.

(Matthew27-3)

Then one of the twelve, called Judas Iscariot, went unto the chief priests, And said unto them, What will ye give me, and I will deliver him unto you? And they covenanted with him for thirty pieces of silver. (Matthew26-14)

Then Judas, which had betrayed him, when he saw that he was condemned, repented himself, and brought again the thirty pieces of silver to the chief priests and elders, Saying, I have sinned in that I have betrayed the innocent blood. And they said, What is that to us? see thou to that. And he cast down the pieces of silver in the temple, and departed, and went and hanged himself. And the chief priests took the silver pieces, and said, It is not lawful for to put them into the treasury, because it is the price of blood. And they took counsel, and bought with them the potter's field, to bury strangers in. Wherefore that field was called, The field of blood, unto this day.

About 1,000 years before Christ, David the 2ⁿᵈ king of Israel and the centering figure of I and II Samuel of Old Testament described the prosecution of Jesus Christ's as following.

(Psalms22-1)   My God, my God, why hast thou forsaken me? why art thou so far from helping me, and from the words of my roaring? O my God, I cry in the daytime, but thou hearest not; and in the night season, and am not silent.......But I am a worm, and no man; a reproach of men, and despised of the people. All they that see me laugh me to scorn: they shoot out the lip, they shake the head saying, He trusted on the LORD that he would deliver him: let him deliver him, seeing he delighted in him......
Many bulls have compassed me: strong bulls of

Bashan have beset me round. They gaped upon me with their mouths, as a ravening and a roaring lion. I am poured out like water, and all my bones are out of joint: my heart is like wax; it is melted in the midst of my bowels. My strength is dried up like a potsherd; and my tongue cleaveth to my jaws; and thou hast brought me into the dust of death. For dogs have compassed me: the assembly of the wicked have inclosed me: they pierced my hands and my feet. I may tell all my bones: they look and stare upon me. They part my garments among them, and cast lots upon my vesture. But be not thou far from me, O LORD: O my strength, haste thee to help me. Deliver my soul from the sword; my darling from the power of the dog.

The bulls and dogs here mean the chief priests' group who turned Jesus Christ to death and the Roman soldiers who prosecuted him. Now let's look at the actual scene of Jesus Christ's crucifixion through New Testament.

(Matthew 27-27)
Then the soldiers of the governor took Jesus into the common hall, and gathered unto him the whole band of soldiers. And they stripped him, and put on him a scarlet robe. And when they had platted a crown of thorns, they put it upon his head, and a reed in his right hand: and they bowed the knee before him, and mocked him, saying, Hail, King of the Jews! And they spit upon him, and took the reed, and smote him on the head. And after that they had mocked him, they took the robe off from him, and put his own raiment on him, and led him away to crucify him. And as they came out, they found a man of Cyrene, Simon by name: him they compelled to bear his cross. And when they were come unto a

place called Golgotha, that is to say, a place of a skull, They gave him vinegar to drink mingled with gall: and when he had tasted thereof, he would not drink. And they crucified him, and parted his garments, casting lots: that it might be fulfilled which was spoken by the prophet, They parted my garments among them, and upon my vesture did they cast lots. And sitting down they watched him there; And set up over his head his accusation written, THIS IS JESUS THE KING OF THE JEWS. Then were there two thieves crucified with him, one on the right hand, and another on the left. And they that passed by reviled him, wagging their heads, And saying, Thou that destroyest the temple, and buildest it in three days, save thyself. If thou be the Son of God, come down from the cross. Likewise also the chief priests mocking him, with the scribes and elders, said, He saved others; himself he cannot save. If he be the King of Israel, let him now come down from the cross, and we will believe him. He trusted in God; let him deliver him now, if he will have him: for he said, I am the Son of God. The thieves also, which were crucified with him, cast the same in his teeth. Now from the sixth hour there was darkness over all the land unto the ninth hour. And about the ninth hour Jesus cried with a loud voice, saying, Eli, Eli, lama sabachthani? that is to say, My God, my God, why hast thou forsaken me? Some of them that stood there, when they heard that, said, This man calleth for Elias. And straightway one of them ran, and took a spunge, and filled it with vinegar, and put it on a reed, and gave him to drink. The rest said, Let be, let us see whether Elias will come to save him. Jesus, when he had cried again with a loud voice, yielded up the ghost.

(John 19-23)   Then the soldiers, when they had crucified Jesus, took his garments, and made four parts, to every soldier a part; and also his coat: now the coat was without seam, woven from the top throughout. They said therefore among themselves, Let us not rend it, but cast lots for it, whose it shall be: that the scripture might be fulfilled, which saith, They parted my raiment among them, and for my vesture they did cast lots. These things therefore the soldiers did.

The prophet Isaiah (B.C.739-B.C.680) who was born in a high rank family prophesied that the Jesus Christ was to be born from a virgin as following.

(Isaiah7-14)   Therefore the Lord himself shall give you a sign; Behold, a virgin shall conceive, and bear a son, and shall call his name Immanuel.

Here the Immanuel means "God is with us".
The actual birth of Jesus Christ described in the New Testament is as following.

(Matthew 1-18)   Now the birth of Jesus Christ was on this wise: When as his mother Mary was espoused to Joseph, before they came together, she was found with child of the Holy Ghost. Then Joseph her husband, being a just man, and not willing to make her a publick example, was minded to put her away privily. But while he thought on these things, behold, the angel of the Lord appeared unto him in a dream, saying, Joseph, thou son of David, fear not to take unto thee Mary thy wife: for that which is conceived in her is of the Holy Ghost. And she shall bring forth a son, and thou shalt call his name

JESUS: for he shall save his people from their sins. Now all this was done, that it might be fulfilled which was spoken of the Lord by the prophet, saying, Behold, a virgin shall be with child, and shall bring forth a son, and they shall call his name Emmanuel, which being interpreted is, God with us. Then Joseph being raised from sleep did as the angel of the Lord had bidden him, and took unto him his wife: And knew her not till she had brought forth her firstborn son: and he called his name JESUS.

The prophet Micah (BC 739-BC 697) prophesied the Jesus Christ was to be born in Bethlehem where David the 2nd king of Israel was born.

(Micah 5-2)   But thou, Bethlehem Ephratah, though thou be little among the thousands of Judah, yet out of thee shall he come forth unto me that is to be ruler in Israel; whose goings forth have been from of old, from everlasting.

Jesus Christ started to preach in Capernaum by the sea in the region of Zebulun and Naptali. This region is the border of Philistine and had suffered seriously from invasions of the aliens many times. The prophet Isaiah prophesied as following that the Jesus Christ will glorify this region by settling down and doing active preaching there.

(Isaiah9-1)   Nevertheless the dimness shall not be such as was in her vexation, when at the first he lightly afflicted the land of Zebulun and the land of Naphtali, and afterward did more grievously afflict her by the way of the sea, beyond Jordan, in Galilee of the nations. The people that walked in darkness have seen a great light: they that dwell in the land of the shadow of death, upon them hath the light shined.

Isaiah prophesied also that Jesus Christ was to be born in the branch of David's family. And Joseph, the father of Jesus Christ, was the 27th descendant of David. The bible reads as following.

(Isaiah 11-1)   And there shall come forth a rod out of the stem of Jesse, and a Branch shall grow out of his roots: And the spirit of the LORD shall rest upon him, the spirit of wisdom and understanding, the spirit of counsel and might, the spirit of knowledge and of the fear of the LORD; And shall make him of quick understanding in the fear of the LORD: and he shall not judge after the sight of his eyes, neither reprove after the hearing of his ears: But with righteousness shall he judge the poor, and reprove with equity for the meek of the earth: and he shall smite the earth with the rod of his mouth, and with the breath of his lips shall he slay the wicked. And righteousness shall be the girdle of his loins, and faithfulness the girdle of his reins. ......And in that day there shall be a root of Jesse, which shall stand for an ensign of the people; to it shall the Gentiles seek: and his rest shall be glorious.

Let's see further what had happened when Mary had Jesus Christ.

(Luke 1-26)   And in the sixth month the angel Gabriel was sent from God unto a city of Galilee, named Nazareth, To a virgin espoused to a man whose name was Joseph, of the house of David; and the virgin's name was Mary. And the angel came in unto her, and said, Hail, thou that art highly favoured, the Lord is with thee: blessed art thou among women. And when she saw him, she was troubled at his saying, and cast in her mind what manner of salutation this should be. And the angel

said unto her, Fear not, Mary: for thou hast found favour with God. And, behold, thou shalt conceive in thy womb, and bring forth a son, and shalt call his name JESUS. He shall be great, and shall be called the Son of the Highest: and the Lord God shall give unto him the throne of his father David: And he shall reign over the house of Jacob for ever; and of his kingdom there shall be no end. Then said Mary unto the angel, How shall this be, seeing I know not a man? And the angel answered and said unto her, The Holy Ghost shall come upon thee, and the power of the Highest shall overshadow thee: therefore also that holy thing which shall be born of thee shall be called the Son of God.

God said about Jesus Christ through the prophets Isaiah and Jeremiah as following. When we read the bible, we can find easily that Jesus Christ was doing what was prophesied about himself in the Old Testament and told the people to know that he was doing that.

(Isaiah 42-1)   Behold my servant, whom I uphold; mine elect, in whom my soul delighteth; I have put my spirit upon him: he shall bring forth judgment to the Gentiles. He shall not cry, nor lift up, nor cause his voice to be heard in the street. A bruised reed shall he not break, and the smoking flax shall he not quench: he shall bring forth judgment unto truth. He shall not fail nor be discouraged, till he have set judgment in the earth: and the isles shall wait for his law. Thus saith God the LORD, he that created the heavens, and stretched them out; he that spread forth the earth, and that which cometh out of it; he that giveth breath unto the people upon it, and spirit to them that walk therein: I the LORD have called thee in righteousness, and will hold thine hand, and will keep thee, and give thee for a covenant of the people, for a light of the Gentiles; To open the blind eyes, to bring out the prisoners from the prison, and them that sit in darkness out of the prison house. I am the LORD: that is my name: and my glory will I not give to another, neither my praise to graven images. Behold, the former things are come to pass, and new things do I declare: before they spring forth I tell you of them.

(Isaiath 49-7) Thus saith the LORD, the Redeemer of Israel, and his Holy One, to him whom man despiseth, to him whom the nation abhorreth, to a servant of rulers, Kings shall see and arise, princes also shall worship, because of the LORD that is faithful, and the Holy One of Israel, and he shall choose thee.

(Jeremiah 33-15) Behold, the days come, saith the LORD, that I will perform that good thing which I have promised unto the house of Israel and to the house of Judah. In those days, and at that time, will I cause the Branch of righteousness to grow up unto David; and he shall execute judgment and righteousness in the land.

To this far, we have examined the prophecies foretold by the prophets in the Old Testament by comparing with the record of what actually had happened about Jesus Christ through the New Testament.

This time we are going to look what John the Baptist witnessed. He was the first prophet in the New Testament and had baptized the people with water just before Jesus Christ came. One day Jesus Christ came to him and he baptized Jesus and witnessed as following as he is the Son of God he had been spoken about.

The First Witness, John the Baptist

(John 1-29)   The next day John seeth Jesus coming unto him, and saith, Behold the Lamb of God, which taketh away the sin of the world. This is he of whom I said, After me cometh a man which is preferred before me: for he was before me. And I knew him not: but that he should be made manifest to Israel, therefore am I come baptizing with water. And John bare record, saying, I saw the Spirit descending from heaven like a dove, and it abode upon him. And I knew him not: but he that sent me to baptize with water, the same said unto me, Upon whom thou shalt see the Spirit descending, and remaining on him, the same is he which baptizeth with the Holy Ghost. And I saw, and bare record that this is the Son of God.

*Apostle John, another John different from the Baptist who baptized Jesus Christ, wrote "**John**" and witnessed Jesus Christ as the Son of God as following.*

John 1-1
In the beginning was the Word, and the Word was with God, and the Word was God. The same was in the beginning with God. All things were made by him; and without him was not any thing made that was made. In him was life; and the life was the light of men. And the light shineth in darkness; and the darkness comprehended it not. There was a man sent from God, whose name was John. The same came for a witness, to bear witness of the Light, that all men through him might believe. He was not that Light, but was sent to bear witness of that Light. That was

the true Light, which lighteth every man that cometh into the world. He was in the world, and the world was made by him, and the world knew him not. He came unto his own, and his own received him not. But as many as received him, to them gave he power to become the sons of God, even to them that believe on his name: Which were born, not of blood, nor of the will of the flesh, nor of the will of man, but of God. And the Word was made flesh, and dwelt among us, (and we beheld his glory, the glory as of the only begotten of the Father,) full of grace and truth. John bare witness of him, and cried, saying, This was he of whom I spake, He that cometh after me is preferred before me: for he was before me. And of his fulness have all we received, and grace for grace. For the law was given by Moses, but grace and truth came by Jesus Christ. No man hath seen God at any time; the only begotten Son, which is in the bosom of the Father, he hath declared him.

Jesus Christ, Testifying Himself

Following is what Jesus Christ is testifying himself.

(John5-30)　I can of mine own self do nothing: as I hear, I judge: and my judgment is just; because I seek not mine own will, but the will of the Father which hath sent me. If I bear witness of myself, my witness is not true. There is another that beareth witness of me; and I know that the witness which he witnesseth of me is true. Ye sent unto John, and he bare witness unto the truth. But I receive not testimony from man: but these things I say, that ye might be saved. He was a burning and a shining light: and ye were willing for a season to rejoice in his light. But I have greater witness than that of John: for the works which the Father hath given me to finish, the same works that I do, bear witness of me, that the Father hath sent me. And the Father himself, which hath sent me, hath borne witness of me. Ye have neither heard his voice at any time, nor seen his shape. And ye have not his word abiding in you: for whom he hath sent, him ye believe not. Search the scriptures; for in them ye think ye have eternal life: and they are they which testify of me. And ye will not come to me, that ye might have life.

Jesus Christ did not just tell the people to believe. He worked lots of miracles to show his being Son of God. He told the people to see what he does and then believe because what he does is what God does through him.

John 10-34   Jesus answered them, Is it not written in your law, I said, Ye are gods? If he called them gods, unto whom the word of God came, and the scripture cannot be broken; Say ye of him, whom the Father hath sanctified, and sent into the world, Thou blasphemest; because I said, I am the Son of God? If I do not the works of my Father, believe me not.

But if I do, though ye believe not me, believe the works: that ye may know, and believe, that the Father is in me, and I in him.

He said people study the bible to believe in God and save oneself but does not come to the savior Jesus Christ himself to get salvation. He taught about this to his disciples as following.

John 14
Let not your heart be troubled: ye believe in God, believe also in me.

In my Father's house are many mansions: if it were not so, I would have told you. I go to prepare a place for you. And if I go and prepare a place for you, I will come again, and receive you unto myself; that where I am, there ye may be also. And whither I go ye know, and the way ye know. Thomas saith unto him, Lord, we know not whither thou goest; and how can we know the way?

Jesus saith unto him, I am the way, the truth, and the life: no man cometh unto the Father, but by me.

If ye had known me, ye should have known my Father also: and from henceforth ye know him, and have seen him.

Philip saith unto him, Lord, shew us the Father, and it sufficeth us.

Jesus saith unto him, Have I been so long time with you, and yet hast thou not known me, Philip? he that hath seen me hath seen the Father; and how sayest thou then, Shew us the Father?

Believest thou not that I am in the Father, and the Father in me? the words that I speak unto you I speak not of myself: but the Father that dwelleth in me, he doeth the works.

Believe me that I am in the Father, and the Father in me: or else believe me for the very works' sake.

Verily, verily, I say unto you, He that believeth on me, the works that I do shall he do also; and greater works than these shall he do; because I go unto my Father.

And whatsoever ye shall ask in my name, that will I do, that the Father may be glorified in the Son.

If ye shall ask any thing in my name, I will do it. If ye love me, keep my commandments. And I will pray the Father, and he shall give you another Comforter, that he may abide with you for ever;

Even the Spirit of truth; whom the world cannot receive, because it seeth him not, neither knoweth him: but ye know him; for he dwelleth with you, and shall be in you.

I will not leave you comfortless: I will come to you.

Yet a little while, and the world seeth me no more; but ye see me: because I live, ye shall live also.

At that day ye shall know that I am in my Father, and ye in me, and I in you. He that hath my commandments, and keepeth them, he it is that loveth me: and he that loveth me shall be loved of my Father, and I will love him, and will manifest myself to him.

Judas saith unto him, not Iscariot, Lord, how is it that thou wilt manifest thyself unto us, and not unto the world?

Jesus answered and said unto him, If a man love me, he will keep my words: and my Father will love him, and we will come unto him, and make our abode with him.

He that loveth me not keepeth not my sayings: and the word which ye hear is not mine, but the Father's which sent me.

These things have I spoken unto you, being yet present with you.

But the Comforter, which is the Holy Ghost, whom the Father will send in my name, he shall teach you all things, and bring all things to your remembrance, whatsoever I have said unto you.

Peace I leave with you, my peace I give unto you: not as the world giveth, give I unto you. Let not your heart be troubled, neither let it be afraid.

Ye have heard how I said unto you, I go away, and come again unto you. If ye loved me, ye would

rejoice, because I said, I go unto the Father: for my
Father is greater than I. And now I have told you
before it come to pass, that, when it is come to pass,
ye might believe.

Hereafter I will not talk much with you: for the
prince of this world cometh, and hath nothing in me.

But that the world may know that I love the
Father; and as the Father gave me commandment,
even so I do.

*Even though the people believed the scripture that a Savior will come to
save them they did not come to the savior. For the same reason, Jesus Christ
repeatedly emphasized of his being Son of God. To make people believe, he
told them to see first what he does and if he does which is possible only by
God then believe he is the Son of God. And then worked such unbelievable
miracles that could not be done if not by God. But still the people didn't
believe him. Following explains the reason well.*

(John 12-37)   And Jesus walked in the temple in
Solomon's porch. Then came the Jews round about
him, and said unto him, How long dost thou make
us to doubt? If thou be the Christ, tell us plainly.
Jesus answered them, I told you, and ye believed not:
the works that I do in my Father's name, they bear
witness of me. But ye believe not, because ye are not
of my sheep, as I said unto you.

(John 10-23)
But though he had done so many miracles before
them, yet they believed not on him: That the saying
of Esaias the prophet might be fulfilled, which he
spake, Lord, who hath believed our report? and
to whom hath the arm of the Lord been revealed?
Therefore they could not believe, because that Esaias
said again, He hath blinded their eyes, and hardened

their heart; that they should not see with their eyes, nor understand with their heart, and be converted, and I should heal them.

Jesus Christ preached everything in parables so that not everybody can understand it. He answered when asked about it by the disciples as following.

(Matthew 13-10)   And the disciples came, and said unto him, Why speakest thou unto them in parables? He answered and said unto them, Because it is given unto you to know the mysteries of the kingdom of heaven, but to them it is not given. For whosoever hath, to him shall be given, and he shall have more abundance: but whosoever hath not, from him shall be taken away even that he hath. Therefore speak I to them in parables: because they seeing see not; and hearing they hear not, neither do they understand. And in them is fulfilled the prophecy of Esaias, which saith, By hearing ye shall hear, and shall not understand; and seeing ye shall see, and shall not perceive:

For this people's heart is waxed gross, and their ears are dull of hearing, and their eyes they have closed; lest at any time they should see with their eyes, and hear with their ears, and should understand with their heart, and should be converted, and I should heal them. But blessed are your eyes, for they see: and your ears, for they hear. For verily I say unto you, That many prophets and righteous men have desired to see those things which ye see, and have not seen them; and to hear those things which ye hear, and have not heard them."

Jesus Christ proving being Son of God

Now, then let's see how he tried to prove his being Son of God with one good practical example. Following is what and how he did when he brought the dead Lazarus back to life.

(John 11-1)

Now a certain man was sick, named Lazarus, of Bethany, the town of Mary and her sister Martha.

(It was that Mary which anointed the Lord with ointment, and wiped his feet with her hair, whose brother Lazarus was sick.)

Therefore his sisters sent unto him, saying, Lord, behold, he whom thou lovest is sick.

When Jesus heard that, he said, This sickness is not unto death, but for the glory of God, that the Son of God might be glorified thereby.

Now Jesus loved Martha, and her sister, and Lazarus.

When he had heard therefore that he was sick, he abode two days still in the same place where he was. *(He waited until Nazarus die so he can reveal the glory of God.)*

Then after that saith he to his disciples, Let us go into Judaea again.

His disciples say unto him, Master, the Jews of late sought to stone thee; and goest thou thither again?

Jesus answered, Are there not twelve hours in the day? If any man walk in the day, he stumbleth not, because he seeth the light of this world.

But if a man walk in the night, he stumbleth, because there is no light in him.

These things said he: and after that he saith unto

them, Our friend Lazarus sleepeth; but I go, that I may awake him out of sleep.

Then said his disciples, Lord, if he sleep, he shall do well. Howbeit Jesus spake of his death: but they thought that he had spoken of taking of rest in sleep.

Then said Jesus unto them plainly, Lazarus is dead.

And I am glad for your sakes that I was not there, to the intent ye may believe; nevertheless let us go unto him.

Then said Thomas, which is called Didymus, unto his fellowdisciples, Let us also go, that we may die with him.

Then when Jesus came, he found that he had lain in the grave four days already.

Now Bethany was nigh unto Jerusalem, about fifteen furlongs off:

And many of the Jews came to Martha and Mary, to comfort them concerning their brother.

Then Martha, as soon as she heard that Jesus was coming, went and met him: but Mary sat still in the house.

Then said Martha unto Jesus, Lord, if thou hadst been here, my brother had not died.

But I know, that even now, whatsoever thou wilt ask of God, God will give it thee.

Jesus saith unto her, Thy brother shall rise again.

Martha saith unto him, I know that he shall rise again in the resurrection at the last day.

Jesus said unto her, I am the resurrection, and the life: he that believeth in me, though he were dead, yet shall he live:

And whosoever liveth and believeth in me shall never die. Believest thou this? She saith unto him,

Yea, Lord: I believe that thou art the Christ, the Son of God, which should come into the world.

And when she had so said, she went her way, and called Mary her sister secretly, saying, The Master is come, and calleth for thee.

As soon as she heard that, she arose quickly, and came unto him.

Now Jesus was not yet come into the town, but was in that place where Martha met him.

The Jews then which were with her in the house, and comforted her, when they saw Mary, that she rose up hastily and went out, followed her, saying, She goeth unto the grave to weep there.

Then when Mary was come where Jesus was, and saw him, she fell down at his feet, saying unto him, Lord, if thou hadst been here, my brother had not died. When Jesus therefore saw her weeping, and the Jews also weeping which came with her, he groaned in the spirit, and was troubled,

And said, Where have ye laid him? They said unto him, Lord, come and see. Jesus wept. Then said the Jews, Behold how he loved him!

And some of them said, Could not this man, which opened the eyes of the blind, have caused that even this man should not have died?

Jesus therefore again groaning in himself cometh to the grave. It was a cave, and a stone lay upon it.

Jesus said, Take ye away the stone. Martha, the sister of him that was dead, saith unto him, Lord, by this time he stinketh: for he hath been dead four days.

Jesus saith unto her, Said I not unto thee, that, if thou wouldest believe, thou shouldest see the glory of God?

Then they took away the stone from the place

where the dead was laid. And Jesus lifted up his eyes, and said, Father, I thank thee that thou hast heard me.

And I knew that thou hearest me always: but because of the people which stand by I said it, that they may believe that thou hast sent me.

And when he thus had spoken, he cried with a loud voice, Lazarus, come forth. And he that was dead came forth, bound hand and foot with graveclothes: and his face was bound about with a napkin. Jesus saith unto them, Loose him, and let him go.

Jesus Christ reflecting himself the Son of God

Following is what happened just before Jesus Christ was crucified.

(Matthew 26:20)
Now when the evening had come, he sat down with the twelve. And as they did eat, he said, Verily I say unto you, that one of you will betray me.

And they were exceeding sorrowful, and began every one of them to say unto him, Lord, is it I?

And he answered and said, He that dippeth his hand with me in the dish, the same shall betray me.

The Son of man goeth as it is written of him: but woe unto that man by whom the Son of man is betrayed! it had been good for that man if he had not been born.

Then Judas, which betrayed him, answered and said, Master, is it I? He said unto him, Thou hast said.

And as they were eating, Jesus took bread, and

blessed it, and brake it, and gave it to the disciples, and said, Take, eat; this is my body.

And he took the cup, and gave thanks, and gave it to them, saying, Drink ye all of it; For this is my blood of the New Testament, which is shed for many for the remission of sins.

But I say unto you, I will not drink henceforth of this fruit of the vine, until that day when I drink it new with you in my Father's kingdom.

And when they had sung an hymn, they went out into the mount of Olives.

Then saith Jesus unto them, All ye shall be offended because of me this night: for it is written, I will smite the shepherd, and the sheep of the flock shall be scattered abroad.

But after I am risen again, I will go before you into Galilee.

Peter answered and said unto him, Though all men shall be offended because of thee, yet will I never be offended.

Jesus said unto him, Verily I say unto thee, That this night, before the cock crow, thou shalt deny me thrice.

Peter said unto him, Though I should die with thee, yet will I not deny thee.

Likewise also said all the disciples.

Then cometh Jesus with them unto a place called Gethsemane, and saith unto the disciples, Sit ye here, while I go and pray yonder.

And he took with him Peter and the two sons of Zebedee, and began to be sorrowful and very heavy.

Then saith he unto them, My soul is exceeding sorrowful, even unto death: tarry ye here, and watch with me.

And he went a little further, and fell on his face,

and prayed, saying, O my Father, if it be possible, let this cup pass from me: nevertheless not as I will, but as thou wilt.

And he cometh unto the disciples, and findeth them asleep, and saith unto Peter,

What, could ye not watch with me one hour?

Watch and pray, that ye enter not into temptation: the spirit indeed is willing, but the flesh is weak.

He went away again the second time, and prayed, saying, O my Father, if this cup may not pass away from me, except I drink it, thy will be done.

And he came and found them asleep again: for their eyes were heavy.

And he left them, and went away again, and prayed the third time, saying the same words.

Then cometh he to his disciples, and saith unto them, Sleep on now, and take your rest: behold, the hour is at hand, and the Son of man is betrayed into the hands of sinners.

Rise, let us be going: behold, he is at hand that doth betray me.

And while he yet spake, lo, Judas, one of the twelve, came, and with him a great multitude with swords and staves, from the chief priests and elders of the people.

Now he that betrayed him gave them a sign, saying, Whomsoever I shall kiss, that same is he: hold him fast.

And forthwith he came to Jesus, and said, Hail, master; and kissed him.

And Jesus said unto him, Friend, wherefore art thou come? Then they came up and laid hands on Jesus and took him.

And, behold, one of them which were with Jesus stretched out his hand, and drew his sword, and struck a servant of the high priest's, and smote off his ear.

Then said Jesus unto him, Put up again thy sword into his place: for all they that take the sword shall perish with the sword.

Thinkest thou that I cannot now pray to my Father, and he shall presently give me more than twelve legions of angels?

But how then shall the scriptures be fulfilled, that thus it must be?

In that same hour said Jesus to the multitudes, Are ye come out as against a thief with swords and staves for to take me? I sat daily with you teaching in the temple, and ye laid no hold on me.

But all this was done, that the scriptures of the prophets might be fulfilled. Then all the disciples forsook him, and fled.

And they that had laid hold on Jesus led him away to Caiaphas the high priest, where the scribes and the elders were assembled.

But Peter followed him afar off unto the high priest's palace, and went in, and sat with the servants, to see the end.

Now the chief priests, and elders, and all the council, sought false witness against Jesus, to put him to death; But found none: yea, though many false witnesses came, yet found they none. At the last came two false witnesses, And said, This fellow said, I am able to destroy the temple of God, and to build it in three days.

And the high priest arose, and said unto him, Answerest thou nothing? what is it which these witness against thee?

But Jesus held his peace. And the high priest answered and said unto him, I adjure thee by the living God, that thou tell us whether thou be the Christ, the Son of God.

Jesus saith unto him, Thou hast said: nevertheless I say unto you, Hereafter shall ye see the Son of man sitting on the right hand of power, and coming in the clouds of heaven. Then the high priest rent his clothes, saying, He hath spoken blasphemy; what further need have we of witnesses? behold, now ye have heard his blasphemy.

What think ye? They answered and said, He is guilty of death.

Then did they spit in his face, and buffeted him; and others smote him with the palms of their hands, Saying, Prophesy unto us, thou Christ, Who is he that smote thee?

Now Peter sat without in the palace: and a damsel came unto him, saying, Thou also wast with Jesus of Galilee.

But he denied before them all, saying, I know not what thou sayest.

And when he was gone out into the porch, another maid saw him, and said unto them that were there, This fellow was also with Jesus of Nazareth.

And again he denied with an oath, I do not know the man.

And after a while came unto him they that stood by, and said to Peter, Surely thou also art one of them; for thy speech bewrayeth thee.

Then began he to curse and to swear, saying, I know not the man. And immediately the cock crew.

And Peter remembered the word of Jesus, which said unto him, Before the cock crow, thou shalt deny me thrice. And he went out, and wept bitterly."

Jesus Christ prayed unto the Father in heaven that he does not like to die so please do not leave him alone to die. But he wanted the father in heaven accomplishes what the father wanted not what Jesus Christ himself wanted. The father in heaven killed him as planned and Jesus Christ said just before he breathed the last breath as:

(John 19:28)   After this, Jesus knowing that all things were now accomplished, that the scripture might be fulfilled, saith, I thirst…….. It is finished: and he bowed his head, and gave up the ghost.

Here 'it is finished' means God accomplished his plan on Jesus Christ or Jesus Christ finished the work imposed on his life as God planned.

Jesus Christ obeyed God that he has to die as written in the Old Testament.

As Jesus Christ said clearly that he came to this world to accomplish God's will, we can easily see that he was performing his life only to accomplish as written about himself in the bible.

And the scripture was fulfilled as Matthew wrote.

(Matthew 20:28)   Even as the Son of man came not to be ministered unto, but to minister, and to give his life a ransom for many.

This means he came to accomplish God's Will imposed on him, not to accomplish his own will, as foretold by the prophet Isaiah as following.

(Isaiah 53)
Who has believed our message?
And to whom has the arm of the Lord been revealed?
For He grew up before Him like a tender shoot, And like a root out of parched ground; He has no stately form or majesty That we should look upon him. Nor appearance that we should be attracted to him.

He was despised and forsaken of men, a man of sorrows, and acquainted with grief; and like one from whom men hide their face, he was despised, and we did not esteem him.

Surely our griefs he himself bore, and our sorrows he carried; yet we ourselves esteemed him stricken, smitten of God, and afflicted.

But he was pierced through for our transgressions. He was crushed ofr our iniquities; the chastening for our well-being fell upon him, and by his scourging we are healed.

All of us like sheep have gone astray, each of us has turned to his own way, but the lord has caused the iniquity of us all to fall on him.

He was oppressed and he was afflicted, yet he did not open his mouth; like a lamb that is led to slaughter, and like a sheep that is silent before its shearers, so he did not open his mouth.

By oppression and judgment he was taken away; and as for his generation, who considered that he was cut off out of the land of the loveing, for the transgression of my people to whom the strike was due?

His grave was assigned of with wicked men, yet he was with a rich man in his death, because he had done no violence, nor was there any deceit in his mouth.

But the Lord was pleased to crush him, putting him to grief; If he would render himself as a guilt offering, he will see his offspring, he will prolong his days, and the good pleasure of the Lord will prosper in his hand.

As a result of the anguish of his soul, he will see it and be satisfied; by his knowledge the righteous one, my servant, will justify the many, as he will bear their iniquities.

Therefore, I will allot him a portion with the great, and he will divide the booty with the strong; because he poured out himself to death, and was numbered with the transgressors; yet he himself bore the sin of many, and interceded for the transgressors.

Then, why did God sent the own son to this world? What is he going to be and what is he going to do? God showed it clearly to us through Isaiah as following.

(Isaiah 9)
For a child will be born to us, a son will be given to us; and the government will rest on his shoulders; and his name will be called wonderful counselor, mighty God, eternal father, prince of peace. There will be no end to the increase of his government or of peace, on the throne of David and over his kingdom, to establish it and to uphold it with justice and righteousness from then on and forevermore. The zeal of the Lord of hosts will accomplish this.

In another chapter, he said:

(Isaiah 55)
Ho! Every one who thirsts, come to the waters; and you who have no money come buy and eat. Come, buy wine and milk without money and without cost.

Why do you spend money for what is not bread, and your wages for what does not satisfy? Listen carefully to me, and eat what is good, and delight yourself in abundance.

Incline your ear and come to me. Listen, that you may live; and I will make an everlasting covenant with you, according to the faithful mercies shown to David.

Behold, I have make him a witness to the peoples, a leader and commander for the peoples. Behold, you will call a nation you do not know, and a nation which knows you not will run to you, because of the Lord your God, even the Holy One of Israel; for he has glorified you.

And the disciple John said:

(John 3)
For God so loved the world, that he gave his only begotten Son, that whosoever believeth in him should not perish, but have everlasting life.

For God sent not his Son into the world to condemn the world; but that the world through him might be saved.

He that believeth on him is not condemned: but he that believeth not is condemned already, because he hath not believed in the name of the only begotten Son of God.

And this is the condemnation, that light is come into the world, and men loved darkness rather than light, because their deeds were evil.

For every one that doeth evil hateth the light, neither cometh to the light, lest his deeds should be reproved.

But he that doeth truth cometh to the light, that his deeds may be made manifest, that they are wrought in God.

He said in another chapter:

Then spake Jesus again unto them, saying, I am the light of the world: he that followeth me shall not walk in darkness, but shall have the light of life. (John 8)

And also, in another chapter he said:

(John 15)

I am the true vine, and my Father is the husbandman.

Every branch in me that beareth not fruit he taketh away: and every branch that beareth fruit, he purgeth it, that it may bring forth more fruit. Now ye are clean through the word which I have spoken unto you.

Abide in me, and I in you. As the branch cannot bear fruit of itself, except it abide in the vine; no more can ye, except ye abide in me.

I am the vine, ye are the branches: He that abideth in me, and I in him, the same bringeth forth much fruit: for without me ye can do nothing.

If a man abide not in me, he is cast forth as a branch, and is withered; and men gather them, and cast them into the fire, and they are burned.

If ye abide in me, and my words abide in you, ye shall ask what ye will, and it shall be done unto you.

Herein is my Father glorified, that ye bear much fruit; so shall ye be my disciples. As the Father hath loved me, so have I loved you: continue ye in my love. If ye keep my commandments, ye shall abide in my love; even as I have kept my Father's commandments, and abide in his love.

These things have I spoken unto you, that my joy might remain in you, and that your joy might be full.

This is my commandment, That ye love one another, as I have loved you. Greater love hath no man than this, that a man lay down his life for his friends. Ye are my friends, if ye do whatsoever I command you.

Henceforth I call you not servants; for the servant knoweth not what his lord doeth: but I have called you friends; for all things that I have heard of my Father I have made known unto you.

Ye have not chosen me, but I have chosen you, and ordained you, that ye should go and bring forth fruit, and that your fruit should remain: that whatsoever ye shall ask of the Father in my name, he may give it you. These things I command you, that ye love one another.

If the world hate you, ye know that it hated me before it hated you.

If ye were of the world, the world would love his own: but because ye are not of the world, but I have chosen you out of the world, therefore the world hateth you.

Remember the word that I said unto you, The servant is not greater than his lord. If they have persecuted me, they will also persecute you; if they have kept my saying, they will keep yours also.

But all these things will they do unto you for my name's sake, because they know not him that sent me.

If I had not come and spoken unto them, they had not had sin: but now they have no cloke for their sin.

He that hateth me hateth my Father also.

If I had not done among them the works which none other man did, they had not had sin: but now have they both seen and hated both me and my Father.

But this cometh to pass, that the word might be fulfilled that is written in their law, They hated me without a cause.

But when the Comforter is come, whom I will send unto you from the Father, even the Spirit of truth, which proceedeth from the Father, he shall testify of me:

And ye also shall bear witness, because ye have been with me from the beginning.

Our Faith and Jesus Christ

Following scriptures show us the clear direction that our faith should grow in. Let's see what it says first.

(Luke12)
I am come to send fire on the earth; and what will I, if it be already kindled?

But I have a baptism to be baptized with; and how am I straitened till it be accomplished!

Suppose ye that I am come to give peace on earth? I tell you, Nay; but rather division:

For from henceforth there shall be five in one house divided, three against two, and two against three.

The father shall be divided against the son, and the son against the father; the mother against the daughter, and the daughter against the mother; the mother in law against her daughter in law, and the daughter in law against her mother in law.

And he said also to the people, When ye see a cloud rise out of the west, straightway ye say, There cometh a shower; and so it is.

And when ye see the south wind blow, ye say, There will be heat; and it cometh to pass.

Ye hypocrites, ye can discern the face of the sky and of the earth; but how is it that ye do not discern this time?

Nowadays, most people's common "Believe in God" means "Blessed are those who does good and cursed are those who does evil". But Jesus Christ says nay to this idea. He said he came to bring fire and division instead of peace and unification, which most of us can not understand. Normal idea we have about Jesus Christ is "good, peace, mercy, forgive, blessing, everyone's savior, unification in one, etc."

Especially, we, our generation is witnessing the above scriptures.

Jesus Christ said he is the Son of God and the savior. And the same Jesus Christ said, he came to bring the fire and division to the same people who believed Jesus Christ would save them. He also said the great distress is prearranged in this world before the salvation. I would like to say "Believe in God" means "Believe what God says" and "Believe what God says" is "Believe in Jesus Christ" because he came as the Word of God.

"Blessed are those who do good and cursed are those who do evil" is God's policy upon our life in this world but our faith for the salvation can grow only by believing God's word.

As we continue, we are going to study in depth about what God says, however I'd like to summarize what God told us to give the frame of God's words.

1. *We are all destined to die in this world which god gave to Satan.*
2. *Nobody can come to God if God doesn't allow him to come.*
3. *Jesus Christ preached everything in parables so no men other than Sons of God can understand to be healed and saved. He said to leave the evil doers as evil doers and good doers as good doers but to spread the Good News to the end of the world so the lost Sons of God can hear it, know it and be healed to live in hope for salvation not despaired.*
4. *Jesus Christ came first to let people know about the Kingdom of God. He is coming again to restore the government of God.*

   Remember God didn't allow the Israel people to have their own king until the 1st King Saul. God allowed them a king after the badger of Israel people. So, the government today under the catch phrase of "by the people, for the people, of the people" is not the type of ideal government of God. Even though the majority runs the government that does not mean the majority is always right. God is only right and God is always right. Because God created this world as he wanted. Jesus Christ is coming to restore God ruling government.

5. *There is going to be a great distress before the Jesus Christ's returning.*

6. *When Jesus Christ comes again the Sons of God will be moved from the judgment and saved from the 2nd death to live in peace in the Kingdom of God.*

7. *1,000 years after Jesus Christ's returning, men who have ever lived in this world will be resurrected and are going to be judged according to each one's deed.*

First of all, we should not forget the bible is only for the Sons of God.

We, the Sons of God, are only passing this evil world as Jesus Christ said. We are not staying here. He also says there will be a great distress in this evil world, so the Sons of God should stay awoke and discern what hours of the God's schedule on this world we are passing and evade from this soon coming great distress. God talks to the Sons of God spirit to spirit. So, those who do not have the spirit of God can not understand God, the Holy Spirit, and also can not live by God's command.

Let's go back to the scripture again and find out what it says.

(Luke 12:51)
Do you think that I have come to give peace on earth?
No, I tell you, but rather division; for henceforth in one house there will be divided, three against two and two against three; they will be divided, father against son and son against father, mother against daughter and daughter against her mother, mother-in-law against her daughter-in-law and daughter-in-law against her mother-in-law.

As anybody would agree, above scripture describes our life exactly and we ourselves are the witnesses about it. Jesus Christ brought fire to this world and said to the God's people to discern and evade. So, anybody who would be mingled among the people burning oneself in this world won't be the Son of God and anybody who would keep oneself away from it to stand perfect in God would be the Son of God.

That's because if a man could hear god and evade the evil things, that fact proves he has the Spirit of God and those who has the Spirit of God is written in the bible as to be the Son of God. I believe being written in the book of life in heaven means that. As we know everybody dies. So "being perfect" means "being perfect spiritually".

We can tell what time we are passing by the intensity of fire based upon the words written in the bible.

Those social problems like killing, fighting, hatred, destroying, hurting, cheating, doing drug, etc. are the burning fire that Jesus Christ brought into this world and those who participated in it to be burned wouldn't be the Sons of God. So, to be perfect to God we will have to discern and evade oneself from burning. That's the way how God discerns the grain from chaff and that's why Jesus Christ brought the fire into this world.

How can we avoid fighting when somebody hurt us?

Jesus Christ taught us as following.

(Matthew 5-40)
If anyone slaps you on the right cheek, let him slap your left cheek too."

Since the salvation is the matter of each individual, we will have to deal with above examples of killing, hatred, destroying...as relating to each individual's behavior. It is very interesting to find that so many people say that the bible is a kind of one great epic written by a great writer with great talent. They say they believe in God too.

We have examined the Jesus Christ's being Son of God through Old and New Testament. Now, Anyone, who believes Jesus Christ is the Son of God will understand God and learn to fear God. Likewise, anybody who does not believe Jesus Christ is the Son of God can not understand the bible what it says. I would say those people wouldn't be even interested in the Bible.

This could be compared to two people, one with sunglasses and the other one without it. The one with sunglasses can not see the right color and would not believe it is white however somebody tries hard to let him know the color he is looking at is white.

Try harder to let him know it is white, the more it's going to be boring to him.

As the bible says, Jesus Christ worked a lot of miracles to make people believe. But what I've got from him is he talks about God and the words become the truth.

From next chapter I am going to dig the bible and study how God accomplishes. Before that I want to warm up and revive our spirit with couple of pages of words what God told us. That is to get ready for further in-depth study. Because I recall God reveals from faith to faith. I also experienced that finding the books, chapters and clauses made me so tired and boring and which made me not to proceed any more and give up.

So, I tried to make this book not necessary to read the bible together, but I encourage readers to read the bible together if possible, for further solid rock faith for oneself.

Remember we have to listen by our spirit. Otherwise we cannot understand and it's going to be just boring.

Warming Up the Spirit

(Romans 5)
Whosoever believeth that Jesus is the Christ is born of God: and every one that loveth him that begat loveth him also that is begotten of him.

By this we know that we love the children of God, when we love God, and keep his commandments.

For this is the love of God, that we keep his

commandments: and his commandments are not grievous.

For whatsoever is born of God overcometh the world: and this is the victory that overcometh the world, even our faith.

Who is he that overcometh the world, but he that believeth that Jesus is the Son of God?

He that believeth on the Son of God hath the witness in himself: he that believeth not God hath made him a liar; because he believeth not the record that God gave of his Son.

And this is the record, that God hath given to us eternal life, and this life is in his Son.

He that hath the Son hath life; and he that hath not the Son of God hath not life.

These things have I written unto you that believe on the name of the Son of God; that ye may know that ye have eternal life, and that ye may believe on the name of the Son of God.

And this is the confidence that we have in him, that, if we ask any thing according to his will, he heareth us:

And if we know that he hear us, whatsoever we ask, we know that we have the petitions that we desired of him.

All unrighteousness is sin: and there is a sin not unto death.

We know that whosoever is born of God sinneth not; but he that is begotten of God keepeth himself, and that wicked one toucheth him not.

And we know that we are of God, and the whole world lieth in wickedness.

And we know that the Son of God is come, and hath given us an understanding, that we may know him that is true, and we are in him that is true, even in his Son Jesus Christ. This is the true God, and eternal life.

(John 12)
For I have not spoken of myself; but the Father which sent me, he gave me a commandment, what I should say, and what I should speak.

And I know that his commandment is life everlasting: whatsoever I speak therefore, even as the Father said unto me, so I speak.

(Corinthians 3)
Know ye not that ye are the temple of God, and that the Spirit of God dwelleth in you?

If any man defile the temple of God, him shall God destroy; for the temple of God is holy, which temple ye are.

(I Timothy 6)
But godliness with contentment is great gain.

For we brought nothing into this world, and it is certain we can carry nothing out.

And having food and raiment let us be therewith content.

But they that will be rich fall into temptation and a snare, and into many foolish and hurtful lusts, which drown men in destruction and perdition.

For the love of money is the root of all evil: which while some coveted after, they have erred from the faith, and pierced themselves through with many sorrows.

But thou, O man of God, flee these things; and follow after righteousness, godliness, faith, love, patience, meekness.

Fight the good fight of faith, lay hold on eternal

life, whereunto thou art also called, and hast professed a good profession before many witnesses.

I give thee charge in the sight of God, who quickeneth all things, and before Christ Jesus, who before Pontius Pilate witnessed a good confession;

That thou keep this commandment without spot, unrebukeable, until the appearing of our Lord Jesus Christ:

Which in his times he shall shew, who is the blessed and only Potentate, the King of kings, and Lord of lords;

Who only hath immortality, dwelling in the light which no man can approach unto; whom no man hath seen, nor can see: to whom be honour and power everlasting. Amen. Charge them that are rich in this world, that they be not highminded, nor trust in uncertain riches, but in the living God, who giveth us richly all things to enjoy;

That they do good, that they be rich in good works, ready to distribute, willing to communicate;

Laying up in store for themselves a good foundation against the time to come, that they may lay hold on eternal life.

(James 1)
Then when lust hath conceived, it bringeth forth sin: and sin, when it is finished, bringeth forth death.

(John 6)
Labour not for the meat which perisheth, but for that meat which endureth unto everlasting life, which the Son of man shall give unto you: for him hath God the Father sealed.

Then said they unto him, What shall we do, that we might work the works of God?

Jesus answered and said unto them, This is the work of God, that ye believe on him whom he hath sent.

They said therefore unto him, What sign shewest thou then, that we may see, and believe thee? what dost thou work?

Our fathers did eat manna in the desert; as it is written, He gave them bread from heaven to eat.

Then Jesus said unto them, Verily, verily, I say unto you, Moses gave you not that bread from heaven; but my Father giveth you the true bread from heaven.

For the bread of God is he which cometh down from heaven, and giveth life unto the world.

Then said they unto him, Lord, evermore give us this bread.

And Jesus said unto them, I am the bread of life: he that cometh to me shall never hunger; and he that believeth on me shall never thirst.

But I said unto you, That ye also have seen me, and believe not.

All that the Father giveth me shall come to me; and him that cometh to me I will in no wise cast out.

For I came down from heaven, not to do mine own will, but the will of him that sent me.

And this is the Father's will which hath sent me, that of all which he hath given me I should lose nothing, but should raise it up again at the last day.

And this is the will of him that sent me, that every one which seeth the Son, and believeth on him, may have everlasting life: and I will raise him up at the last day.

The Jews then murmured at him, because he said, I am the bread which came down from heaven.

And they said, Is not this Jesus, the son of Joseph,

whose father and mother we know? how is it then that he saith, I came down from heaven?

Jesus therefore answered and said unto them, Murmur not among yourselves.

No man can come to me, except the Father which hath sent me draw him: and I

will raise him up at the last day.

It is written in the prophets, And they shall be all taught of God. Every man therefore that hath heard, and hath learned of the Father, cometh unto me.

Not that any man hath seen the Father, save he which is of God, he hath seen the Father.

Verily, verily, I say unto you, He that believeth on me hath everlasting life. I am that bread of life.

Your fathers did eat manna in the wilderness, and are dead.

This is the bread which cometh down from heaven, that a man may eat thereof, and not die.

I am the living bread which came down from heaven: if any man eat of this bread, he shall live for ever: and the bread that I will give is my flesh, which I will give for the life of the world.

The Jews therefore strove among themselves, saying, How can this man give us his flesh to eat?

53: Then Jesus said unto them, Verily, verily, I say unto you, Except ye eat the flesh of the Son of man, and drink his blood, ye have no life in you.

Whoso eateth my flesh, and drinketh my blood, hath eternal life; and I will raise him up at the last day.

For my flesh is meat indeed, and my blood is drink indeed.

He that eateth my flesh, and drinketh my blood, dwelleth in me, and I in him.

As the living Father hath sent me, and I live by

the Father: so he that eateth me, even he shall live by me.

This is that bread which came down from heaven: not as your fathers did eat manna, and are dead: he that eateth of this bread shall live for ever.

It is the spirit that quickeneth; the flesh profiteth nothing: the words that I speak unto you, they are spirit, and they are life.

(1 Corinthians 8)
But meat commendeth us not to God: for neither, if we eat, are we the better; neither, if we eat not, are we the worse.

(1 Corinthians 6)
But he that is joined unto the Lord is one spirit.

Flee fornication. Every sin that a man doeth is without the body; but he that committeth fornication sinneth against his own body.

What? know ye not that your body is the temple of the Holy Ghost which is in you, which ye have of God, and ye are not your own?

For ye are bought with a price: therefore glorify God in your body, and in your spirit, which are God's.

(Romans 8)
There is therefore now no condemnation to them which are in Christ Jesus, who walk not after the flesh, but after the Spirit.

For the law of the Spirit of life in Christ Jesus hath made me free from the law of sin and death.

For what the law could not do, in that it was weak through the flesh, God sending his own Son in the likeness of sinful flesh, and for sin, condemned sin in the flesh:

That the righteousness of the law might be fulfilled in us, who walk not after the flesh, but after the Spirit.

For they that are after the flesh do mind the things of the flesh; but they that are after the Spirit the things of the Spirit.

For to be carnally minded is death; but to be spiritually minded is life and peace.

Because the carnal mind is enmity against God: for it is not subject to the law of God, neither indeed can be.

So then they that are in the flesh cannot please God.

But ye are not in the flesh, but in the Spirit, if so be that the Spirit of God dwell in you. Now if any man have not the Spirit of Christ, he is none of his.

And if Christ be in you, the body is dead because of sin; but the Spirit is life because of righteousness.

But if the Spirit of him that raised up Jesus from the dead dwell in you, he that raised up Christ from the dead shall also quicken your mortal bodies by his Spirit that dwelleth in you.

Therefore, brethren, we are debtors, not to the flesh, to live after the flesh.

For if ye live after the flesh, ye shall die: but if ye through the Spirit do mortify the deeds of the body, ye shall live.

For as many as are led by the Spirit of God, they are the sons of God.

For ye have not received the spirit of bondage again to fear; but ye have received the Spirit of adoption, whereby we cry, Abba, Father.

The Spirit itself beareth witness with our spirit, that we are the children of God:

And if children, then heirs; heirs of God, and

joint-heirs with Christ; if so be that we suffer with him, that we may be also glorified together.

For I reckon that the sufferings of this present time are not worthy to be compared with the glory which shall be revealed in us.

For the earnest expectation of the creature waiteth for the manifestation of the sons of God.

For the creature was made subject to vanity, not willingly, but by reason of him who hath subjected the same in hope, Because the creature itself also shall be delivered from the bondage of corruption into the glorious liberty of the children of God.

For we know that the whole creation groaneth and travaileth in pain together until now.

And not only they, but ourselves also, which have the firstfruits of the Spirit, even we ourselves groan within ourselves, waiting for the adoption, to wit, the redemption of our body.

For we are saved by hope: but hope that is seen is not hope: for what a man seeth, why doth he yet hope for?

But if we hope for that we see not, then do we with patience wait for it.

Likewise the Spirit also helpeth our infirmities: for we know not what we should pray for as we ought: but the Spirit itself maketh intercession for us with groanings which cannot be uttered.

And he that searcheth the hearts knoweth what is the mind of the Spirit, because he maketh intercession for the saints according to the will of God.

And we know that all things work together for good to them that love God, to them who are the called according to his purpose.

For whom he did foreknow, he also did

predestinate to be conformed to the image of his Son, that he might be the firstborn among many brethren.

Moreover whom he did predestinate, them he also called: and whom he called, them he also justified: and whom he justified, them he also glorified.

This scripture let us know that we are living a predestined way of life and therefore we are not capable of doing any good or bad in our own way. If we become one with Holy Spirit in Jesus Christ, we do holiness and if we become one with evil spirit in Satan, we do evil things. If God predestined the way of our life and we are not capable of doing any good or bad in our own way, why God is going to judge us according to our deed? There couldn't be any reason for the punishment or the prize for our deed. Then what is it? The verse 30 of above scripture has the answer. And following scripture backs it up giving more clear understanding.

(2 Timothy 3)
Now in a large house there are not only gold and silver vessels, but also vessels of wood and of earthenware, and some to honor and some to dishonor.

From this, I came to realize that the punishment or the prizes are not the words from God. Those are from human beings originated by the wicked evil mind. That evil mind causes people to struggle in competition breaking the peace for men made success and that evil mind also causes people to cheat, kill, destroy, ... to succeed or to avoid man made punishment.

Men are not interested in what oneself was made and what one's life was predestined for. All these are described as every kinds of greed that leads to death just like we trash a tool when it does not work as it is designed to work. That wicked and self-centered human mind describes God's gathering of the mean tares to burn and clear off as God punishes and the same God's gathering of the precious Sons of God to let them heir the kingdom of heaven as God awards. The judgment is classifying whether it is of the Holy Spirit or the evil spirit, not to punish or award. It could be expressed that way in this world though. It is about straightening up the road as it should be like John the Baptist said. It is to keep the precious ones and to clear away the trash used for the precious ones, not to punish or award. But be careful not to judge which is precious and which is mean. Because we do not know which is precious and which is mean. It is just like an actor playing a leading role of a beggar in this movie could be only a mean extra in that movie according to the writer, not to the actors.

So, being a king or a beggar does not make one precious or mean.

I would say how a king makes his being a king and how a beggar makes his being a beggar makes one precious or mean. So, appreciating one's being oneself holds the key. Because the appreciation builds and the complaint destroys.

The total idea is:

God created this world as he wanted and planned what to accomplish with it from the beginning. When the harvest comes, god separates the precious grain and the mean tares. The precious ones to keep and the mean tares to throw away.

How God distinguishes? By seeing the fruits what it bears. If it bears fruits of Holy Spirit it is Sons of God and if it does not bear fruits and remain as mean tares of evil spirit it is not Son of God, which was told by following scripture.

Matthew 7-16:
You will know them by their fruits. Grapes are not gathered from thorn bushes, nor figs from thistles, are they?

Even so, every good trees bears good fruit; but the bad tree bears bad fruit. A good tree cannot produce bad fruit, nor can a bad tree produce good fruit.

One interesting thing I found is, the men with evil spirit enjoy evil things like violence, adultery, destruction, lie, murder, competition, lousy music, sex movie ...... while the Sons of God with Holy Spirit do not enjoy these.

All these evil things are burning fires and it doesn't look like punishment to the people with evil mind. They just belong to where they are.

However, even the Sons of God would be burnt and have hard time if they do not wake up to discern and mingle in this burning fire. Jesus Christ came to heal and save those burnt and sick Sons of God. But we have to understand if a patient refuses to admit being sick, the doctor cannot figure out the sickness and heal. So is the repent working.

As Jesus Christ said he came to call the sick people not the healthy people, if one thinks oneself is healthy, he does not need Jesus Christ nor does he need to come to Jesus Christ. As we know, many people are sick not even knowing they are sick. Like only those who feel uncomfortable comes to the doctor, only those who feel uncomfortable about own spirit are to come to Jesus Christ to get healed as Jesus Christ said "no one can come to the father if the father doesn't allow him to come."

So, when someone feels uncomfortable about own spirit that means God allowed him to come to God. In other words, any one spiritually in no need does not need to come to Jesus Christ. That does not necessarily mean he is free of sin though.

3. The way God accomplishes

How God accomplishes

When something unreasonable happens, many people including Christians say: **Why the omnipotent and good God let this happen. Nothing is impossible to him. He created this world with words. When he said 'be there light' and the light happened to exist. Then why he just let this happen. He can protect us with only one word. Then why is this? I know he didn't do this. The Satan did this.**

Which results pulling down God's omnipotence.

Or

God made me as he wanted according to his will and he accomplishes his will through me as he want. Whether I want to do something or not, isn't it him that gave me the mind either way. Being accomplished is his will after all.

Which results denying the life God gave.

To believe God created this world and accomplishes as he wants or to believe God created this world and we accomplish as we want on his creation? This is the matter whether we have God or we had God before but not any more. We know we are alive and we know we were born not because we want. So, we know God created us. Then did God created this world and left to somewhere and we are living as we want or God created this world as he wanted and still working on his creation?

I know I do according to my will and in many cases I even forget the existence of God. And still I find myself doing what I want.

Self-contradictory, huh?

I would take the fact that we can neither give birth to ourselves or we can take our lives away from us as evidence of God's existence.

Even if we kill ourselves, it is not us that take the life away from us.

God takes it away. Let's think about this further with what God said.

It is written in Chapter 1 of Genesis as following.

> **Then God said, "Let there be light"; and there was light.**
>
> **And God saw that the light was good; and God separated the light from the darkness.**
>
> **And God called the light day, and the darkness He called night, And there was evening and there was morning, one day.**

As most of us would have the similar idea, what I felt from this word is that God is omnipotent and he can do whatever he wants just by saying "be there" or "be done".

If there is someone who ever wondered about why would it take God one day to create the light, I might be pretty much relieved. Because that is the topic I am going to talk about now. Saying "let there be light" takes one day?

> **Then God said, "Let there be an expanse in the midst of the waters, and let it separate the waters from the waters."**
>
> **And God made the expanse, and separated the waters which were below the expanse from the waters which were above the expanse; and it was so. And God called the expanse heaven. And there was evening and there was morning, a second day.**

As it would have been done it was done as he said and it took the second day. Not like the first day, he said not just "be there ". He planned saying 'let there be' and worked to accomplish it. The verse 7 "God made expanse..." shows this.

Let's see the third day.

Then God said, "Let the waters below the heavens be gathered into one place, and let the dry land appear"; and it was so.

And God called the dry land earth, and the gathering of the waters He called seas; and God saw that it was good.

Then God said, "Let the earth sprout vegetation, plants yielding seed, and fruit trees bearing fruit after their kind, with seed in them, on the earth"; and it was so.

And the earth brought forth vegetation, plants yielding seed after their kind, and trees bearing fruit, with seed in them, after their kind; and God saw that it was good.

And there was evening and there was morning, a third day.

It was done as God said. Let's see what happened the fourth day.

Then God said, "let there be lights in the expanse of the heavens to separate the day from the night, and let them be for signs, and for seasons, and for days and years; and let them be for lights in the expanse of the heavens to give light on the earth"; and it was so.

And God made the two great lights, the greater light to govern the day, ad lesser light to govern the night; He make the stars also.

And God placed them in the expanse of the heavens to give light on the earth, and to govern the day and the night, and to separate the light from the darkness; and God saw that it was good.

And there was evening and there was morning, a fourth day.

These verses give us to more concrete realization that God worked to accomplish. From this day, our timing concept has come into existence. Remember there was God's timing even before this day. This means God's timing concept is different from our human being's timing concept. With that timing concept, one day had passed and the next fifth day opened.

> Then God said, "Let the waters teem with swarms of living creatures, and let birds fly above the earth in the open expanse of the heavens."
>
> And God created the great sea monsters, and every living creature that moves, with which the waters swarmed after their kind, and every winged vird after its kind; and God saw that it was good.
>
> And God blessed them, saying, "Be fruitful and multiply, and fill the waters in the seas, and let birds multiply on the earth."
>
> And there was evening and there was morning, a fifth day.

Just like we put a couple of fish into a aquarium and take care to have them multiply and fill the basin, God created every kind of living things and gave them ability to multiply and fill this world. Let's see the sixth day of creation.

> Then God said, "Let the earth bring forth living creatures after their kind: cattle and creeping things and beasts of the earth after their kind"; and it was so.
>
> And God made the beasts of the earth after their kind, and the cattle after their kind, and everything that creeps on the ground after its kind; and God saw that it was good.
>
> Then God said, "Let us make man in Our image, according to Our likeness; and let them rule over the fish of the sea and over the birds of the sky and

over the cattle and over all the earth, and over every creeping thing that creeps on the earth."

And God created man in His own image, in the image of God He created him, male and female He created them.

And God blessed them; and God said to them, "Be fruitful and multiply, and fill the earth, and subdue it; and rule over the fish of the sea and over the birds of the sky, and over every living thing that moves on the earth."

Then God said, "Behold, I have given you every plant yielding seed that is on the surface of all the earth, and every tree which has fruit yielding seed; it shall be food for you;

and to every beast of the earth and to every bird of the sky and to every thing that moves on the earth which has life, I have given every green plant for food"; and it was so.

And God saw all that He had made, and behold, it was very good. And there was evening and there was morning, the sixth day.

Thus the heavens and the earth were completed, and all their hosts,

And by the seventh day God completed His work which He had done; and He rested on the seventh day from all His work which He had done.

Then God blessed the seventh day and sanctified it, because in it He rested from all His work which God had created and made.

These verses let us know the creation of material beings without life had been completed at the time of creation. God formed every kind of species with these material things and gave them life to accomplish something that can not be accomplished otherwise without life.

So, that we are alive means we are accomplishing God's plan.

At the same time, that we are alive means we are doing God's job.

Because God is accomplishing God's plan gradually through the life God gave us. The controversy between the evolution and creation could be explained this way.

Life, what does it mean?

God made every material differently and that is each material's characteristics. Likewise, the same life that God put in different formation of material happened to grow to have different characteristics of that formation. The life in plant has the plant's characteristics but it doesn't grow and stay just as it was planted at first. Because it was so made that it can not move freely.

The life in an animal has an animal's characteristics. It grows responding to the reaction caused by moving and thinking freely within the boundary allowed to the animal's body. The life in men also has men's characteristics and grows the same way within the boundary allowed to men's most superior body to every living being. Especially, we call man's superior characteristics as character. God made the body first with dust and breathed the life in it to activate the body. According to the bible, the spirit activates the body. Now we can understand what God breathed into the body is the spirit and the spirit is the life.

So, the body is to build the characteristics of life in it, the spiritual character, by moving and thinking freely but in the boundary given to each body.

In other words, without body and free will our spiritual character can not grow. But again, it has the limit of the physical body and became to have different characteristics of life from one kind to another like animal, fish, bird, bacteria, tree and man. Of those bodies, man's most superior body is to have most superior characteristics and that is the character.

As time goes, our body gets old and becomes not a good place for the spirit to reside, then God takes the spirit away from the body and the body can not do anything. That is what we call death, the death of our physical body. Once the spirit leaves the body, the spirit becomes free from the physical body and is still out there somewhere but without a chance to grow any more because it has no body to respond with. So, the time when the spirit is in the body is so important and precious. That is what we call the lifetime. The time while the life, the spirit, is in the body.

God classifies those grown up spirits into two classes as grain and tare according to the deed they made while they were in physical body. That is what the judgment is all about as the bible says any one whosoever lived in this world will be resurrected and stand before the judgment according to each one's deed. As Jesus Christ said we know the tree by the fruit it bears, each one would be judged by their deed. God would classify each spirit by seeing each one's deed that was expressed by the physical behavior of the body while the spirit, the life, was in it. So, we come to know that the fruit means the deed each one made.

Those spirits bearing good fruits are going to wear everlasting holy body not like our present body and live like we live now but in different way, not in the world like this but in the Kingdom of God without tear or pain or even the death. The old body was not perfect so it had tear and pain.

Hence, this new body, the grown-up Holy Spirit, would wear to activate to be a perfect holy one. No tear, no pain and no limit!

It is interesting to see people say: " What is good about living without pain and tear like a dead man? That doesn't look like alive. It's a ghost."

I don't understand why people like to have pain or tear. Sounds like they do not like to live in paradise. Provably it might be due to the misunderstanding of life.

Following scriptures let us know God created everything on different purpose and gave different meaning and different condition.

(Romans 1-20)
For since the creation of the world His invisible attributes, His eternal power and divine nature, have been clearly seen, being understood through what has been made, so that they are without excuse.

Sometimes ago, I had a chance to see a magician performing magic. A girl disappeared all of a sudden and a bird came out replacing the girl.

Handkerchiefs were coming out of the mouth in a row. I tried to figure out how but in vain.

God also creates something out of nothing like the magician does. The difference is God creates the real and magicians create the false.

When God created this world, God set very accurate and strict conditions to every creature to have them comply with and exist only under that condition. So, each creature cannot survive otherwise. For an instance, the temperature has to be below 0'C to get the ice. To have an egg hatched, a certain period of time has to elapse under a certain environment. To have a healthy baby, 10 months of time and an environment like the mother's womb is needed. To have water, oxygen and hydrogen is needed....

Likewise, if somebody wants to play the piano well one has to practice that much. We can not expect a person who didn't even touch the piano play it well. With the same effort, some person plays well and some other persons don't. That's because God gave different reasons for every existence and so each one's condition is different as well.

A magician can make a bird appear in his palm instantly because it is false. But to place a bird on our palm in real we need to meet the God given conditions for it because it is real. To have a real bird appear in our hand we need to keep accurate temperature, maintain good environment and wait certain period of time until the egg be hatched and then move it to our palm when it was hatched.

God designed everything at the time of creation. Just like we design a car before we make. If we do not follow the instruction, we cannot get the exact car of the design.

So is god's creation. Then what's the difference between God and us? God creates from nothing and we make with something god already created.

God creates life and we can't.

Like God breathes the spirit into the body to activate the body, we connect battery to various things like cars, watches, computers and toys to activate those.

We just copy, imitate and learn from God. That's only possible because God made man in the image of God to raise men to have God's character and acquire many Sons of God doing so.

When we look into the design of a car, we find the better-quality car needs more precise tolerance of specification like 1/1,000 of an inch. When man's design is dealing with 1/1,000 of an inch, God's design has "0" tolerance. Then why some eggs hatch an hour early and some eggs hatch an hour late even they are the same kind?

That's just like we drive faster on the paved road and slow down on the gravel road. God's creation has no tolerance but God gave different environment to each one for different purpose.

To a self-centered man, someone who does well could looks like genius and someone who does poor looks like a fool. But to God, everybody is the same. Because they are all just doing God's job. Someone on the paved road runs faster because they have to do god's job imposed on them that way and someone on the gravel road runs slower because they also have to do God's job imposed on them that way to survive. The fact we should know is God placed a life in a certain environment and condition for a certain purpose. We are only trying to survive freely and by doing so, we are accomplishing the job God imposed on each individual that way.

Upon the completion, God takes our life away for another purpose.

Normally, man has 10 months of pregnancy and each kind of animals has different pregnancy period. This means God created so many different environments and conditions to put the life in for so many different purposes.

In old days people tried to make gold with common materials but in vain. This is a good example trying to convert God's design to man's design.

God created everything upon the condition to meet his design and has kept it without a bit of deviation to prove his word is the only truth. We can see it easily through anything surrounding us. For an example, I have never seen an exception that water boils below 100°C. Try million times under the same condition and you will find the water begins to boil exactly at 100°C. Now try it at high up on the mountain. You will see it boils before it reaches 100°C. Million times of experiment will have the same results.

If someone's body temperature were more or less than 36.5°C then the one would know there must be something wrong with him and tries to take care. That becomes possible only because God has kept his word of creation. That's why we know his word is never changing only truth.

Everything in this world from the smallest virus to the big elephant and even the element of a molecule keeps the condition God gave.

The rules we found out by observing God given conditions are the physics, chemistry, mathematics and biology we are learning at school. As time goes by, this knowledge becomes old one and being revised or new theory comes out. That does not mean God's truth was changed. That just means our observation was not perfect. Man found lots of natural laws. The moon moves around the earth once a month. The earth self rotates once a day. Two units of hydrogen and one unit of oxygen makes one molecule of water...etc. This kind of many natural laws are the conditions God set at the time of creation upon God's design and plan.

You never make water with nitrogen, you never see a dog turning into a cat and you never expect a man live without air or water. From the point that God never changes we can see how perfect God is. In that perfect God's design and plan we are allowed to live. Like an egg could be hatched only when kept for certain period of time under the certain environment. God accomplishes only when the conditions and the plans are met, which is not like the magicians performing magic. So, we say God accomplishes and the magicians perform.

When we stay in God's plan and condition God will accomplish, even we do not ask and if we stay out of God's plan and condition God will not accomplish even if we ask. That is just like the water freezes and turn into ice when the temperature goes down to below 0'C regardless we try or not. How hard we ever try, the water wouldn't turn into ice at temperature of 20°C, which is not his condition given for the ice. Jesus Christ taught this with following scriptures.

Matthew 6-32:
For all theses things the Gentiles eagerly seek; for your heavenly Father knows that you need all these things. But seek first His kingdom and His righteousness; and all these things shall be add to you.

Therefore do not be anxious for tomorrow; for tomorrow will care for itself, Each day has enough trouble of its own.

We are inclined to accept vigorously that God would give us when we pray for it. We are not willing to accept even it implies the same meaning that God would not give when needed not to give to accomplish God's will. This explains well that our self-centered beliefs are not toward God.

John the Baptist who baptized Jesus Christ showed an example about what God Centered belief is. He explained as following when his disciples told him that the people who would come to John the Baptist are now going to Jesus Christ as he began to baptize.

John 3-29:
He who has the bride is the bridegroom; but the bridegroom, who stands and hears him, rejoices greatly because of he bridegroom's voice. And so this joy of mine has been made full.
He must increase, but I must decrease.

Like the water freezes when the temperature goes down to God's given condition of below 0°C and boils when the temperature goes up to God's given condition of above 100°C, so is man's well being.

More people will be hurt in the battlefield and there will be peace among harmonious family. Those who live in a dangerous place will have a dangerous life.

I don't mean to waste time for nothing. I find most of us are not interested in straightening our way of living towards God. We go to church saying that we are going to church to work for God but we are not interested in straightening our way of life. Going to church is one way to go forward closer to God but understanding God is another thing. We are only able to understand God when we awake spiritually. Let's take an example.

Going to a good college is one of the most important things for our children. So, we, parents are concerned about it and pray to God to allow our children be accepted at a good college even they are not qualified or not ready for that college. This is just like praying for water freeze and turn into ice even though the temperature is not below 0°C. It is against God's law.

It is not seeking God's righteousness but seeking own greed. I know a young man going to church to pray to be accepted from a good college.

He was attending every church meeting saying all mighty God gives everything even before he asks if he just believes in God and he did not study to prepare for the college.

This is just like praying to God to turn a stone into water. The bible shows lot of things like this as feeding 5,000 people with two fishes and five loafs of bread, getting water by hitting the rock, dividing the sea with a rod and open dry ground through the midst of the sea...etc. God wants us to live like that and put the life in the body to raise the spiritual character to that of Holy Spirit. However, those things happen only to those who have the Holy Spirit. Until the spirit has the character of Holy Spirit, we are supposed to live to comply with God given condition to raise our spirit. That's the way we raise our spiritual character because that is making oneself comply with God's truth and that is our love to God. That is God's way as Jesus Christ said he was doing lots of miracles to show God was working in him. He did that only to show God to people. He didn't do it to teach people to live like that. He taught that if we have the Holy Spirit, we could do the same thing. He did not teach us to live like that. Seek god's righteousness first then God will add everything needed means that. When he does miracle, he said to the public that he was doing it to show God is working in him. God's way is spiritual way. When we pursue something physically in this world, we have to work physically to accomplish it like we study to enter the college. But when we pursue something spiritual, God works in us and accomplishes like God accomplishes a lot of miracles through Jesus Christ. Jesus Christ taught us to free ourselves from the physical body and pursue spiritual things.

As far as we live in this world, we can not take off the heavy burden of doing things in physically law to accomplish but when we die physically the physical law has nothing to do with us and we are free of it.

That is salvation.

Somebody would say "Didn't you just say praying to God without studying is just like trying to turn the water into ice even though the temperature is not below 0°C?"

I said it. As far as you live under the law of physical world you are bound to it. But when you live a spiritual world you are free from the law.

Ask whatever it is! God will accomplish for you.

Then what's the point?

Follow the physical law and struggle to get? Or get easily just by asking spiritually?

I guess many would say I asked spiritually and it was not accomplished. Why was this?

You cannot ask spiritually as far as you live in physical manner.

You can ask spiritually only when you live in spiritual manner.

That you feel like you asked spiritually means not you asked spiritually.

You have to die about your body to ask spiritually.

The dead man does not know whatever happens to the body.

You have to ignore your body like the dead man and that is dying about physical body. And then you can ask spiritually.

Whatever you ask for your body it is not spiritual.

But when you ask whatever for the sake of accomplishing God's will, it is spiritual. God will accomplish it in spiritual way.

I want to point one thing that the law God gave us is not how God accomplishes. It is to train us to have God's character.

It is to let us know what God is, what the truth is.

Think about the world with full of the spirit without God's character. That's hell.

It's about having more Sons of God for the expansion of God himself.

So, I am saying this world is not a real world. It's a world to practice God given law to have the character of God.

Therefore, obeying God's law is righteous. By doing that our character grows in God.

Someone would say again, "What are you talking about? To struggle to obey the law and get or just ask spiritually and get?"

I am saying both.

Obey God's law until you die with all your heart and life to get God's character and when it comes to your physical limit give up your body and ask God spiritually. Then God will give you. The earlier you understand the earlier you can believe and give up your body to ask spiritually and get easily. That's the way you give your heavy burden to God.

When you have God's character you become to believe, whatever you ask it is given to you.

Always remember that there is real limitless world beyond this physical world and don't be afraid of the physical death. That's when your spirit becomes free from your body.

But don't neglect to raise your character because God won't use non-godly spirit for spiritual godly world. Don't kill your body, because through the body you can raise your spiritual character. When you get God's character, God will take your body away from you. You have only limited time. Don't pollute your body because your body is the house of your spirit.

God's truth doesn't discriminate between good or bad person. It is always truth.

If someone who is bad to our eye seeks God's righteousness he will accomplish and if someone who is good to our eye seeks own greed he will not accomplish.

This means the one who looks righteous to our eye is not always righteous but the one who seeks God's righteousness is righteous and the one who looks evil to our eye is not always evil but the one who seeks own greed is evil. Therefore, the one who prays for his own child be accepted from a good college even though he didn't prepare for the college may look righteous to our eye but not to God. It is pursuing one's own greed. It's not righteous to God.

We creatures are living on this never changing God's truth. God allowed us to move freely in God's law and accomplishes only those that meet God's law and leads us to come forward to know God's wisdom and God's character.

This is just like we sow the field with seeds and wait until it grows to bear fruit. We do not take care one by one to sprout. We take care the seedbed as a whole like God gives rain and air to anybody without any discrimination between good and bad to our eye. Each seed sprouts to grow freely and we choose only the ones we want. The good seed sprouts good and the bad seed sprouts bad. We can not make a bad seed sprouts good or good seed sprouts bad. God only can do it but we can distinguish it by what it sprouts.

So is the faith and the faith is not for everyone.

We were also sown in this world to sprout and grow freely. That's the reason why God gave life. And God selects those grown ups to God's character. Those are sons of God. We all are just staying in God and all are accomplishing God's Will regardless it looks good or bad to our eye. Like every fruit is not the same, there are Sons of God and Sons of something else. Every kinds of seeds sprout and grow and when the harvest time comes, God distinguishes by the fruit it bore. Following scriptures tell us about it.

(Mark 4:26)
And He was saying, "The kingdom of God is like a man who casts seed upon th soil; and goes to bed at night and gets up by day, and the seed sprouts up and grows how, he himself does not know.

The soil produces crops by itself; first the blade, then the head, then the mature grain in the head. But when the crop permits, he immediately puts in the sickle, because the harvest has come."

Here the kingdom of God means the kingdom where God's law prevails. In that kingdom, things are only to happen based upon God's law as God planned and designed not like the magicians perform magic. In that kingdom, Sons of God does not feel bound because they have the same character God has. God completed the natural law about material things at the time of creation and thereafter God is now trying to accomplish God's law about living beings, especially human beings, for the expansion of God. God created material things and wanted to fill the material things with the life of god's character to make the creation more valuable like God made man with dust and breathed the life into the body saying "conquer and fill the earth".

Following scriptures also gives the same idea.

(Matthew 13)
He presented another parable to them, saying, The kingdom of heaven may be compared to a man who sowed good seed in his field.

But while men were sleeping, his enemy came and sowed tares also among the wheat, and went away.

But when the wheat sprang up and bore grain, then the tares became evident also.

And the slaves of the landowner came and said to him, 'Sir, did you not sow good seed in your field? How then does it have tares?

And he said to them, 'An enemy has done this!' And the slaves said to him, 'Do you want us, then, to go and gather them up?'

But he said, 'No; lest while you are gathering up the tares, you may root up the wheat with them.

Allow both to grow together until the harvest; and in the time of the harvest I will say to the reapers, First gather up the tares and bind them in bundles to burn them up; but gather the wheat into my barn.

God imposed God's will to everything at the time of creation and likewise God imposed God's will to our spirit residing in our body too. Man's spirit also grows like our body grows. As I mentioned before, the characteristics of the growing spirit is called man's character. Water temperature doesn't go down to 0°C from 70°C all of a sudden to turn into ice. And it must be water to be turned into ice. Likewise, man's spirit also performs good or evil accordingly. But remember it's good or bad to us not to God. Those who God chose as sons of God perform the good and build good characters and classified as Sons of God. Those who God chose as tares perform evil and build evil characters. And God sends those Sons of God to Jesus Christ to teach them.

Jesus Christ says as following.

(Matthew 7)
You will know them by their fruits, Grapes are not gathered from thorn bushes, nor figs from thistles, are they?

Even so, every good tree bears good fruit; but the bad tree bears bad fruit.

A good tree cannot produce bad fruit, nor can a bad tree produce good fruit.

(John 5-29)
and shall come forth; those who did the good deeds to a resurrection of life, those who committed the evil deeds to a resurrection of judgment.

God designed this world upon his willingness and created to fit that design. There is nothing bad to God. Everything is good in God.

Because God is the only good, only truth and God created everything good to God. If a man criticizes somebody, he is doing man's job with man's character to be called man's child and if a man appreciates everything happening to him, he is doing God's job with God's character to be called God's child. Because everything happening in this world is God's job again. So, the appreciation bears precious fruit and criticism or complaint bears bad fruit of mean tares. Remember everything is good to God because all mighty God accomplishes what God wants and that is good. The life is the process for either the good tree grows until bear good fruits of appreciation or the bad tree grows until bear bad fruits of complaints to show each one's being mean tares or grain.

Every children of man are to be judged by their deeds. Because they did man's job to accomplish man's world that man rules despite God gave life to accomplish God's world. Or because they complained God is accomplishing God's world that God rules as God designed at the time of creation. Every children of God will be moved or saved from judgment because they did God's job. How? Their appreciation proves it as written as following.

(Thessalonians 5)
Rejoice always;
pray without ceasing in everything give thanks; for this is God's will for you in Christ Jesus.

(Matthew 7)

Do not judge lest you be judged.

For in the way you judge, you will be judged; and by your standard of measure, it will be measured to you.

And who do you look at the speck that is in your brother's eye, but do not notice the log that is in your own eye?

Or how can you say to your brother, 'Let me take the speck out of your eye,' and behold, the log is in your own eye?

(Matthew 5)

But I say to you, love your enemies, and pray for those who persecute you in order that you may be sons of your Father who is in heaven; for He causes His sun to rise on the evil and the good, and sends rain on the righteous and the unrighteous.

And behold, one came to Him and said, "Teacher, what good thing shall I do that I may obtain eternal life?"

And He said to him, "Why are you asking Me about what is good? There is only One who is good; but if you wish to enter into life keep the commandments."

Even there is nothing bad in God there is something precious and something not precious to God like we do have something precious or not precious. However, God told us no one was born as precious as following.

(Matthew 19)

as it is written, "There is none righteous, not even one;

There is none who understands, There is none who seeks for God;

All have turned aside, together they have become useless;

There is none who does good, There is not even one."

Here "does good" means obey God's law or obey to God. That's because God is good.

So, we, men, are all destined to be judged and classified as not precious and to be burned. Hence, when we cut off a tree in the middle of it and graft a persimmon tree to it, it bears persimmon. The same way, when God (not we) cut off our spirit and grafts God's spirits on to us we become to bear precious fruits of God's child. So, the purpose of our life is to build our spiritual character to that of God's children.

Let's discuss about it with the title of Born Again and Salvation.

Born Again and Salvation

"We got to be born again. Otherwise we can not go into the kingdom of God. So, Let's be born again"

This is very frequently told by many church leaders to encourage the people and also well-grounded to following scriptures.

> **(John 3:3~8)**
> **Jesus answered and said unto him, Verily, verily, I say unto thee,**
> **Except a man be born again, he cannot see the kingdom of God.**
> **Nicodemus saith unto him, How can a man be born when he is old?**
> **Can he enter the second time into his mother's womb, and be born?**
> **Jesus answered, Verily, verily, I say unto thee, Except a man be born of water and of the Spirit, he cannot enter into the kingdom of God.**

That which is born of the flesh is flesh; and that which is born of the Spirit is spirit.

Marvel not that I said unto thee, Ye must be born again.

The wind bloweth where it listeth, and thou hearest the sound thereof, but canst not tell whence it cometh, and whither it goeth: so is every one that is born of the Spirit.

Let's think about our birth.

Were we born ourselves as we wanted? No.

Were we born as a boy or a girl as we wanted? No.

Were we born as white, black or yellow as we wanted? No.

Were we born as a child of a rich man or a poor man as we wanted? No.

Who gave us birth? Did our parents? Yes, to man's children and No to God's children.

God gives birth to God's children and men give birth to men's children.

Like we were not born because we wanted, we can not be born again because we want. Only God gives birth to those God wants. We can not save ourselves. God saves!

As the above scripture says while the first born is born of flesh, the son of man, the second born is born of sprit, the Son of God. The first-born Jesus Christ was son of man and the second born resurrected Jesus Christ was the first fruit of man, the Son of God. Man couldn't do this. So, God came as a man and showed how to do this. That's Jesus Christ.

As God told us, everybody is to be born with spirit. The spirit vitalizes the flesh and the vitalized flesh is called living being. That is oneself.

That spirit is to sleep until it comes to the limit of physical body. And something happens that the flesh can not solve by itself. After struggling desperately, the vitalized flesh is to realize the existence of creator God and asks help in despair. At that time some spiritual things that cannot be explained otherwise happen and solve the problem. Experiencing this unusual happening, the vitalized flesh come to realize it has something in it that it didn't know and begins to wake up to know it is the spirit.

Since the vitalized flesh came to know the spiritual being is bigger, more powerful and last forever, it values the spiritual beings more than the physical beings and begins to pursue spiritual beings. This means the spirit in the body has just woke up from long sleep since the birth when the spirit was planted in our body.

Jesus Christ implied men has never dying spirit in him as following:

(Luke 12:4)
And I say unto you my friends, Be not afraid of them that kill the body, and after that have no more that they can do.

But I will forewarn you whom ye shall fear: Fear him, which after he hath killed hath power to cast into hell; yea, I say unto you, Fear him.

Since the spirit had been grown up in its sleep in the flesh(body), the old spirit has the non-spiritual character like animal.

To grow to have the character of Holy Spirit, the old spirit with the character of flesh has to be removed or cut off in the middle of it.

Just like we transplant the intestines when it is too sick to be cured. Which is expressed as being baptized with water. Now it should be grafted with Spirit of God. That is being born again with Holy Spirit and the Holy Spirit is the Spirit of God. Being one in God means this. This kind of things does not happen to the animal. The reason? God made man only in the image of God.

This is being dead to the body and alive to the spirit. Being grafted with the Holy Sprit, our spiritual life grows to bear good fruit of deed.

This spirit is the precious spirit. The bible tells us about it as following.

John 12-24:
Truly, truly, I say to you, unless a grain of wheat falls into the earth and dies, it remains by itself alone; but if it dies, it bears much fruit.

He who loves his life loses it; and he who hates his life in this world shall keep it to life eternal.

Even though a man was born again to a man of spirit, the spirit feels the same way as before because the spirit still resides in the same body.

The difference is when this man was not born again, he did not know about the spiritual life and live pursuing the physical needs. But after he was born again spiritually, he knows that he is everlasting spiritual life and becomes to live pursuing the spiritual needs instead. In other words, the man of flesh pursues the physical well being and the man of spirit pursues the spiritual well being. The man of flesh builds only his physical character which would not last forever and disappear together with the body when the body was destroyed. As the body dies or be destroyed, the remaining spirit is to be classified as mean tare and burned forever because of its worthless spirit. It is never dying worthless life that's going to be thrown into everlasting lake of fire.

On the other hand, the man of spirit builds his spiritual character and to be classified as Sons of God to wear a new holy body to be revived and saved to live in the kingdom of God. These things are not going to happen until the harvest when the Jesus Christ comes again. Until then people are to live mixed together just like every kind of grasses growing in the field until the harvest.

But we have to remember the flesh is the house of spirit and the spiritual character can grow only when it is in the flesh responding to the physical movements in physical limit. So, our life in this world is important that way. Undergoing a severe ordeal is also a necessary process for the spirit to be a Son of God like the iron stone needs to pass through the hot furnace to be tempered to be good steel.

When we read the bible, we can easily find that the bible is God's word to children of God. So, to speak, God's talking to God's children.

That's why Jesus Christ said everything in parables so others cannot understand. It is not hidden in the closet or safe so others can not see it. It is opened to everybody as Jesus Christ ordered his disciples to propagate the Gospel to the end of the world but only Sons of God understand and follow. Those only can learn from Jesus and those are Sons of God. So propagating God's word is calling lost and sick God's children. Once they hear the voice, they come forward like the lost sheep come forward to the shepherd's voice.

I would say propagating the Gospel is the mission given to us but to make people believe or not is another story. It is in the hand of God. We should rather be very careful to propagate what exactly the Gospel is, not to make the Sons of God be confused. Because Jesus Christ said as the harvest comes the Satan would know their time wouldn't last long and try to deceive the whole world even the Sons of God.

It is interesting to see how the missionary works are being made these days. Because most of them are trying to save more people, all of the people if possible, and to unify the world in one under the name of Jesus Christ as Constantinus the Great of Rome did before. Which is exactly the opposite of what Jesus Christ said. He said he brought fire and division instead of peace and unification. We can not alter the way God put in front of us.

The prophet Isaiah also said anybody who is away from God can not understand God's word because God blinded him.

Anyway, the bible says it's only for God's children.

John 6:65
And he said, Therefore said I unto you, that no man can come unto me, except it were given unto him of my Father.

Thessalonians II 3:2
And that we may be delivered from unreasonable and wicked men: for all men have not faith.

Now we know we have spirit in us. Then how can we live by spirit or grow our spiritual character to have the character of God to be called Sons of God? It is only possible by killing one's own physical desire and put the Holy Spirit instead in that place and let it grow to bear fruit of good behavior to God not to us.

In Genesis it says:

Genesis 6:1
And it came to pass, when men began to multiply on the face of the earth, and daughters were born unto them,

That the sons of God saw the daughters of men that they were fair; and they took them wives of all which they chose.

And the LORD said, My spirit shall not always strive with man, for that he also is flesh: yet his days shall be an hundred and twenty years.

From this time, the spirit of God, the Holy Spirit, wouldn't be with men and men could not know about the spirit. After thousands of years this Holy Spirit came down upon God's son Jesus Christ as a dove with a voice as following.

"As soon as Jesus was baptized, he came up out of the water. Then heaven was opened to him, and he saw the Spirit of God coming down like a dove and lighting on him. And then a voice said from heaven, "This is my own Son, with whom I am well pleased." (Matthew 3-16)

God prophesied this already through the prophet Isiah 600 years ago before Jesus Christ's coming as following.

Isaiah 42:1
Behold my servant, whom I uphold; mine elect, in whom my soul delighteth; I have put my spirit upon him: he shall bring forth judgment to the Gentiles.

Jesus Christ also said witnessing himself as:

Jesus answered him: "I am the way, I am the truth, I am the life; no one goes to the Father except by me." (John 14-6)

So, born again does not necessarily mean the spirit has been saved.
Born again means the spirit is now grafted to Holy Spirit and has a chance to grow to be Son of God. Even the born- again spirit has to grow

to bear good fruit to be saved. Because God said the trees without fruit will be cut and burned. Now, let's move to another scripture.

John 5:24
Verily, verily, I say unto you, He that heareth my word, and believeth on him that sent me, hath everlasting life, and shall not come into condemnation; but is passed from death unto life.

Looks like asking someone a question of "Have you been saved?" and seeing how he responds to that question became a common procedure to know if one has firm belief to God.

If one answers "Yes, I have been saved" then the one is regarded as a firm believer and if one says "I do not know." then the one is regarded as not a firm believer toward God.

This is called the conviction of salvation and every Christian is requested to have this conviction of salvation because it is said to represent the amount of one's belief.

Let's think about this. This idea came from following scriptures.

Romans 10:10
For with the heart man believeth unto righteousness; and with the mouth confession is made unto salvation.

I experienced a preacher asking me "Do you believe in Jesus Christ? If so, then say yes."

He continued soon after I said Yes,

"Now since you have confessed with your mouth that Jesus Christ is your personal savior you have been saved being moved from death to life just now. So, do not doubt a bit that you have eternal life and have peace in mind" implying that I just got the eternal life which I didn't have.

I would ask, even if I have the eternal life, what is good about having the eternal life if the eternal life suffers forever? I don't think it is salvation.

We have the eternal life, the spirit, in us already as we discussed before.

The salvation is saving this eternal life from suffering which is due to the imperfect body in this world and due to the non-Godly character, that wouldn't fit in the coming spiritual world.

We can not get the perfect body by ourselves unless God gives us just like we could not come to this world in this imperfect body and just like we can not change our imperfect body to perfect body even one stripe of our hair.

So, every effort to save oneself from this imperfect body will fail if it's not by belief. Someone would say even the believer dies.

That's right.

Even the believer dies, the physical death, but they believe the word of God that God will raise them in perfect holy body because of their belief just like God raised Jesus Christ for his belief toward God which is written in the Bible. God accomplished what God planned on Jesus Christ and Jesus Christ believed it.

So, Jesus Christ is the first ripe fruit. The same way God would accomplish what we believe. If we believe eternal life in perfect holy body God will accomplish eternal life in perfect holy body and if we don't believe eternal life in perfect body God will accomplish something else what we believe and the eternal life will suffer in imperfect body forever.

So, the word "Your belief will save your spirit" stands.

Many people say salvation is so easy to get.

They say "Just say I believe in Jesus Christ, then you are saved. It's that easy. It doesn't cost you anything. Why don't you just say yes and live in peace?"

But the bible says it is not. Why?

Let's see why.

As we discussed before, believing in God is the only condition for our salvation as Jesus told us "your belief will save you".

Jesus Christ said:

Matthew 5:44
But I say unto you, Love your enemies, bless them that curse you, do good to them that hate you, and pray for them which despitefully use you, and persecute you; That ye may be the children of your

Father which is in heaven: for he maketh his sun to rise on the evil and on the good, and sendeth rain on the just and on the unjust.

Do you believe this? He told us:

Matthew 10:36
And a man's foes shall be they of his own household.

Together with above words we can easily induce that our wife, husband, sons, daughters, father and mother would be our own foes and we should love them.

However, what I see is the majority does not love these enemies. The majorities do not love their husband, wife and divorce or fight each other. It's hard to see a normal family these days. Each one loves oneself more than these enemies God gave them and split themselves into pieces to avoid suffering from each other. This is evading God's training.

The husband loves oneself more than his wife and divorces, husband and wife love themselves more than their parents and persecute the old parents, parents love their own child and try to kick out the daughters-in-law or sons-in-law. The children ignore their parents and pursue their own pleasure embarrassing their parents, which is just the opposite of the word God told us to do. That is disobedience.

God said these enemies are the crosses given to us to carry.
It's written in the bible as:

Matthew 10:37
He that loveth father or mother more than me is not worthy of me: and he that loveth son or daughter more than me is not worthy of me.

And he that taketh not his cross, and followeth after me, is not worthy of me.

He also said as following

Matthew 10:39
He that findeth his life shall lose it: and he that
loseth his life for my sake shall find it.

Can you kill yourself for another life? I know many kills oneself in desperate to escape from this world not in hope for another life.

The bible says to try to give up your life to get another life and even hate your life to long for another eternal life which Jesus let us know.

Do you believe that?

That's why I say it is not going to be easy to get salvation. It is not going to be only very difficult but also it is going to be very dangerous. For it is a matter of life or death.

However, it is so much precious that one would invest all of one's possession to pursue as written in the bible as:

Matthew 13:44
Again, the kingdom of heaven is like unto treasure
hid in a field; the which when a man hath found,
he hideth, and for joy thereof goeth and selleth all
that he hath, and buyeth that field.
Again, the kingdom of heaven is like unto a
merchant man, seeking goodly pearls: Who, when
he had found one pearl of great price, went and sold
all that he had, and bought it.

I would say it is like exchanging our present corruptible life with the everlasting life in the future. That's why the salvation can not be made without belief. Because nobody would even try to give up own life without belief that he has eternal spiritual life in him and he is going to save that life exchanging with the physical corruptible life.

Those who does not know this and kill oneself in desperate to escape from this world would also be burned in fire for sure. Because these people also did not believe what God says.

The faith is to believe what God said. We can measure the size of our faith by checking how much do we believe God's words without doubt.

As the bible says "God reveals from faith to faith", I know that God accomplishes as to one's belief. As far as the belief is concerned, I agree with this preacher who asked to confess with my mouth. What I want to point is not what this preacher said to me. It is whether my belief toward Jesus Christ is really the belief that I confessed with my mouth.

We could understand what the problem would this be if we look back upon what Peter the most beloved disciple of Jesus Christ did when Jesus Christ had been arrested to be crucified. He denied that he is one of the disciples three times before the cock crew after a couple of hours even he swore to Jesus Christ that he would follow even to the death.

Romans 3:20
Therefore by the deeds of the law there shall no flesh be justified in his sight: for by the law is the knowledge of sin.

But now the righteousness of God without the law is manifested, being witnessed by the law and the prophets; Therefore we conclude that a man is justified by faith without the deeds of the law.

As above scripture let us know, our deeds do not save us.

But when we think that the deed is the fruit of the spirit and the spirit is going to be saved or judged, we come to understand that we could know whether someone would be saved or judged by seeing the deed not by the confession one makes with mouth.

To explain it reverse, our belief towards God leads us to grow to have good character of Holy Spirit and that fact saves us from judgment. Confession is accepting we need to be cured like the patient comes to the doctor to be cured. Deed is only the fruit of spiritual character that God would see to it to distinguish grain from mean tare. Apostle Paul let us know that the belief makes our belief grow and when the belief reaches to the belief we confessed with our mouth, that belief in Jesus Christ gives us wisdom to save ourselves as following. And the wisdom is the word of God.

Romans 1:17
For therein is the righteousness of God revealed from faith to faith: as it is written, The just shall live by faith.

Timothy II 3:15
And that from a child thou hast known the holy scriptures, which are able to make thee wise unto salvation through faith which is in Christ Jesus.

So, our faith grows not by saying that we believe in Jesus Christ but by believing in Jesus Christ. And believing in Jesus Christ means believe what he told us and follow it.

But, because of the fact that the belief grows by belief, so many people are inclined to believe and follow anybody for no reason like the blind following the blind. There should be some good reason to believe and to follow. That's why we need to dig the bible and study. By doing so, the Holy Spirit in us adds faith to our faith and our faith grows.

Let's remember that our spirit grows in Jesus Christ to have the character of Holy Spirit and that it does not turn into a good spirit all of a sudden just by saying with our mouth that we accept Jesus Christ as our personal savior. But every firm believer accepts and says Jesus Christ is their personal savior. Those with great faith would save oneself from the big distress with great wisdom and those with small faith would save oneself from small troubles with small wisdom and fall into big troubles when the big distress comes.

As we discussed in the previous chapter about how God accomplishes, God does not accomplish like the magicians perform cheating, the magic. When we believe without a doubt that what we believe is God's will, then God gives us wisdom to get it. The belief without any doubt does not come by just saying we believe. It comes only by grafting the Holy Spirit to our spirit. It grows to understand God's will and understanding God makes us believe more and leads us to firm belief.

When we recall God is not for the dead but for the alive, we could understand that we believe in God not only to save our spirit after our body is destroyed but also to save ourselves from every kind of troubles caused by the sin in this world.

In a word our faith towards God means we are having God's limitless wisdom to save ourselves from every trouble. The final destination of the faith is saving our spirit from endless trouble and pain.

Everybody has different motives to come to believe in Jesus Christ.

Like the bad man who came to believe when he was nailed together with the Jesus Christ. Or like the disciple Thomas who believed after he inserted his finger into Jesus Christ's side. Or like the Apostle Paul who came to realize God's existence and believed due to the strange experience that happened when he was on the way to Damascus to bring the Christians bound to Jerusalem.

Like these people, every believer has some kind of experience to go the way of believers. But the size of each individual's faith is different, which means every faith is different.

We should be very watchful about our faith because even Peter, the most beloved disciple, who learned and saw what Jesus Christ did for three years did not know his own faith and denied Jesus Christ three times in fear of death.

I found something common among them, which is still common in this modernized world.

We come to find or realize the existence of God only through each one's physical limit. Like the one who is about to undergo a dangerous operation, the one whose tire has just popped out on the highway, the one who has a trouble child and does not know what to do and the one who is about to executed… Not everyone does though. Only those God chosen Sons of God experience God.

Jesus Christ said as following.

Matthew 5:3
Blessed are the poor in spirit: for theirs is the kingdom of heaven.

Blessed are they that mourn: for they shall be comforted.

Blessed are the meek: for they shall inherit the earth.

Blessed are they which do hunger and thirst after righteousness: for they shall be filled.

Blessed are the merciful: for they shall obtain mercy.

Blessed are the pure in heart: for they shall see God.

Blessed are the peacemakers: for they shall be called the children of God.

Blessed are they which are persecuted for righteousness' sake: for theirs is the kingdom of heaven.

Blessed are ye, when men shall revile you, and persecute you, and shall say all manner of evil against you falsely, for my sake.

When the disciple Thomas said he wouldn't believe if he does not put his finger into Jesus Christ's side and see, Jesus Christ said those who did not see but believed are more blessed as following.

John 20:27
Then saith he to Thomas, Reach hither thy finger, and behold my hands; and reach hither thy hand, and thrust it into my side: and be not faithless, but believing.

And Thomas answered and said unto him, My Lord and my God.

Jesus saith unto him, Thomas, because thou hast seen me, thou hast believed: blessed are they that have not seen, and yet have believed.

God gave us life to move and think freely to have our spirit grow to the character of Holy Spirit. In next chapter, I am going to confess my faith based upon my bible understanding under the title of Free Will that is causing a lot of controversy among believers.

Following is the scripture that represents my understanding about Free Will. It says:

Proverbs 16:1
The preparations of the heart in man, and the answer of the tongue, is from the LORD.

All the ways of a man are clean in his own eyes; but the LORD weigheth the spirits.

Commit thy works unto the LORD, and thy thoughts shall be established. The LORD hath made all things for himself: yea, even the wicked for the day of evil.

Every one that is proud in heart is an abomination to the LORD:

though hand join in hand, he shall not be unpunished.

By mercy and truth iniquity is purged: and by the fear of the LORD men depart from evil.

When a man's ways please the LORD, he maketh even his enemies to be at peace with him.

Better is a little with righteousness than great revenues without right.

A man's heart deviseth his way: but the LORD directeth his steps.

Most of the brethren in Jesus Christ say: "Since God is good, God manages every good thing and since the Satan is bad every evil thing are managed by Satan."

But above scripture says God created everything. Even the evil people were created proper for the evil days, and when the time comes God will gather every evil people together with Satan and lock up in the second death. God created everyone properly for God's use and each one lives in God's will as given to each one as God wants. Let's see my confession on this through next chapter.

4. Free Will

Following is my confession about what I found and made three years ago when God gave me the pleasure of understanding the bible and prompted me to write this book.

I hope everybody could taste the same pleasure I had.

Since God allowed each one different size of faith and different kind of benefits according to God's necessity, it is quite natural that each one understand the same Words of God differently. In that sense I do not intend to force anybody to accept my faith.

I just hope readers have a good chance to examine own faith to find the faith God allowed and go the way God gave to each one.

———•—•—•———

My Confession

I believe God created everything as God wanted and so God accomplishes as God planned. Therefore, I know what I am saying now is not what I am saying but God made me appropriately and is accomplishing his will through me.

To men's eye, Pharaoh the king of Egypt did evil things to the Israel people but the bible says God made his mind hard and let him do it to spread the name of God to the world.

Just like Pharaoh did God's job not knowing he was doing that, I know God is doing God's job through me. The only thing that I do not know is what God is doing for.

Somebody would say, "Then you are not alive but just a robot."

And would also say,

"Do you believe God to be a robot? I believe to be forgiven of my sin and save my life."

You fool, why don't you know we are free only in God and if God does not allow us, we can not even come to believe. If someone put the only bridge in front of me and I have no choice other than passing over the bridge not deviating to the right or left, then am I a robot? We could be alive and free only in God. Just like the ice turns into water as soon as the temperature goes up above 0'C which is God's will, we die as soon as we are out of God and do not comply with God's will.

In God there is Life and Freedom, and out of God there is death and bondage.

Can you live without your heart beating regularly? Then who gave your heartbeat? God did. You can live as far as your heart continues beating and you are free as much as your heart beating.

How can we, the creature, understand why God make one-person blind from the birth and the other person a king? All these mean God is accomplishing God's will through these people. We did not come to this world as a blind or a king because we wanted. That we are living in this world means we are in God already.

The problem is we do not believe we are in God.

Each one was made appropriately to each one and collaborates each other to accomplish one ultimate God's will. And God is the only truth. That is Good.

Everything in this world does not go as you want because God make this world as God wanted. God did not make this world as you wanted. So, don't bother yourself to accomplish your own will. You may feel like you are accomplishing your own will but that's only because what God did is what you like. Once you believe you are accomplishing your own will, then you are getting closer to death. That's because you are accomplishing your own will when you are supposed to accomplish God's will as he planned. And you are not going to be needed in his plan any more.

We all were sent over to this world to accomplish God's will. So, that you believe you accomplished your will means you admit you committed sin against God. So, denying oneself is good and pursuing oneself is sin. And everybody is dying pursuing own will.

That's what bible says as:

Romans 6:23
The wages of sin is death.

We better be careful not to be haughtily minded and say: "I will accomplish God's Will."

You can not make even one stripe of your hair white or black and you can not stop your heartbeat even for a second. Because you are just like the dust or the fog that would disappear after a short period of time and can not be found nowhere.

Why don't you know what you are doing right now is God's job?

You don't know why God made you.

Whether to make you the president of the United States or a king like the Pharaoh or a beggar like the Lazarus. How can we measure the depth of God? How could we know whether God would prearrange my son blind from the birth? Isn't that why every parent worry about their babies to be born newly?

Our creator God told us not to swear as following.

Matthew 5:34
But I say unto you, Swear not at all; neither by heaven; for it is God's throne: Nor by the earth; for it is his footstool: neither by Jerusalem; for it is the city of the great King. Neither shalt thou swear by thy head, because thou canst not make on hair white or black.

But let your communication be, Yea, yea; Nay, nay: for whatsoever is more than these cometh of evil.

That's because God is the only one who accomplishes God's will.

He is the one who manages everything upon his will.

There are two kinds of people among those who think they are achieving with their own will.

Ones are those who are in God and always appreciate to know that whatever they do it is God's job. They never fail and always accomplish because everything is God's job and God accomplishes everything. They know it could be dirty and mean job or it could be nice and clean job. They know it is their job and God's job also, so they are free from the law which God prepared for the disobedient people, but still they are fulfilling the law because they are in God. They can appreciate because they know they never fail and their life is always achieving and successful regardless of it's being miserable, poor or rich. Because they are accomplishing what God had planned upon them and it would never fail.

The other ones are those who do not realize God made them and think they are doing their job with their own will. Since these people do not believe they are in God, their job could not be God's job and the results are not going to be the one they want. They appreciate when the results come out as they like and complain when it was not like what they want.

God prepared the law to judge if these people did God's job with the life God gave them to do God's job. Since they do not think they are in God they are not free from the law. They worry how could they free themselves from this snare.

So, the appreciation is obeying God and the complaint is disobeying God.

Those who are in God appreciate and look for God's will more to get more.

While those who are not in God does not know God and can not pursue God's will.

They hear but do not understand. They see but do not know what it is. They are only eager to look for their own which does not exist and loose even what they have as the bible says.

Regardless of people's being this or that, God accomplishes like God rains not only to the good people but also to the bad people to our eye. Giving the air and let the people breathe it regardless of their being good or bad, God is righteous.

It's us that are binding ourselves to our own greed only to accomplish own will and bring oneself to the law to suffer.

Talking in the way of this world, the bad people know they have the law to keep but since the law troubles them they try to hide and avoid punishment. But still the law troubles them and finally they go to jail, loose the freedom.

When we are in God, God's will accomplish through us. We do not realize the law and so we are free from the law. When we are not in God, God takes our freedom away and put us under the law. Jesus Christ said none is righteous.

Even though we know accomplishing God's Will is Good, our canal mind does not want to stay in God and try to accomplish own will which do not even exist. This evil mind puts us under the law like the law puts the criminal in the jail taking the freedom away and finally takes our life away like a condemned criminal being executed.

Jesus Christ said, not believing the creator God is sin. He also said doing God's job is to believe in God.

Those who believe in God are already living in the Kingdom of God.

Because Kingdom of God is where God's will accomplish. Since God's will is one's own will in there, everything accomplishes without fail to those who believe they are in God. But those who do not believe in God are living in the hell already even they are living in the same place because nothing but only God's will accomplish.

Since their will is not God's will, they come to find they accomplished nothing.

They struggle to accomplish and finally die. So, I would call it as Kingdom of Death or Kingdom of Void. That's why Jesus said the Kingdom of Heaven cannot be said to be here or there, it is among you.

I would like to point one thing here.

If we believe we are in God, then we are living in the Kingdom of God. Then why do we still have pain and tear?

God put our spirit in imperfect body to train our spirit and to let us know what it is living in the hell to make our spirit long for the painless eternal life in the Kingdom of God.

We still have pain and tear because of that imperfect body but when the time comes, God is going to wear us with perfect Holy Body and we wouldn't be bordered by the desire of body. We are going to live in perfect peace without pain and tear. So even the born-again people who grew up to have the Holy Spirit will have to wait until that time.

Jesus Christ came to let us know this telling to spread the good news about the "Kingdom of God".

One would say, "So I know I was born again and I am in heaven now. But you know I forget the very next day that I was born again and pursue my bodily desire again.

I repeat this. Then am I going back and forth between heaven and hell?"

Remember this world is not real. It looks like real but it's not. Just like a magician performs magic, everything disappears the next second.

Looks like we have parents, sons, daughters, house, gold, good position... But where can you find them after a certain period of time? You don't even find yourself. You find yourself dead, not only yourself but also everything. You are disappeared. It's not a real world!

We are just passing this fake world practicing our faith to God. And the time for the real world hasn't come yet.

We are living the fake world, the hell. (I am going to discuss about this hell in detail later in the chapter of Resurrection and Salvation.) We are on the field just like a racer practicing and waiting for the real game.

Nobody knows who would win or loose until the game is over.

Likewise, nobody knows whether one would be saved or not until the harvest. But we know what to do to win the game. Only practice!

The same way we have to practice our faith to God to win the salvation and live in the real world. That's what we are repeating.

When you practice stretching the left leg more, then you are going to use that technique at the game to win. Just like that, when you practice something in this world spiritually you are going to use that in the real world too. But when you practice physical things you can not use that technique in the real world because the bible says the real world is not a physical world. It's a spiritual world.

You are not taking with you what you've earned to the game.

Like the car, gold or any possession.

Same way, you are not taking those things to the heaven.

But again, you are taking what you have practiced to heaven for your spirit to use it like the player would use the skill he had practiced. That's what the bible says as:

Matthew 6:19

Lay not up for yourselves treasures upon earth, where moth and rust doth corrupt, and where thieves break through and steal:

But lay up for yourselves treasures in heaven, where neither moth nor rust doth corrupt, and where thieves do not break through nor steal:

For where your treasure is, there will your heart be also.

Our heart is there where we have invested and so is our practice. If we practice the spiritually, we are going to long for the spiritual world more.

Then what can we practice for our spirit? Spiritual things!

Pray, appreciate, love, sacrifice....

Practice how to pray and learn how to communicate with God. That's how you get the power of God. That way you come to understand God.

Practice appreciation to learn how to make God's accomplishment to your own. That way you can be one with God and satisfied to be happy.

Practice to love even the enemy. That is learning how to show your love to God. Because every happening is God's job and that way you show your love to God. Practice sacrifice to learn how to help God accomplish God's will. That way you know you are doing God's job.

Studying the bible is like joining the camp to practice and win.

Since practicing God's will is practicing killing oneself, no one other than the born-again people would like to believe the word of God in Jesus and do this. Because those who were not born again can not believe what God said and they would not practice killing themselves to get the real world which looks not real to them because it's not visible.

108

It looks even stupid to them.

That's why the scripture "Your belief will save your spirit" stands.

Bound in the physical body, these spiritually born-again people practice their belief towards God in pain and tear due to the imperfect body like the racers practice in pain and tear.

Since the racers practice for the physical things, they win the physical things.

Same way, those who practice spiritual things win the spiritual world of Kingdom of God. When the body is destroyed, they rest doing nothing until the harvest and be resurrected in a holy body like Jesus Christ revived to live in peace forever without pain or tear like an angel in the heaven.

Thanks, God, for revealing yourself to us.

Before, we were not born again and we were imprisoned in our body. We worked on the bodily desire struggling with the heavy burden the body put on us.

Now after we were born again, we came to know God accomplishes through us and we have nothing to accomplish but being made by God. We are now able to take off our heavy burden of accomplishing our bodily desire and rest leaving that heavy burden unto God. Only God's will be accomplished. Amen.

Jesus Christ asks to have only the spiritual desire, which is light and easy as following.

Matthew 11:28
Come unto me, all ye that labour and are heavy laden, and I will Give you rest. Take my yoke upon you, and learn of me; for I am meek and lowly In heart: and ye shall find rest unto your souls.
For my yoke is easy, and my burden is light.

Jesus Christ explained it as following.

Matthew 6:25

Therefore I say unto you, Take no thought for your life, what ye shall eat, or what ye shall drink; nor yet for your body, what ye shall put on. Is not the life more than meat, and the body than raiment?

Behold the fowls of the air: for they sow not, neither do they reap, nor gather into barns; yet your heavenly Father feedeth them. Are ye not much better than they?

Which of you by taking thought can add one cubit unto his stature?

And why take ye thought for raiment? Consider the lilies of the field, how? They do not sow, or reap, or gather into barns, yet your heavenly Father feeds them.

And yet I say unto you, That even Solomon in all his glory was not arrayed like one of these. Wherefore, if God so clothe the grass of the field, which to day is, and to morrow is cast into the oven, shall he not much more clothe you, O ye of little faith?

Therefore take no thought, saying, What shall we eat? or, What shall we drink? or, Wherewithal shall we be clothed? (For after all these things do the Gentiles seek:) for your heavenly Father knoweth that ye have need of all these things.

But seek ye first the kingdom of God, and his righteousness; and all these things shall be added unto you. Take therefore no thought for the morrow: for the morrow shall take thought for the things of itself. Sufficient unto the day is the evil thereof.

Let's take pity for those unbelievers.

Those with heavy burden of accomplishing one's own desire were not made different from us. We men are all made with the same soil and destined to be burned and return to soil.

The only difference is, with the same soil, God made one precious to do the precious job and the other one ungracious to do God's ungracious job.

We have nothing to be proud of ourselves about our doing God's precious job because it's not us that are doing it. God does. So, the glory is only with God. Only God's compassion accomplishes.

The righteous God made everybody disobedient by giving the fruit of good and evil and put everybody under the judgment of death.

And said with compassion to the people who are destined to die as "Anybody who would believe that Jesus Christ is the Son of God would come to God and get the key to heaven and save oneself."

For the sake of God's only son and for the glory for him, God set up a rule to kill anybody who does not respect his only son Jesus Christ just like everyone respect God.

Jesus Christ forgave anybody who would come to him for the life of his spirit, and those forgiven respects Jesus Christ and follow him to save his life of spirit.

How could there be compassion where there is no sin!

God's compassion added for the benefit of the people by giving the law and making the sin more sinful. Those forgiven more loved Jesus Christ more than those forgiven less.

As the sin gets more serious more people came to Jesus Christ for forgiveness and respected more because they were forgiven the death penalty. As the sin played the king in death, the mercy played the king in righteousness and let the Jesus Christ be the first-born Son of many sons to be. As we admit Jesus Christ as the Son of God, Jesus Christ will recognize us as his sheep and lead us to save from the sin like a shepherd leads his sheep saving them from wolves

The next is to believe Jesus Christ was alive from dead. By doing so we are having the promise of resurrection that God would raise us from the dead like God raised Jesus Christ from the dead.

Being the truth of God's Will is like this, when we keep God's law God would recognize us as Sons of God like a shepherd recognizes his sheep. But those saying they know God and do not keep God's law are liars. They are adding sin to their sin by lying to God. Anyone who knows God should keep God's law and it is said by following scripture.

John I 3:22
And whatsoever we ask, we receive of him, because we keep his commandments, and do those things that are pleasing in his sight.

And this is his commandment, That we should believe on the name of his Son Jesus Christ, and love one another, as he gave us commandment.

And he that keepeth his commandments dwelleth in him, and he in him.

And hereby we know that he abideth in us, by the Spirit which he hath given us.

Beloved, believe not every spirit, but try the spirits whether they are of God:because many false prophets are gone out into the world.

Hereby know ye the Spirit of God: Every spirit that confesseth that Jesus Christ is come in the flesh is of God:

And every spirit that confesseth not that Jesus Christ is come in the flesh Is not of God: and this is that spirit of antichrist, whereof ye have heard that should come; and even now already is it in the world.

As Apostle Paul said we creature were made subject to vanity, not willingly but as God reasoned it. And God subjected the same in hope because we creature also shall be delivered from the bondage of corruption into the glorious liberty of the children of God.

We have to know one thing that this true freedom was allowed only to those God had chosen and those who believe in Jesus Christ.

Knowing that we are just weak creatures God had mercy on us to show God's will in advance through the bible and let us not be hopeless in despair or afraid. Let's take off all the heavy burdens. Leave it to God and stay in peace. God will accomplish.

We feel like we are alive because we are moving around. But everything we see is vanity returning to the soil and disappears. That shows us we are already in death as Jesus Christ said to his disciple as following.

Matthew8-22

And another of his disciples said unto him, Lord, suffer me first to go and bury my father. But Jesus said unto him, Follow me; and let the dead bury their dead.

Jesus Christ concluded the unbelievers as dead and he is asking us not to set the goal in this world of death because it is void and vanity.

He is asking us to look for the Kingdom of God instead.

The depth of God's wisdom and the abundance of knowledge, who could ever measure it!

Who could ever find his way!

Who knew his mind and who could teach him?

Who could dare to say "I gave him first and now I am going to get it back from him"?

We all are just getting from him.

He reasoned everything. He made everything and everything goes back to him.

Glory shall be with God forever.

Apostle Paul showed that it is God, not us, that accomplishing as following.

Romans 9:10

And not only this; but when Rebecca also had conceived by one, even by our father Isaac; (For the children being not yet born, neither having done any good or evil, that the purpose of God according to election might stand, not of works, but of him that calleth;) It was said unto her, The elder shall serve

the younger. As it is written, Jacob have I loved, but Esau have I hated.

What shall we say then? Is there unrighteousness with God?

God forbid.

For he saith to Moses, I will have mercy on whom I will have mercy, and I will have compassion on whom I will have compassion.

So then it is not of him that willeth, nor of him that runneth, but of God that showeth mercy.

For the scripture saith unto Pharaoh, Even for this same purpose have I raised thee up, that I might show my power in thee, and that my name might be declared throughout all the earth.

Therefore hath he mercy on whom he will have mercy, and whom he will he hardeneth. Thou wilt say then unto me, Why doth he yet find fault? For who hath resisted his will?

Nay but, O man, who art thou that repliest against God? Shall the thing formed say to him that formed it, Why hast thou made me thus?

Hath not the potter power over the clay, of the same lump to make one vessel unto honour, and another unto dishonour?

What if God, willing to show his wrath, and to make his power known, endured with much longsuffering the vessels of wrath fit to destruction:

And that he might make known the riches of his glory on the vessels of mercy, which he had afore prepared unto glory,

We do not know whether God made us precious to do God's precious job and inherit the Kingdom of God with glory or not precious to do God's mean job and be burnt like trash after use. But I know God accomplishes what we believe in God.

Following shows us about it.

Matthew 17:14
And when they were come to the multitude, there came to him a certain man, kneeling down to him, and saying, Lord, have mercy on my son: for he is a lunatic, and sore vexed: for ofttimes he falleth into the fire, and oft into the water. And I brought him to thy disciples, and they could not cure him.

Then Jesus answered and said, O faithless and perverse generation, how long shall I be with you? how long shall I suffer you? bring him hither to me.

And Jesus rebuked the devil; and he departed out of him: and the child was cured from that very hour.

Then came the disciples to Jesus apart, and said, Why could not we cast him out?

And Jesus said unto them, Because of your unbelief: for verily I say unto you, If ye have faith as a grain of mustard seed, ye shall say unto this mountain, Remove hence to yonder place; and it shall remove; and nothing shall be impossible unto you.

Then what is faith? Apostle Paul says:

Hebrews 11:1
Now faith is the substance of things hoped for, the evidence of things not seen.

Now we know God accomplishes through us what we believe and make us precious or not precious according to our belief. When we believe in God, we are going to be God's precious one and when we believe something else, we are going to be something else not precious.

Someone would say "I believe in God and I murdered somebody. Am I still precious?"

I would say this man is lying. These are those that saying "I believe, I really believe" and do not know what they believe. As Jesus Christ told us belief without deed is dead belief. People in God fulfill the law not knowing even what the law is, like the good people fulfill the law not knowing there is law about it. The good people fulfill the law because they are good not because they try to observe the law.

Brothers! Do not follow this world. Be renewed and transformed to know what God's whole goodness is. Do not think more than given and behave wisely with as much belief as given to you. As we have many limbs in our body every limb is not the same and each limb works their own different job. Likewise, we are all given different benefits from God. Shouldn't we work as much as given to us? If you were given teaching then teach, if servicing, then serve, if ruling then rule diligently, if relief work then relieve sincerely, and if authority then authorize dignity...

Knowing that everything is God's job how can you judge others? Don't you know we all are doing God's job? Know that you are judging God by judging someone's job. The same way, you should know that you are looking down upon God when you look down upon others. Know that you love God when you love your enemy because God made them to do something you don't know. So, loving your enemy proves your love to God.

To the people in God, nothing is bad because God is holy and God made everything.

Anybody who would think something is bad is saying God is bad and he is not in God.

There couldn't be judgment for the people in God because they are doing God's job.

How could God judge those who does God's job. There is nothing bad in God because God is good. Anybody in God is precious and all those are brothers born in spirit.

Let's discern spiritual beings from physical beings with spiritual eye.

Know the tree with the fruit it bears. Any tree that does not sprout from the belief and bears not righteous fruit of good deed will be gathered and burned. Because these are the mean tares and the fruit shows what the tree is.

Should the trees from the seed of belief sprout and bear righteous fruits of good deed ten times, hundred times and inherit the kingdom of God with glory.

But how can I sow seed on me. If the farmer sow seed on me then I am going to sprout and grow to bear fruit. When the harvest comes and the fruit is ripe enough, God will gather them to keep for future use.

Thanks, God, for allowing me understanding. Everything is yours and everything is on you my father. Now I know and just pray your will be accomplished through me wholly. Amen.

March 1997
Dae Young Choe

Free in God's will

That we live means we are free and that we are like dust or fog means we are not free. We discussed about each one in the chapter of Free Will and the Meaning of Life. It contradicts each other giving lots of conflicts to the people who want to be in God.

The bible says both and we are going to think about what it is.

> **John 9:1**
> **And as Jesus passed by, he saw a man which was blind from his birth. And his disciples asked him, saying, Master, who did sin, this man, or his parents, that he was born blind?**
>
> **Jesus answered, Neither hath this man sinned, nor his parents: but that the works of God should be made manifest in him.**

Everyone comes into this world with a certain job God imposed on each one.

As the above scripture says God reveals God's will through each one and differently.

When we think about this blind man, we know he did not want to be born as blind from the birth. He has nothing to do about it but just to be born like that. Under the given condition of blindness this man struggles freely to survive. That this man was born blind is what God imposed on him to reveal God's will. So, this man is just like dust or fog that cannot avoid what God imposes on him.

And the struggle this man makes to survive is the expression of this man's free will responding to his blindness.

Like a dumb express signaling by hand, the struggle of this blind man is the expression of his life responding to God's will imposed on him.

Our life is our response to God's will imposed unto each one. It is like talking to God.

So, if we pursue God's will through our life then we are praying always.

We cannot refuse what God imposes on us every second and that means we are only such an existence like dust or fog. God put the life, the spirit, in such existence to have them move around freely and accomplish God's will. And God's will is raising our spirit to let us live in spiritual world of the Kingdom of God. Since the spirit could only grow through physical distress like the iron stone needs to pass through hot furnace to make good steel, God had to plant the spirit into the body and put in this satanic physical world to have them pass through the hot furnace of this world.

The limit of this satanic world is the death of flesh, the departure of the spirit from the flesh.

We are responding to the hot furnace in the limit of death and grow until that time.

If we try to stand out of this satanic world, we have troubles and when we jump out of this world we fail to survive and die. So, our freedom has the limit of death and we are all imprisoned in the world of death. As we grow spiritually by passing through the furnace we begin to long for the real spiritual world where there is no pain and tear and death. All want to grow over the death. But as soon as we try to jump out of this world to go into the real spiritual world, we come to face the death and give up to jump in fear of death and doubt the existence of spiritual world. Which shows one was not grown up spiritually enough to jump yet. Don't be confused about what the death here means.

Physically dead person does not care what happens to his body. So, if a person ignores the physical necessity thoroughly, then he is as good as dead.

I found out one interesting thing.

When one says in normal fashion that above blind man failed to survive and died, everybody without one exception would say "Oh! What a poor thing".

But Jesus Christ says to this blind man "Do not try to survive in this world of death. If you try to survive you will have to carry the heavy burden with you and as the result you are going to die still remaining blind."

It's not only to this blind man. It's to everybody who lives in this world.

Jesus said God gave this world to Satan. This world is the world Satan manages.

If a world is managed be Satan, it'll surely be a hell! (I'll talk about this in detail later.)

I would say nobody would believe this world is the hell even though it is written in the bible as hell.

Even though you love this world and succeed to survive, you are still going to die and your success will vanish. But if you hate your life in this world and give up to live in this world aiming the kingdom of heaven, you can use your physical life to get spiritual growth and jump out of this world to save yourself and get your eye opened. Give up your physical desire and use your physical life to pursue spiritual things.

That is jumping out of this world.

Who would believe God made you blind to make you hate your life and pursue spiritual things and thus encourage you to jump out of this world? In many places in the bible, God implies these things as following.

Mark 8:35

For whosoever will save his life shall lose it; but whosoever shall lose his life for my sake and the gospel's, the same shall save it.

For what shall it profit a man, if he shall gain the whole world, and lose his own soul? Or what shall a man give in exchange for his soul?

Mark 10:43
But so shall it not be among you: but whosoever will be great among you, shall be your minister: And whosoever of you will be the chiefest, shall be servant of all.

Matthew 5:4
Blessed are they that mourn: for they shall be comforted.

Blessed are they which are persecuted for righteousness' sake: for theirs is the kingdom of heaven.

Blessed are ye, when men shall revile you, and persecute you, and shall say all manner of evil against you falsely, for my sake.

Many preachers say it is so easy to enter the kingdom of God as just saying with our mouth "I believe in Jesus Christ and admit him as my personal savior".

But that exact Jesus Christ says as following asking to give up this world.

Mark 10:19
Thou knowest the commandments, Do not commit adultery, Do not kill, Do not steal, Do not bear false witness, Defraud not, Honour thy father and mother.

And he answered and said unto him, Master, all these have I observed from my youth. *(This man observed every law.)*

Then Jesus beholding him loved him, and said unto him, One thing thou lackest: go thy way, sell whatsoever thou hast, and give to the poor, and thou shalt have treasure in heaven: and come, take up the cross, and follow me.

And he was sad at that saying, and went away grieved: for he had great possessions.

(But this man failed to give up this world.)

And Jesus looked round about, and saith unto his disciples, How hardly shall they that have riches enter into the kingdom of God!

And the disciples were astonished at his words. But Jesus answereth again, and saith unto them, Children, how hard is it for them that trust in riches to enter into the kingdom of God!

(The richer the harder to give up.)

It is easier for a camel to go through the eye of a needle, than for a rich man to enter into the kingdom of God.

(Giving up own possession and pursuing invisible Kingdom of God is harder than a camel goes through the eye of a needle.)

And they were astonished out of measure, saying among themselves, Who then can be saved? And Jesus looking upon them saith, With men it is impossible, but not with God: for with God all things are possible.

Then Peter began to say unto him, Lo, we have left all, and have followed thee.

And Jesus answered and said, Verily I say unto you, There is no man that hath left house, or brethren, or sisters, or father, or mother, or wife, or children, or lands, for my sake, and the gospel's, But he shall receive an hundredfold now in this time, houses, and brethren, and sisters, and mothers, and children, and lands, with persecutions; and in the world to come eternal life.

But many that are first shall be last; and the last first.

(The one who struggled to be the first in this world might be the first one in this world but he is going to be

*the last in the spiritual world. Because he neglected to
raise his spirit.)*

Here I want to make one thing very clear.

*We can see many religious groups or individuals commit suicide these
days saying they are killing themselves to go to heaven as written in the bible.*

*How could a person who was not born again understand God? How
could this people understand God and grow up spiritually to be Sons of
God to enter the kingdom of God?*

They do it because they do not understand God.

*Committing suicide is nothing but giving up this physical world and
spiritual world as well. That's one other way how the Satan manages this
world and keeps people in death. That is exactly "a blind leading the blind."*

*Killing oneself is not committing suicide. The biblical meaning of
killing oneself written in the bible is giving up pursuing physical things for
this world and pursuing the spiritual things for the Kingdom of God. It is
killing the physical desire.*

*Remember, once our body is destroyed the spirit loses the chance to
grow to fit into the heaven over the world of death and God only judge
who would fit to the heaven.*

*We have to know Satan is holding us as hostages threatening us with
our physical life if we might jump out to accomplish God's will over the
limit of death. That's his duty given by God and that's how he tests each
belief of individual spirit over the world of death.*

*We have to understand the death, the Satan threatening with, is just
the death of physical body. Which is the departure of the spirit from the
body. Due to the misunderstanding we are afraid of what we actually hope,
the spiritual freedom.*

*If our spirit doesn't grow over the limit of death, we cannot live the real
world of spiritual life and remain in this fake physical world. It is ironical
that God asks us not to pursue physical desire and at the same time trains
us by way of the physical distress. Anyway, every good and bad thing to
men's eye collaborate each other and make one good, God's truth.*

Again, it is possible only to those who believe there is spiritual world.

Jesus Christ taught us about it and proved it by rising again from the death.

So, Jesus Christ is the way, the truth and the life.

We have to learn from him directly not from others, nobody.

Everything happening to us second by second is God's imposing to us to accomplish God's will and everything we do is doing God's job responding to what God imposed.

So, that we are living means we are doing God's job and God's job is raising our spirit. The only problem is we do not believe God's word, the Jesus Christ. The bible says Jesus came as a word. So, believe in Jesus Christ means believe what he said.

Our spirit grows by way of free expression upon God's will to bear fruits of truth and this is how God accomplishes. The truth is those who did evil collects evil things and those who did good collects good things. Through the bible God showed God's will clearly to have men bear fruits abundantly. So regardless of one's being precious or not precious if a precious one doesn't bear fruits as much, he will be classified as mean tare and burned.

If a not precious one to men's eye bears fruits he will be classified as grain and inherit the Kingdom of God.

So, it's not the matter of being precious doing nice and clean job or being not precious doing dirty job in this world. It's the matter of bearing good fruits or not. That shows our spiritual growth.

But there will be troubles to those who think oneself was made precious. Because these people have to work harder to bear more fruits as much as made precious.

And those who think were made not precious for God's dirty job has to know they are also doing God's job. Everyone wants to do God's precious job. But God only gives the job to each one. Therefore, blessed are those who love God in thirsty of God's words and follow God's word. God will give the eye to these people to distinguish which is precious and which is not precious. The bible says Jesus Christ came as the word of God as following.

John 1:1
**In the beginning was the Word, and the Word was
with God, and the Word was God. And the Word
was made flesh, and dwelt among us, and we beheld
his glory, the glory as of the only begotten of the
Father,) full of grace and truth.**

*So, Sons of God shouldn't deplore about being disabled or having some
difficulties.*

*Rather, we should take our difficulties as blessed and appreciate as
God loves us more and wants to accomplish greater things having us bear
more fruits.*

*The greater thing God wants to accomplish through us is to raise Sons
of God and save from this fake, physical and corruptible world to make us
live in real, spiritual, non-corruptible world, the Kingdom of God.*

*Those who were given easy job and enjoying the comfort of life should
take it as cursed or God does not love them, neither wants to accomplish a
great job through them. Those should watch themselves.*

John 8:32
**And ye shall know the truth, and the truth shall
make you free.**

**They answered him, We be Abraham's seed, and
were never in bondage to an man: how sayest thou,
Ye shall be made free? Jesus answered them, Verily,
verily, I say unto you, Whosoever committet sin is
the servant of sin. And the servant abideth not in
the house for ever: but the Son abideth ever.**

**If the Son therefore shall make you free, ye shall
be free indeed.**

*As we discussed in this chapter, we are free only in the limit of death
in this world. To be in absolute free, we need to be one in God.*

*The only condition for that is to believe the existence of Kingdom of
God without any doubt. Once we believe, the belief frees us from the death*

and make us not to fear the physical death to lead us to the same will God has and we become one with God.

We are going to pursue the spiritual world and God is going to raise us spiritually to let us live in spiritual world as Sons of God. Being one is just like a sports team. Unless the coach and the player become one, the harder the coach tries the harder the player will resist and the team can not make a good record. The goal can be achieved only mutual belief that they are doing for each other's good even if the practice is terribly hard.

John 17:20

Neither pray I for these alone, but for them also which shall believe on me through their word;

That they all may be one; as thou, Father, art in me, and I in thee, that they also may be one in us: that the world may believe that thou hast sent me. And the glory which thou gavest me I have given them; that they may be one, even as we are one:

I in them, and thou in me, that they may be made perfect in one; and that the world may know that thou hast sent me, and hast loved them, as thou hast loved me.

Father, I will that they also, whom thou hast given me, be with me where I am; that they may behold my glory, which thou hast given me: for thou lovedst me before the foundation of the world.

But we have to remember that the sound belief is not going to happen suddenly. It grows as our physical bodies pass through the hot furnace of this world. We can experience the spiritual existence only when we come to the limit of our physical capability. So the more you deny yourself and give up, the more you can experience the spiritual existence and it builds your belief towards God.

John 15:1

I am the true vine, and my Father is the husbandman.

Every branch in me that beareth not fruit he taketh away: and every branch that beareth fruit, he purgeth it, that it may bring forth more fruit. Now ye are clean through the word which I have spoken unto you.

Abide in me, and I in you. As the branch cannot bear fruit of itself, except it abide in the vine; no more can ye, except ye abide in me.

I am the vine, ye are the branches: He that abideth in me, and I in him, the same bringeth forth much fruit: for without me ye can do nothing.

If a man abide not in me, he is cast forth as a branch, and is withered; and men gather them, and cast them into the fire, and they are burned.

If ye abide in me, and my words abide in you, ye shall ask what ye will, and it shall be done unto you.

We are nothing but the dust or fog and we cannot avoid what God gives us every second.

But when we deny ourselves and love God more than ourselves, then we become one with God and have the whole spirit like God has and be pleased at God's accomplishment through us.

We are not supposed to complain about the difficulties happening around us.

Rather, we should have the idea that we are helping God in solving God's difficult problems together with God being one in God.

Then, when we ask, God is going to give whatever it is to accomplish his will and we are going to grow spiritually and bear fruit of good deed.

Knowing that people would be confused between denying oneself and denying life itself, Jesus Christ made it clear as following to the people who say:

God knows everything and does everything as he likes and accomplishes as he pleases through us. So, what can I do and what can I accomplish? We are just like the dust or the fog. Whether I want to do something or not, isn't it he that gave me that mind? Everything is useless. Wouldn't my effort be ended to no purpose after all?

(Matthew 25:14)

For the kingdom of heaven is as a man travelling into a far country, who called his own servants, and delivered unto them his goods.

And unto one he gave five talents, to another two, and to another one; to every man according to his several ability; and straightway took his journey.

Then he that had received the five talents went and traded with the same, and made them other five talents. And likewise he that had received two, he also gained other two. But he that had received one went and digged in the earth, and hid his lord's money. After a long time the lord of those servants cometh, and reckoneth with them. And so he that had received five talents came and brought other five talents, saying, Lord, thou deliveredst unto me five talents: behold,I have gained beside them five talents more. His lord said unto him, Well done, thou good and faithful servant: thou hast been faithful over a few things, I will make thee ruler over many things: enter thou into the joy of thy lord.

He also that had received two talents came and said, Lord, thou deliveredst unto me two talents: behold, I have gained two other talents beside them.

His lord said unto him, Well done, good and faithful servant; thou hast been faithful over a few things, I will make thee ruler over many things:

enter thou into the joy of thy lord. Then he which had received the one talent came and said, Lord, I knew thee that thou art an hard man, reaping where thou hast not sown, and gathering where thou hast not strowed: And I was afraid, and went and hid thy talent in the earth: lo, there thou hast that is thine.

His lord answered and said unto him, Thou wicked and slothful servant, thou knewest that I reap where I sowed not, and gather where I have not strowed: Thou oughtest therefore to have put my money to the exchangers, and then at my coming I should have received mine own with usury.

Take therefore the talent from him, and give it unto him which hath ten talents.

For unto every one that hath shall be given, and he shall have abundance: but from him that hath not shall be taken away even that which he hath. And cast ye the unprofitable servant into outer darkness: there shall be weeping and gnashing of teeth.

Denying oneself is denying one's physical desire and we should not neglect to raise our spirit to the Holy Spirit. Working for the physical desire will be ended to no purpose and working for the spiritual desire will lead you to real freedom and real life in the Kingdom of God.

5. God's Job

God's job and men's job

That God allowed life to our flesh means God wanted to do God's some precious job through some flesh and also God wanted to do God's some mean job through some other flesh. Either way it should be God's job for sure.

Before we proceed further, I'd like to think about what is precious job or mean job in biblical respect.

In normal fashion, when somebody killed a real bad person he is regarded as a righteous man and if somebody killed an innocent man he is regarded as a bad man. The point is not only why one killed somebody. Rather it depends more on which ruler was used to measure it.

Since everybody's interests lay only on each one's own profit, everybody come to judge the opponents to protect their own profit.

So, a good man in this side turns out to be a bad man to that side and a bad man in that side turns out to be a good man to this side. Not to mention about the wars, the trials, the businesses, every competition what so ever are the same. Even the love affairs between lovers are not the exception. Who acquires the name of good man? The winner does.

There couldn't be any good job or bad job. There is only meaningless job. That is mean job of the winner or the looser.

That's because no absolute ruler is available for those who live by man made law.

And that's because everybody lives for one's own profit creating other one's disadvantage due to the limit of this physical world like the lions, profit by eating other weak animals.

So, the only way to do the meaningful job is living in limitless spiritual world.

Then the limitless God will be the ultimate ruler and we can measure with that ultimate and never changing ruler, the truth, with full of meaning. That is precious job.

If God says it is this, then it is going to be this. And if God says it is that, then it's going to be that. It never changes and God proves it by keeping his words since the creation as never changing truth. The natural phenomenon proves for sure that God's law for the nature never changes. Now, God is going to prove God's law for human beings never changes.

In this world, the same incident can be interpreted as good or bad according to which side you are in or which law is applied to you.

But in God's spiritual world, God is the only law and there is no this side or that side.

There is only one side of God.

Being one in God means this.

God gives a very clear ruler, the truth, so that everybody can measure oneself with that absolute ruler and behave as God wants and that way everybody accomplishes God's will. It's not liked the law in this world that one incident appears good to someone and bad to another causing lots of trouble and division.

It is possible only in spiritual world on behalf of its limitlessness.

You never can be one in one law in this world due to the physical limit as we discussed several times. We know world leaders are pursuing one unified government for the peace.

I know it is not going to happen unless we kill our physical desire and live by spiritual desire. I also know it's not going to happen in this physical world due to its physical limit.

One world without freedom, without peace could happen though.

Now we know what is precious job and what is mean job.

Also, we know regardless we do mean job or precious job, it is God's job. When we recall God blinded those unbelievers so they could not *understand the bible and the bible is only for the Sons of God, we can easily come to the conclusion that God let the Sons of God do the precious job telling through the bible. Those unbelievers would do the mean job because they do not understand the bible and they would think keeping the law is doing good job. But we know their law is changing endlessly.*

It is interesting to know that the evil doers do not believe or understand the bible. Neither they are interested in Bible!

Murder or cheating is definitely a sin to normal people and also were written in the Ten Commandments not to.

But, next three incidents are from many other incidents written in the bible, which shows God commanded God's own people to kill, cheat and take away, which is contrary to God's own commandments. What does this mean? Let's discuss about it with some cases as following.

———•—•—•———

When Israel people were wandering at the wild plain followings had happened.

Numbers 25:1

And Israel abode in Shittim, and the people began to commit whoredom with the daughters of Moab.

And they called the people unto the sacrifices of their gods: and the people did eat, and bowed down to their gods.

And Israel joined himself unto Baalpeor: and the anger of the LORD was kindled against Israel.

And the LORD said unto Moses, Take all the heads of the people, and hang them up before the LORD against the sun, that the fierce anger of the LORD may be turned away from Israel.

And Moses said unto the judges of Israel, Slay ye every one his men that were joined unto Baalpeor.

And, behold, one of the children of Israel came

and brought unto his brethren a Midianitish woman in the sight of Moses, and in the sight of all the congregation of the children of Israel, who were weeping before the door of the tabernacle of the congregation.

And when Phinehas, the son of Eleazar, the son of Aaron the priest, saw it, he rose up from among the congregation, and took a javelin in his hand; And he went after the man of Israel into the tent, and thrust both of them through, the man of Israel, and the woman through her belly. So the plague was stayed from the children of Israel.

And those that died in the plague were twenty and four thousand.

And the LORD spake unto Moses, saying, Phinehas, the son of Eleazar, the son of Aaron the priest, hath turned my wrath away from the children of Israel, while he was zealous for my sake among them, that I consumed not the children of Israel in my jealousy.

Wherefore say, Behold, I give unto him my covenant of peace:

And he shall have it, and his seed after him, even the covenant of an everlasting priesthood; because he was zealous for his God, and made an atonement for the children of Israel.

Now the name of the Israelite that was slain, even that was slain with the Midianitish woman, was Zimri, the son of Salu, a prince of a chief house among the Simeonites.

And the name of the Midianitish woman that was slain was Cozbi, the daughter of Zur; he was head over a people, and of a chief house in Midian. And the LORD spake unto Moses, saying, Vex the Midianites, and smite them: For they vex you with their wiles, wherewith they have beguiled you in the matter of Peor, and in the matter of Cozbi, the daughter of a prince of Midian, their sister, which was slain in the day of the plague for Peor's sake.

The same God who gave Ten Commandments to Moses ordered the same Moses to vex and slay the Moab people thoroughly.

Ahab was a King of Israel and he was so bad as written as following and his wife was such an evil also as to kill his own people to take their possessions.

Kings I 21:26
And he did very abominably in following idols, according to all things as did the Amorites, whom the LORD cast out before the children of Israel.

God allowed one of the angels to cheat the king Ahab to get him killed as following.

Kings I 22:20
And the LORD said, Who shall persuade Ahab, that he may go up and fall at Ramothgilead? And one said on this manner, and another said on that manner. And there came forth a spirit, and stood before the LORD, and said, I will persuade him.

And the LORD said unto him, Wherewith? And he said, I will go forth, and I will be a lying spirit in the mouth of all his prophets. And he said, Thou shalt persuade him, and prevail also: go forth, and do so.

The king Ahab was cheated and killed as God said.

The same God who gave Ten Commandments told the Angel to cheat the king Ahab and kill.

———•—•—•—•—

When Moses delivered the Israel people from Egypt, God hardened Egyptian king Pharaoh's heart not to free the Israel people. And God killed every first born of Pharaoh's from maidservants to the beast including Pharaoh's own son.

On the other hand, God told Moses:

Exodus 11:2
Speak now in the ears of the people, and let every man borrow of his neighbour, and every woman of her neighbour, jewels of silver, and jewels of gold. And the LORD gave the people favour in the sight of the Egyptians.

God instructed Moses to ask Pharaoh's people and take as much valuables as possible. The Israel people would never have returned the borrowed gold, silver and the jewels.

Exodus 12:12
For I will pass through the land of Egypt this night, and will smite all the firstborn in the land of Egypt, both man and beast; and against all the gods of Egypt I will execute judgment: I am the LORD.

And the blood shall be to you for a token upon the houses where ye are: and when I see the blood, I will pass over you, and the plague shall not be upon you to destroy you, when I smite the land of Egypt.

And this day shall be unto you for a memorial; and ye shall keep it a feast to the LORD throughout your generations; ye shall keep it a feast by an ordinance for ever.

(The "Pass Over" we keep as an important annual event is from this)

———•—■—•—■—•———

Let's see one more incident.

> **Samuel I 15:3**
> **Now go and smite Amalek, and utterly destroy all that they have, and spare them not; but slay both man and woman, infant and suckling, ox and sheep, camel and ass.** *(God commanded to kill everything.)*
> **But Saul and the people spared Agag, and the best of the sheep, and of the oxen, and of the fatlings, and the lambs, and all that was good, and would not utterly destroy them: but every thing that was vile and refuse, that they destroyed utterly.**
> **Then came the word of the LORD unto Samuel, saying, It repenteth me that I have set up Saul to be king: for he is turned back from following me, and hath not performed my commandments. And it grieved Samuel; and he cried unto the LORD all night.**
> **And Saul said unto Samuel, I have sinned: for I have transgressed commandment of the LORD, and thy words: because I feared the people, and obeyed their voice.**

(Today's democracy is not the one God like. Because it's foundation stands on the fear of the people saying "by the people, for the people, of the people. Watch that today's Christian ministry is also performed based on this democracy.)

> **Now therefore, I pray thee, pardon my sin, and turn again with me, that I may worship the LORD. And Samuel said unto Saul, I will not return with thee:**

**for thou hast rejected the word of the LORD, and
the LORD hath rejected thee from being king over
Israel.**

———•——•—•——

What do these examples teach us? Following scripture has the answer.

Mark 12:28
**And one of the scribes came, and having heard
them reasoning together, and perceiving that he
had answered them well, asked him, Which is the
first commandment of all? And Jesus answered him,
The first of all the commandments is, Hear, O Israel;
The Lord our God is one Lord: And thou shalt love
the Lord thy God with all thy heart, and with all thy
soul, and with all thy mind, and with all thy strength:
this is the first commandment. And the second is
like, namely this, Thou shalt love thy neighbour as
thyself. There is none other commandment greater
than these.**

*As is written in the bible, the first commandment "Love your God
with all your heart, your soul, and your strength" has the priority to all
other commandments.*

*That means we are all bound to God's law and die as the result. But,
before that, our love to God will free us from God's law.*

The above examples explain it explicitly.

*Above examples of "The law says do not kill and God commanded to
kill" has been solved as following.*

*The people who try to keep the law will not kill but the people who
love God will kill.*

*Those who try to keep the law die because the law is not possible to keep
in this world. While those who loved God and obeyed to kill are going to be
forgiven of their violating the law and live by the favor of God's compassion.*

One thing we have to be very careful is "Is the command really a command from God?" That's what God says about "wake up and discern."

Only those who have the Holy Spirit can discern because the Holy Spirit is God. Whatever God says, it is good because God is good. When God says it is good, it is good this time and God says another next time it is good also. It is God who decides which is good and which is not good. God is not bound to the law. God is absolute. Following scripture shows what that means.

Deuteronomy 32:39
See now that I, even I, am he, and there is no god with me: I kill, and I make alive; I wound, and I heal: neither is there any that can deliver out of my hand. For I lift up my hand to heaven, and say, I live for ever.

If I whet my glittering sword, and mine hand take hold on judgment; I will render vengeance to mine enemies, and will reward them that hate me.

The law is for the people who live in this physical world. But those who are dead about physical body are free from the law and their spirit lives. Because they are dead about the law which God gave to govern the physical world for the training of the sons of God. It shows God's character anyway.

I hear that some religious community that are said to believe in Jesus Christ do not join the military because they can not kill obeying God's law and they even runaway causing lots of troubles to themselves. But we have to remember many people like Moses, Joshua and David killed so many people and God said they are righteous and they are in heaven with Jesus Christ now.

Abraham, we call him as the ancestor of believers, tried to kill even his own son responding to God's command to offer him.

I hope readers do not misunderstand me because I know what I am saying now looks pretty much encouraging to people to kill.

I remember a young man wrote me a letter when he was serving the army in Bosnia. He was a very religious man. He wrote he was thinking about something very seriously. He said the training officers at the camp told him that he had to think about clear reason for killing opponents in advance otherwise when something happens abruptly, he cannot pull the trigger decisively and hesitate to be killed by the opponents.

Good example of misunderstanding the bible!

These kinds of misunderstandings work as a gridlock in having the perfect wisdom of God. This kind of shortsighted understanding keeps the people in meanness, holding them not to grow brave or wise.

Why then Jesus Christ taught people as:

Matthew 5:39

But I say unto you, That ye resist not evil: but whosoever shall smite thee on thy right cheek, turn to him the other also. And if any man will sue thee at the law, and take away thy coat, let him have thy cloak also. And whosoever shall compel thee to go a mile, go with him twain. Give to him that asketh thee, and from him that would borrow of thee turn not thou away.

As the salvation, born again and forgiveness... are personal matters of each individual, our faith is personal as the above scripture says. God's Ten Commandments are the same case. God is talking to us directly not via somebody else.

God has some precious job and not precious job even when it is about the group relations like nation to nation. Those who believes in God have the spirit of God and know which side is God's precious job and which is God's not precious job. Just like someone who wouldn't compel anybody to go a mile would not like to take part in God's ungracious job. Likewise, when some righteous man saw unrighteous things, he could kill the unrighteous man to take part of God's precious side and still remain righteous man like Moses. Yet, most Christians say, "Jesus said to forgive and love even your enemy".

Forgiveness can be made only when someone asks compassion about something what he did wrong. You can forgive someone only when he comes to you for forgiveness. You can not say you forgave someone who ran away after killing your son for money and now threatening your life for more money. Forgiveness can be made only when he comes to you for your compassion. Where there is forgiveness, there should be some repent.

Jesus said to love even your enemy. This also could be explained with the same sense as following. It is written in the bible as:

Corinthians I 13:1
If I speak in the tongues of men and of angels, but have not love, I am a noisy gong or a clanging cymbal. And if I have prophetic powers, and understand all mysteries and all knowledge, and if I have all faith, so as to remove mountains, but have not love, I am nothing. If I give away all I have, and if I deliver my body to be burned, but have not love, I gain nothing. Love is patient and kind; love is not jealous or boastful; it is not arrogant or rude. Love does not insist on its own way; it is not irritable or resentful; it does not rejoice at wrong, but rejoices in the right. Love bears all things, believes all things, hopes all things, endures all things. Love never ends; as for prophecies, they will pass away; as for tongues, they will cease; as for knowledge, it will pass away. For our knowledge is imperfect and our prophecy is imperfect; but when the perfect comes, the imperfect will pass away. When I was a child, I spoke like a child, I thought like a child, I reasoned like a child; when I became a man, I gave up childish ways.

Is our "love" the same love with the "love" in the bible?
The "love" is translated as "Charity" in the bible King James Version.
Looks like most of the people in our generation do not know what the "love" is. We are just expressing that we love for what we like. As the Apostle Paul said, we should give up our childish ways of love. That way

139

we are to grow spiritually. Thereafter, we will be able to love our enemy and pray for them. We are not going to like our enemy. We are going to love them. When Moses delivered Israel people from the Egyptian, there must be good men and bad men in Moses's side and also there must be good men and bad men in Egyptians also. All of the Moses's people were alive and most of the Egyptians were died regardless of their being good or bad. Moses believed God and knew God's plan while Egyptians did not believe God and did not know God's plan. That was the reason. Believers are to know God's plan and do God's precious job and grow spiritually. How? Believe what God said through the bible. Think about this. What if Moses refused to go to Paraoh to ask to release the Israel people and what if Moses refused to perform God's power of killing all of the Egyptian's first-born sons. Would God's plan be accomplished? Many would say God would accomplish it in certain way anyhow. I'm saying that was God's certain way.

Jesus Christ commanded to love your neighbor saying when you love your neighbor you are accomplishing all the commandments in Old Testament.

Accomplishing Old Commandments does not mean accomplishing New Commandments.

Jesus gave us new commandment of "Love each other" saying all the commandments are in there.

So, accomplishing New Testament is accomplishing Old Testament as well.

We are living the age of New Testament. That means we are living the spiritual age of God's plan and we are to live the life of New Testament God told us.

Read the bible carefully and you will find the bible is the timetable of God's plan or the history of men written in advance in reverse order.

Now we know why we have to live like we are doing God's job.

Every happening is God's job

Whatever we do, it's God's job.

However, God let the Satan do the mean job through mean people and gave this physical world to Satan for that mean job. And also, the bible says Satan loves those who struggle for the success in his satanic world. That is God's mean job.

Now, I'd like to talk about the reality of our physical life in this world and think about "why", "for what", and "how" about our life by reflecting it to the mirror of bible.

A woman said a burglar came in her store and killed her husband and baby for seventy dollars in the cash register and ran away. Her neighbor told her who did it but he did not want to testify at the court because he was afraid of the retaliation. Now, that bad man is walking around her store and she can not do anything about it. Are you saying this is God's job?

The tragic Oklahoma federal building explosion which took away so many young lives, the collapse of the Sam Poong department store that killed hundreds of people in Korea, six million of Jewish holocaust, over 50% of divorce rate, deadly famine in many countries....

Are you saying all these are God's job? Let's see what the bible says.

In Job's day, God allowed Satan to take away all the possessions from Job whom God said righteous man. Satan killed all of his children and let him scratch the itching of skin disease off all over his body with a piece of tile.

In Elisha's day, when Israel was surrounded by Syria followings had happened.

Kings II 6:24

And it came to pass after this, that Benhadad king of Syria gathered all his host, and went up, and besieged Samaria. And there was a great famine in Samaria: and, behold, they besieged it, until an ass's head was sold for four score pieces of silver, and the fourth part of a cab of dove's dung for five pieces of silver. And as the king of Israel was passing by upon

the wall, there cried a woman unto him, saying, Help, my lord, O king. And he said, If the LORD do not help thee, whence shall I help thee? out of the barnfloor, or out of the winepress? And the king said unto her, What aileth thee? And she answered, This woman said unto me, Give thy son, that we may eat him to day, and we will eat my son to morrow. So we boiled my son, and did eat him: and I said unto her on the next day, Give thy son, that we may eat him: and she hath hid her son.

And the bible says this famine was also of God as following.

Kings II 6:33
And while he yet talked with them, behold, the messenger came down unto him: and he said, Behold, this evil is of the LORD; what should I wait for the LORD any longer?

Who made the earthquake happen in San Francisco and who made the riot broke out in Los-Angeles? And who sent own son to be crucified and die for our sin. God did all these! We are just his creature and do not understand why God is doing these. Because of our arrogance we are holding ourselves away from God and imprisoned in the world of death to live a meaningless life and find nothing when die. Why don't we realize that we are living the world God prearranged for the disobedient people? We are passing this world and only experiencing the things that are happening in this world of death. Why don't we understand God put us in this evil world to let us know what the hell is and make us long for the Kingdom of God? It's not because your two-year old innocent child did something wrong and it's not because your righteous husband sinned. It's just because we fell into this physical evil world and live together with the evil people. God sent own son to let us know that and taught how to save ourselves from this evil world.

Bible says God gave this world to Satan and it is not the place for the

Sons of God. He says: "Don't try to stay there! Just try to get out of there! Satan is only able to hold you in this world by grabbing your physical body. Why do you follow your body? Satan is holding your body. Don't you see it turns out to be just nothing but a handful of soil? Everything in this world is nothing. It's false! It's not real! It's cheating you. Do not love it! Rather, hate it! Do not serve your body. It's keeping you in that hell. Rather use it as a slave for your spirit. But you don't know how. So, I am sending you my son Jesus Christ. Learn from him!"

Let's think about following example Jesus Christ showed.

Luke 16:20

And there was a certain beggar named Lazarus, which was laid at his gate, full of sores, And desiring to be fed with the crumbs which fell from the rich man's table: moreover the dogs came and licked his sores. And it came to pass, that the beggar died, and was carried by the angels into Abraham's bosom: the rich man also died, and was buried; 16:23 And in hell he lift up his eyes, being in torments, and seeth Abraham afar off, and Lazarus in his bosom. And he cried and said, Father Abraham, have mercy on me, and send Lazarus, that he may dip the tip of his finger in water, and cool my tongue; for I am tormented in this flame. But Abraham said, Son, remember that thou in thy lifetime receivedst thy good things, and likewise Lazarus evil things: but now he is comforted, and thou art tormented. And beside all this, between us and you there is a great gulf fixed: so that they which would pass from hence to you cannot; neither can they pass to us, that would come from thence. Then he said, I pray thee therefore, father, that thou wouldest send him to my father's house: For I have five brethren; that he may testify unto them, lest they also come into this place of torment. Abraham saith unto him, They

have Moses and the prophets; let them hear them. And he said, Nay, father Abraham: but if one went unto them from the dead, they will repent. And he said unto him, If they hear not Moses and the prophets, neither will they be persuaded, though one rose from the dead.

This rich man was such a righteous man to our eyes as to allow the beggar to be laid at the front door of his house everyday and eat something coming out from his house. But Jesus said this righteous (?) rich man is in the hell to suffer and the lazy beggar is in the heaven.

When we recall "God gave this world to Satan" and "being loved by this world is being loved by Satan and being hated by God", we come to understand that being rich and succeed in this world means being hated by God. How can we understand this?

Aren't we going to church to pray God for our children's success, for the successful business, for the better position and for the better life?

We are praying to fill our storage, we are praying to multiply our business, we are praying for our health, for the peace, for the unification...

Nobody pray for God's will be accomplished.

What if God's will is destroying like God destroyed Roman Empire?

What if God's will is division like God divided Israel into two pieces of Judah and Israel? And what if God's will is war like God ordered Israel to conquer the land of Canaan?

I do not see anybody who prays God's will be accomplished through oneself.

Everybody just pray for own well being or for own group's well being so they could have surplus to help others. Why don't they understand a tiger's profit hurts other weak animals? They pray for more profit to help others. Why don't they understand more profit would hurt more people? God says to kill oneself to help others instead of making more profit.

Then how can we survive? Jesus said:

(Luke 12:22)

And he said unto his disciples, Therefore I say unto you, Take no thought for your life, what ye shall eat; neither for the body, what ye shall put on. The life is more than meat, and the body is more than raiment. Consider the ravens: for they neither sow nor reap; which neither have storehouse nor barn; and God feedeth them: how much more are ye better than the fowls? And which of you with taking thought can add to his stature one cubit? If ye then be not able to do that thing which is least, why take ye thought for the rest? Consider the lilies how they grow: they toil not, they spin not; and yet I say unto you, that Solomon in all his glory was not arrayed like one of these. If then God so clothe the grass, which is to day in the field, and to morrow is cast into the oven; how much more will he clothe you, O ye of little faith? And seek not ye what ye shall eat, or what ye shall drink, neither be ye of doubtful mind. For all these things do the nations of the world seek after: and your Father knoweth that ye have need of these things.

But rather seek ye the kingdom of God; and all these things shall be added unto you. Fear not, little flock; for it is your Father's good pleasure to give you the kingdom.

That we live or die in this world is not up to us. It's in the hand of God and he knows what we need to live or to die. And he will accomplish as he planned. We are living just as much as we are allowed to.

Jesus Christ taught us how to pray as following.

Luke 11:1

And it came to pass, that, as he was praying in a certain place, when he ceased, one of his disciples

said unto him, Lord, teach us to pray, as John also taught his disciples. And he said unto them, When ye pray, say, Our Father which art in heaven, Hallowed be thy name. Thy kingdom come. Thy will be done, as in heaven, so in earth. Give us day by day our daily bread. And forgive us our sins; for we also forgive every one that is indebted to us. And lead us not into temptation; but deliver us from evil.

And showed us a good example of pursuing God's will when he was about to be crucified. He prayed for God's will be accomplished instead of his own will as following

Luke 22:40

And when he was at the place, he said unto them, Pray that ye enter not into temptation. And he was withdrawn from them about a stone's cast, and kneeled down, and prayed, Saying, Father, if thou be willing, remove this cup from me: nevertheless not my will, but thine, be done.

Again, we have to understand God accomplishes what God planned and we are living to accomplish God's plan not for our well being.

So, I believe the fundamental attitude of our Christian toward God must be like an actor in a drama. The actor enjoys his role in the drama regardless it is a happy drama or a sad drama. The actor's interest is not in himself. Rather, he is more interested in his role of the drama.

Regardless of the role given to each one, trying to perform God's given role better is doing precious job and trying to find out other role than God given is doing mean job. Appreciating the role makes one do the role better and complaining for another role makes one perform the role poorly.

God let us know "Blessed are those poor than the rich, blessed are those sad than the happy and blessed are those lower than the higher" with the example of a beggar Lazarus.

Why is it like that? We know everybody loses everything when die.

So, the more you possess, the more you don't want to lose.

The richer, higher, healthier and happier you are, the more you don't want to die to get a new life and therefore you don't long for a new life and neglect to pursue it and at last loose your life in this world.

The poorer, lower, sad and sicker you are, the more you don't like this world and even hate. Those are going to long for the new life and pursue it and get new everlasting life. Apostle Paul confessed it as following.

Philippians 3:7
But whatever gain I had, I counted as loss for the sake of Christ. Indeed I count everything as loss because of the surpassing worth of knowing Christ Jesus my Lord. For his sake I have suffered the loss of all things, and count them as refuse, in order that I may gain Christ

I would say if someone is happy and nothing is short why would he look for some other world? But those who believe there is something bigger over the horizon looks for it. In next chapter we are going to discuss about the foundation our faith built on.

Confirming our Faith

Let's go ahead to reconfirm if our faith stands on God's words one by one.

I'd like to do this job for a couple of bible scriptures.

Because confirming jobs on biblical stand point needs time to taste the scriptures. So, let's take time to read the bible.

James 1:9
Let the brother of low degree rejoice in that he is exalted:
But the rich, in that he is made low: because as the flower of the grass he shall pass away. For the sun is no sooner risen with a burning heat, but it

withereth the grass, and the flower thereof falleth, and the grace of the fashion of it perisheth: so also shall the rich man fade away in his ways.

———•———•—•—•———

James 4:4
Ye adulterers and adulteresses, know ye not that the friendship of the world is enmity with God? whosoever therefore will be a friend of the world is the enemy of God.

Considering God expressed himself as groom to men, here the adultery means someone who believes something else than God. Since the belief causes the deed, when someone believes that he is doing his own job, he is adulterous to God. And when someone believes he does God's job with appreciation he becomes one with God like a man and a woman becomes one by the marriage when they swear to live for the other each other.

———•———•—•—•———

James 4:8
Draw nigh to God, and he will draw nigh to you. Cleanse your hands, ye sinners; and purify your hearts, ye double minded. Be afflicted, and mourn, and weep: let your laughter be turned to mourning, and your joy to heaviness. Humble yourselves in the sight of the Lord, and he shall lift you up.

———•———•—•—•———

James 5:1
Go to now, ye rich men, weep and howl for your miseries that shall come upon you. Your riches are corrupted, and your garments are motheaten. Your gold and silver is cankered; and the rust of them shall

be a witness against you, and shall eat your flesh as it were fire. Ye have heaped treasure together for the last days. Behold, the hire of the labourers who have reaped down your fields, which is of you kept back by fraud, crieth: and the cries of them which have reaped are entered into the ears of the Lord of sabaoth. Ye have lived in pleasure on the earth, and been wanton; ye have nourished your hearts, as in a day of slaughter.

———•——•——•———

Isaiah 45:7
I form the light, and create darkness: I make peace, and create evil: I the LORD do all these things. Drop down, ye heavens, from above, and let the skies pour down righteousness: let the earth open, and let them bring forth salvation, and let righteousness spring up together; I the LORD have created it. Woe unto him that striveth with his Maker! Let the potsherd strive with the potsherds of the earth. Shall the clay say to him that fashioneth it, What makest thou? or thy work, He hath no hands? Woe unto him that saith unto his father, What begettest thou? or to the woman, What hast thou brought forth? Thus saith the LORD, the Holy One of Israel, and his Maker, Ask me of things to come concerning my sons, and concerning the work of my hands command ye me. I have made the earth, and created man upon it: I, even my hands, have stretched out the heavens, and all their host have I commanded.

God who makes peace and creates evil also planned at the time of creation that Jesus Christ be sold by one of his disciples and let the people know saying that God will take away his beloved one and the sheep will be dispersed. That the Israel people will be delivered after serving Egyptians for four hundred years was also planned and known to Abraham already hundreds of years before that happened.

James 4:14
Whereas ye know not what shall be on the morrow. For what is your life? It is even a vapour, that appeareth for a little time, and then vanisheth away. For that ye ought to say, If the Lord will, we shall live, and do this, or that. But now ye rejoice in your boastings: all such rejoicing is evil. Therefore to him that knoweth to do good, and doeth it not, to him it is sin.

———•——•—•——•———

Isaiah 46:10 Declaring the end from the beginning, and from ancient times the things that are not yet done, saying, My counsel shall stand, and I will do all my pleasure:

God created men to accomplish what God wants according to God's plan, not what men want according to men's plan.

———•——•—•——•———

John I 3:23
And this is his commandment, That we should believe on the name of his Son Jesus Christ, and love one another, as he gave us commandment. And he that keepeth his commandments dwelleth in him, and he in him. And hereby we know that he abideth in us, by the Spirit which he hath given us.

———•——•—•——•———

4:1

Beloved, believe not every spirit, but try the spirits whether they are of God: because many false prophets are gone out into the world.

———•—■—•—•———

John I 4:5

They are of the world: therefore speak they of the world, and the world heareth them. We are of God: he that knoweth God heareth us; he that is not of God heareth not us. Hereby know we the spirit of truth, and the spirit of error. Beloved, let us love one another: for love is of God; and every one that loveth is born of God, and knoweth God. He that loveth not knoweth not God; for God is love. In this was manifested the love of God toward us, because that God sent his only begotten Son into the world, that we might live through him. Herein is love, not that we loved God, but that he loved us, and sent his Son to be the propitiation for our sins. Beloved, if God so loved us, we ought also to love one another. No man hath seen God at any time. If we love one another, God dwelleth in us, and his love is perfected in us. Hereby know we that we dwell in him, and he in us, because he hath given us of his Spirit. And we have seen and do testify that the Father sent the Son to be the Saviour of the world. Whosoever shall confess that Jesus is the Son of God, God dwelleth in him, and he in God. And we have known and believed the love that God hath to us. God is love; and he that dwelleth in love dwelleth in God, and God in him. Herein is our love made perfect, that we may have boldness in the day of judgment: because as he is, so are we in this world. There is no fear in love;

but perfect love casteth out fear: because fear hath torment. He that feareth is not made perfect in love. We love him, because he first loved us. If a man say, I love God, and hateth his brother, he is a liar: for he that loveth not his brother whom he hath seen, how can he love God whom he hath not seen? And this commandment have we from him, That he who loveth God love his brother also.

—————•—•———•———

Timothy II 2:20
But in a great house there are not only vessels of gold and of silver, but also of wood and of earth; and some to honour, and some to dishonour. If a man therefore purge himself from these, he shall be a vessel unto honour, sanctified, and meet for the master's use, and prepared unto every good work. Flee also youthful lusts: but follow righteousness, faith, charity, peace, with them that call on the Lord out of a pure heart.

—————•—•———•———

Matthew 5:33
Again, ye have heard that it hath been said by them of old time, Thou shalt not forswear thyself, but shalt perform unto the Lord thine oaths: But I say unto you, Swear not at all; neither by heaven; for it is God's throne: Nor by the earth; for it is his footstool: neither by Jerusalem; for it is the city of the great King. Neither shalt thou swear by thy head, because thou canst not make one hair white or black. But let your communication be, Yea, yea; Nay, nay: for whatsoever is more than these cometh of evil.

John 3:27
John answered and said, A man can receive nothing,
except it be given him from heaven.

(John, the Baptist who baptized Jesus Christ said.)

Deuteronomy 18:21
And if thou say in thine heart, How shall we know
the word which the LORD hath not spoken? When
a prophet speaketh in the name of the LORD, if the
thing follow not, nor come to pass, that is the thing
which the LORD hath not spoken, but the prophet
hath spoken it presumptuously: thou shalt not be
afraid of him.

Deuteronomy 8:12
Lest when thou hast eaten and art full, and hast
built goodly houses, and dwelt therein; And when
thy herds and thy flocks multiply, and thy silver
and thy gold is multiplied, and all that thou hast
is multiplied; Then thine heart be lifted up, and
thou forget the LORD thy God, which brought
thee forth out of the land of Egypt, from the house
of bondage; Who led thee through that great and
terrible wilderness, wherein were fiery serpents, and
scorpions, and drought, where there was no water;
who brought thee forth water out of the rock of
flint; Who fed thee in the wilderness with manna,
which thy fathers knew not, that he might humble

thee, and that he might prove thee, to do thee good at thy latter end; And thou say in thine heart, My power and the might of mine hand hath gotten me this wealth. But thou shalt remember the LORD thy God: for it is he that giveth thee power to get wealth, that he may establish his covenant which he sware unto thy fathers, as it is this day.

Romans 14:23
for whatsoever is not of faith is sin.

It's not good or evil because it looks good or evil to human. It is good when it is of faith. And it is evil if it is not of faith. To believe that God reasoned everything is faith. Every happening is meaningful for those because God reasoned it and there is no failure to them, good or bad to human eye, because God accomplishes what God planned.

Those who believe God reasoned everything would pursue God's will. And those others would pursue something else.

John 8:29
And he that sent me is with me: the Father hath not left me alone; for I do always those things that please him. As he spake these words, many believed on him. Then said Jesus to those Jews which believed on him, If ye continue in my word, then are ye my disciples indeed; And ye shall know the truth, and the truth shall make you free.

John 6:28
**Then said they unto him, What shall we do, that
we might work the works of God? Jesus answered
and said unto them, This is the work of God, that
ye believe on him whom he hath sent.**

*Jesus did not say to do. He said to believe! This means it's not us who
accomplishes. It's God that accomplishes in us*

———•——•—•———

Hebrews 11:1
**Now faith is the substance of things hoped for, the
evidence of things not seen. For by it the elders
obtained a good report. Through faith we understand
that the worlds were framed by the word of God, so
that things which are seen were not made of things
which do appear.**

*Things that are seen look like all to unbelievers. But there is a world
that is not seen like there is a world that is seen. Like you know there is
something more than you can imagine beyond the horizon, there are limitless
miles over your vision. Know what you see is just a few miles. There are
millions of miles over it*

———•——•—•———

Luke 7:41
**There was a certain creditor which had two debtors:
the one owed five hundred pence, and the other
fifty. And when they had nothing to pay, he frankly
forgave them both. Tell me therefore, which of them
will love him most? Simon answered and said, I
suppose that he, to whom he forgave most. And he
said unto him, Thou hast rightly judged. Wherefore I**

say unto thee, Her sins, which are many, are forgiven;
for she loved much: but to whom little is forgiven,
the same loveth little.

*Those who know oneself sinned are blessed because they are going to
be forgiven.*

*But those who believe not guilty will be judged whether they are guilty
or not indeed.*

Hebrews 10:36
**For ye have need of patience, that, after ye have done
the will of God, ye might receive the promise.**

*For the promise of Kingdom of God we need to do God's will and wait
until Jesus Christ's 2nd coming. Believe in God is doing God's job.*

John 8:12
**Then spake Jesus again unto them, saying, I am the
light of the world: he that followeth me shall not
walk in darkness, but shall have the light of life.**

John 8:24
**ye shall die in your sins: for if ye believe not that
I am he, ye shall die in your sins. I do nothing of
myself; but as my Father hath taught me, I speak
these things.**

*Jesus said he does only what God taught to. He said he is not doing his
job. He said he is doing God's job.*

Luke 12:15

for a man's life consisteth not in the abundance of the things which he   possesseth. And he spake a parable unto them, saying, The ground of a certain rich man brought forth plentifully: And he thought within himself, saying, What shall I do, because I have no room where to bestow my fruits? And he said, This will I do: I will pull down my barns, and build greater; and there will I bestow all my fruits and my goods. And I will say to my soul, Soul, thou hast much goods laid up for many years; take thine ease, eat, drink, and be merry. But God said unto him, Thou fool, this night thy soul shall be required of thee: then whose shall those things be, which thou hast provided? So is he that layeth up treasure for himself, and is not rich toward God. And he said unto his disciples, Therefore I say unto you, Take no thought for your life, what ye shall eat; neither for the body, what ye shall put on. The life is more than meat, and the body is more than raiment. Consider the ravens: for they neither sow nor reap; which neither have storehouse nor barn; and God feedeth them: how much more are ye better than the fowls? And which of you with taking thought can add to his stature one cubit? If ye then be not able to do that thing which is least, why take ye thought for the rest? Consider the lilies how they grow: they toil not, they spin not; and yet I say unto you, that Solomon in all his glory was not arrayed like one of these. If then God so clothe the grass, which is to day in the field, and tomorrow is cast into the oven; how much more will he clothe you, O ye of little faith? And seek not ye what ye shall eat, or what ye shall drink, neither be ye of doubtful mind. For all these things do the nations of the world seek after: and your Father knoweth that ye have need of these things. But rather seek ye the kingdom of God; and all these things shall be added unto you. Fear not, little flock; for it is your Father's good pleasure to give you the kingdom. Sell that ye have, and give alms; provide yourselves bags which wax not old, a treasure in the heavens that faileth not, where no thief approacheth, neither moth corrupteth. For where your treasure is, there will your heart be also. Let your loins be girded about, and your lights burning;

———•——•——•———

Corinthians I 2:10
But God hath revealed them unto us by his Spirit: for the Spirit searcheth all things, yea, the deep things of God. For what man knoweth the things of a man, save the spirit of man which is in him? even so the things of God knoweth no man, but the Spirit of God.

Those who were not born again with Holy Spirit can not understand God.

———•——•——•———

Luke 17:6
And the Lord said, If ye had faith as a grain of mustard seed, ye might say unto this sycamine tree, Be thou plucked up by the root, and be thou planted in the sea; and it should obey you.

———•——•——•———

Luke 17:7
But which of you, having a servant plowing or
feeding cattle, will say unto him by and by, when he
is come from the field, Go and sit down to meat? And
will not rather say unto him, Make ready wherewith
I may sup, and gird thyself, and serve me, till I have
eaten and drunken; and afterward thou shalt eat
and drink? Doth he thank that servant because he
did the things that were commanded him? I trow
not. So likewise ye, when ye shall have done all
those things which are commanded you, say, We
are unprofitable servants: we have done that which
was our duty to do.

God reminds us that we are just a creature made to do God's job.

Romans 1:17
For therein is the righteousness of God revealed
from faith to faith: as it is written, The just shall
live by faith.

The faith makes the faith grow and the faith saves the spirit.

Isaiah 44:6
Thus saith the LORD the King of Israel, and his
redeemer the LORD of hosts; I am the first, and I am
the last; and beside me there is no God. And who, as
I, shall call, and shall declare it, and set it in order
for me, since I appointed the ancient people? and
the things that are coming, and shall come, let them
show unto them. Fear ye not, neither be afraid: have

not I told thee from that time, and have declared it?
ye are even my witnesses. Is there a God beside me?
yea, there is no God; I know not any.

*God had chosen Israel people as the witness to show his being only God
to everybody.*

———•—◦—•———

Isaiah 59:1
Behold, the LORD'S hand is not shortened, that
it cannot save; neither his ear heavy, that it cannot
hear: But your iniquities have separated between
you and your God, and your sins have hid his face
from you, that he will not hear.

———•—◦—•———

Ecclesiastes 3:1
To everything there is a season, and a time to every
purpose under the heaven: A time to be born, and a
time to die; a time to plant, and a time to pluck up
that which is planted; A time to kill, and a time to
heal; a time to break down, and a time to build up; A
time to weep, and a time to laugh; a time to mourn,
and a time to dance; A time to cast away stones, and
a time to gather stones together; a time to embrace,
and a time to refrain from embracing; A time to get,
and a time to lose; a time to keep, and a time to cast
away; A time to rend, and a time to sew; a time to
keep silence, and a time to speak; A time to love, and
a time to hate; a time of war, and a time of peace.
What profit hath he that worketh in that wherein he
laboureth? I have seen the travail, which God hath
given to the sons of men to be exercised in it. He hath

made everything beautiful in his time: also he hath set the world in their heart, so that no man can find out the work that God maketh from the beginning to the end. I know that there is no good in them, but for a man to rejoice, and to do good in his life. And also that every man should eat and drink, and enjoy the good of all his labour, it is the gift of God. I know that, whatsoever God doeth, it shall be for ever: nothing can be put to it, nor any thing taken from it: and God doeth it, that men should fear before him. That which hath been is now; and that which is to be hath already been; and God requireth that which is past. And moreover I saw under the sun the place of judgment, that wickedness was there; and the place of righteousness, that iniquity was there. I said in mine heart, God shall judge the righteous and the wicked: for there is a time there for every purpose and for every work. I said in mine heart concerning the estate of the sons of men, that God might manifest them, and that they might see that they themselves are beasts. For that which befalleth the sons of men befalleth beasts; even one thing befalleth them: as the one dieth, so dieth the other; yea, they have all one breath; so that a man hath no preeminence above a beast: for all is vanity. All go unto one place; all are of the dust, and all turn to dust again. Who knoweth the spirit of man that goeth upward, and the spirit of the beast that goeth downward to the earth?

We creatures are only to do what God designed us and planned upon us. So free yourself from you. There is not you. What you think about yourself is false and you are going to prove it yourself when you die.

Ecclesiastes 3:10
I have seen the travail, which God hath given to
the sons of men to be exercised in it. He hath made
everything beautiful in his time: also he hath set the
world in their heart, so that no man can find out the
work that God maketh from the beginning to the
end. I know that there is no good in them, but for a
man to rejoice, and to do good in his life. And also
that every man should eat and drink, and enjoy the
good of all his labour, it is the gift of God. I know
that, whatsoever God doeth, it shall be for ever:
nothing can be put to it, nor any thing taken from it:
and God doeth it, that men should fear before him.

*Everything was made proper for each one and does God's job accordingly.
We have nothing to do more or less, but God gave us a gift that we can
enjoy in our labor.*

—————•━━•━•━•—————

Ecclesiastes 12:13
Let us hear the conclusion of the whole matter: Fear
God, and keep his commandments: for this is the
whole duty of man. For God shall bring every work
into judgment, with every secret thing, whether it
be good, or whether it be evil.

*So, whatever you do always do it as God would do. Do your job like
you do God's job.*

—————•━━•━•━•—————

John I 2:3
And hereby we do know that we know him, if we
keep his commandments. He that saith, I know

him, and keepeth not his commandments, is a liar, and the truth is not in him. But whoso keepeth his word, in him verily is the love of God perfected: hereby know we that we are in him. He that saith he abideth in him ought himself also so to walk, even as he walked.

———•——•—•——•———

Romans 12:3

For I say, through the grace given unto me, to every man that is among you, not to think of himself more highly than he ought to think; but to think soberly, according as God hath dealt to every man the measure of faith.

———•——•—•——•———

Mark 8:35

For whosoever will save his life shall lose it; but whosoever shall lose his life for my sake and the gospel's, the same shall save it. For what shall it profit a man, if he shall gain the whole world, and lose his own soul? Or what shall a man give in exchange for his soul? Whosoever therefore shall be ashamed of me and of my words in this adulterous and sinful generation; of him also shall the Son of man be ashamed, when he cometh in the glory of his Father with the holy angels.

———•——•—•——•———

Luke 14:26

If any man come to me, and hate not his father, and mother, and wife, and children, and brethren, and sisters, yea, and his own life also, he cannot be my disciple. And whosoever doth not bear his cross, and come after me, cannot be my disciple.

———•━•●•━•———

Romans 14:8
For whether we live, we live unto the Lord; and whether we die, we die unto the Lord: whether we live therefore, or die, we are the Lord's. Romans I know, and am persuaded by the Lord Jesus, that there is nothing unclean of itself: but to him that esteemeth any thing to be unclean, to him it is unclean.

Everyone is doing God's job. If you judge anybody for any reason you are judging God.

———•━•●•━•———

John 6:38
For I came down from heaven, not to do mine own will, but the will of him that sent me.

———•━•●•━•———

Jesus said to all of his disciples before crucified, and the followings are what they said.

John 13:19
Now I tell you before it come, that, when it is come to pass, ye may believe that I am he. Verily, verily, I say unto you, that one of you shall betray me.

Judas Iscariot, one of the disciples betrayed him.

———•━•●•━•———

Luke 9:22
Saying, The Son of man must suffer many things, and be rejected of the elders and chief priests and scribes, and be slain, and be raised the third day.

———•━●━•———

Matthew 26:39
And ...... prayed, saying, O my Father, if it be possible, let this cup pass from me: nevertheless not as I will, but as thou wilt.

———•━●━•———

Mark 14:29
But Peter said unto him, Although all shall be offended, yet will not I.

And Jesus saith unto him, Verily I say unto thee, That this day, even in this night, before the cock crow twice, thou shalt deny me thrice.

But he spake the more vehemently, If I should die with thee, I will not deny thee in any wise. Likewise also said they all.

Even the most beloved Peter denied as following when Jesus was arrested.

Matthew 26:69
Now Peter sat without in the palace: and a damsel came unto him, saying, Thou also wast with Jesus of Galilee. But he denied before them all, saying, I know not what thou sayest. And when he was gone out into the porch, another maid saw him, and said unto them that were there, This fellow was also with Jesus of Nazareth. And again he denied with an oath, I do not know the man. And after a while came unto

him they that stood by, and said to Peter, Surely thou also art one of them; for thy speech bewrayeth thee. Then began he to curse and to swear, saying, I know not the man. And immediately the cock crew. And Peter remembered the word of Jesus, which said unto him, Before the cock crow, thou shalt deny me thrice. And he went out, and wept bitterly.

———•—■•■—•———

When God allowed Satan to take away all of Job's possession, Job did not complain.
He said:

Job 1:21
And said, Naked came I out of my mother's womb, and naked shall I return thither: the LORD gave, and the LORD hath taken away; blessed be the name of the LORD.

And the bible described sin as following.

Job 1:22
In all this Job sinned not, nor charged God foolishly.

This shows that complaining about what God does is the sin.
So, the bad behavior itself is not sin but the fruit of complaint.
That fruit shows one's being man of physical body or man of spirit.
As the situation became worse Job's wife also mocked him.
And Job explained again what sin is as following.

Job 2:9
Then said his wife unto him, Dost thou still retain thine integrity? curse God, and die. But he said unto her, Thou speakest as one of the foolish women speaketh. What? shall we receive good at the hand

of God, and shall we not receive evil? In all this did
not Job sin with his lips.

———•——•——•———

God said this mind and this attitude of Job is righteous.
Job's friend who came to relieve Job said about Job's this attitude.

Job 22:1
Then Eliphaz the Temanite answered and said, Can
a man be profitable unto God, as he that is wise may
be profitable unto himself? Is it any pleasure to the
Almighty, that thou art righteous? or is it gain to
him, that thou makest thy ways perfect?

This is the same thing that was discussed at the previous chapter as "We
are like dust or fog and we cannot do nothing on our own will. Whether we
want to do something or we don't want to do something, isn't that the mind
God gave?" This idea comes from the lack of understanding the meaning
of life God gave to accomplish God's will.
Later, God said it's not righteous.

Job 42:7
And it was so, that after the LORD had spoken
these words unto Job, the LORD said to Eliphaz
the Temanite, My wrath is kindled against thee, and
against thy two friends: for ye have not spoken of
me the thing that is right, as my servant Job hath.

Job showed us the attitude toward God should be as following.

Job 23:10
But he knoweth the way that I take: when he hath
tried me, I shall come forth as gold. My foot hath
held his steps, his way have I kept, and not declined.
Neither have I gone back from the commandment

of his lips; I have esteemed the words of his mouth more than my necessary food. But he is in one mind, and who can turn him? and what his soul desireth, even that he doeth. For he performeth the thing that is appointed for me: and many such things are with him. Therefore am I troubled at his presence: when I consider, I am afraid of him.

I believe this is the faith.

———•—•—•———

Proverbs 27:1
Boast not thyself of to morrow; for thou knowest not what a day may bring forth.

———•—•—•———

Solomon, the king of wisdom, said:

Ecclesiastes 1:2
Vanity of vanities, saith the Preacher, vanity of vanities; all is vanity.

What profit hath a man of all his labour which he taketh under the sun?

———•—•—•———

Ecclesiastes 4:1
So I returned, and considered all the oppressions that are done under the sun: and behold the tears of such as were oppressed, and they had no comforter; and on the side of their oppressors there was power; but they had no comforter. Wherefore I praised the dead which are already dead more than the living which are yet alive. Yea, better is he than both

they, which hath not yet been, who hath not seen the evil work that is done under the sun. Again, I considered all travail, and every right work, that for this a man is envied of his neighbour. This is also vanity and vexation of spirit. The fool foldeth his hands together, and eateth his own flesh. Better is an handful with quietness, than both the hands full with travail and vexation of spirit. Then I returned, and I saw vanity under the sun. There is one alone, and there is not a second; yea, he hath neither child nor brother: yet is there no end of all his labour; neither is his eye satisfied with riches; neither saith he, For whom do I labour, and bereave my soul of good? This is also vanity, yea, it is a sore travail.

Ecclesiastes 5:18
Behold that which I have seen: it is good and comely for one to eat and to drink, and to enjoy the good of all his labour that he taketh under the sun all the days of his life, which God giveth him: for it is his portion. Every man also to whom God hath given riches and wealth, and hath given him power to eat thereof, and to take his portion, and to rejoice in his labour; this is the gift of God. For he shall not much remember the days of his life; because God answereth him in the joy of his heart.

Ecclesiastes 9:1
For all this I considered in my heart even to declare all this, that the righteous, and the wise, and their works, are in the hand of God: no man knoweth

either love or hatred by all that is before them. All things come alike to all: there is one event to the righteous, and to the wicked; to the good and to the clean, and to the unclean; to him that sacrificeth, and to him that sacrificeth not: as is the good, so is the sinner; and he that sweareth, as he that feareth an oath. This is an evil among all things that are done under the sun, that there is one event unto all: yea, also the heart of the sons of men is full of evil, and madness is in their heart while they live, and after that they go to the dead.

Ecclesiastes 9:9
Live joyfully with the wife whom thou lovest all the days of the life of thy vanity, which he hath given thee under the sun, all the days of thy vanity: for that is thy portion in this life, and in thy labour which thou takest under the sun. I returned, and saw under the sun, that the race is not to the swift, nor the battle to the strong, neither yet bread to the wise, nor yet riches to men of understanding, nor yet favour to men of skill; but time and chance happeneth to them all. For man also knoweth not his time: as the fishes that are taken in an evil net, and as the birds that are caught in the snare; so are the sons of men snared in an evil time, when it falleth suddenly upon them.

The "Vanity" is the word that repeats all through the **Ecclesiastes.** *God says chasing your physical desire is vanity so get out of the world of vanity* *and labor joyfully as God gave as your portion. It is God's commandment and keeping God's commandment is our life.*

Solomon closed this **Ecclesiastes** *as following.*

> **Ecclesiastes 12:13**
> Let us hear the conclusion of the whole matter: Fear God, and keep his commandments: for this is the whole duty of man. For God shall bring every work into judgment, with every secret thing, whether it be good, or whether it be evil.

———•—•—•———

Now I am going to think about what the life itself is from next chapter after rearranging our relationship to God as following.

> **Isaiah 10:15**
> Shall the ax boast itself against him that heweth therewith? or shall the saw magnify itself against him that shaketh it? as if the rod should shake itself against them that lift it up, or as if the staff should lift up itself, as if it were no wood.

———•—•—•———

> **Isaiah 29:15**
> Woe unto them that seek deep to hide their counsel from the LORD, and their works are in the dark, and they say, Who seeth us? and who knoweth us? Surely your turning of things upside down shall be esteemed as the potter's clay: for shall the work say of him that made it, He made me not? or shall the thing framed say of him that framed it, He had no understanding? Surely your turning of things upside down shall be esteemed as the potter's clay: for shall

the work say of him that made it, He made me not?
or shall the thing framed say of him that framed it,
He had no understanding?

———•━•━•———

Jeremiah 18:1
The word which came to Jeremiah from the LORD,
saying, Arise, and go down to the potter's house, and
there I will cause thee to hear my words. Then I went
down to the potter's house, and, behold, he wrought
a work on the wheels. And the vessel that he made
of clay was marred in the hand of the potter: so he
made it again another vessel, as seemed good to the
potter to make it. Then the word of the LORD came
to me, saying, O house of Israel, cannot I do with
you as this potter? saith the LORD. Behold, as the
clay is in the potter's hand, so are ye in mine hand,
O house of Israel.

6. About Life

What's Life

John 1:1
In the beginning was the Word, and the Word was with God, and the Word was God. The same was in the beginning with God.

All things were made by him; and without him was not any thing made that was made. In him was life; and the life was the light of men.

———•—•—•———

Genesis 1:26
And God said, Let us make man in our image, after our likeness: and let them have dominion over the fish of the sea, and over the fowl of the air, and over the cattle, and over all the earth, and over every creeping thing that creepeth upon the earth. So God created man in his own image, in the image of God created he him; male and female created he them. And God blessed them, and God said unto them, Be fruitful, and multiply, and replenish the earth, and subdue it: and have dominion over the fish of the sea, and over the fowl of the air, and over every living thing that moveth upon the earth.

———•—•—•———

Genesis 2:7
And the LORD God formed man of the dust of the ground, and breathed into his nostrils the breath of life; and man became a living soul.

———•━•■━•——

When God formed a man with dust and breathed the life into the man, the man became a living soul. In American Standard Version, "the living soul" is translated as "the living being". And we can assume the life is something that activates the body to move.

Jesus said as:

John 6:63
It is the spirit that gives life, the flesh is of no avail; the words that I have spoken to you are spirit and life.

So, we come to know that something God breathed into body is spirit and the spirit is life. When we recall the word is God and God is spirit, we can understand that God breathed himself into the body. So, God is living in our body. When God breathed the life into man, man became a living being or living soul.

Likewise, when God formed a dog, cat, bird, sneak, rabbit, bacteria and tree…and breathed the life into each of those, each one became a living being and worked appropriately as each one was made.

The lives breathed into each body are actually the same except that each life was breathed into different body. As the life itself implies, the life is life and has nothing to do with death. In other word, it never dies. This means the living beings are made with two things of body and the spirit that activates the body to move. And the spirit has the life. So, we have never dying everlasting life in us already.

Somebody would say "Then why every living being dies?"

That does not mean the spirit is dying. It means the spirit that activates the body leaves the body. That is what we call the death. So, the body is nothing but the dust.

But God worked out with the dust to make very surprising bodies with the endless knowledge and wisdom and breathed the life into it to use the body to accomplish what God wants. And each body began to work appropriately as God designed on them.

Like the bacteria spoil things, trees grow and bear fruits, bees fly around to help trees bear fruit... and men subdue and exercise dominion over every living being. If we analyze the bodies, we find each body is composed of different kind of materials. Like the steel lasts longer than the paper, each body's life period was decided accordingly. When it is damaged and fails to sustain, God takes the spirit away from the body but still the spirit remains as life without body and cannot do anything like the battery without car.

Being breathed into the body means it was imprisoned in the body and it can not come out of the body by itself. It can exercise the life only through the body. This is the physical reason why I say we are free only in God's will. That's what we call alive.

That way it does God's job not knowing that it is doing God's job.

Many people say the difference between men and animals is that men have spirit and animals don't. King Solomon said about this:

Ecclesiastes 3:18
I said in my heart with regard to the sons of men that God is testing them to show them that they are but beasts. For the fate of the sons of men and the fate of beasts is the same; as one dies, so dies the other. They all have the same breath, and man has no advantage over the beasts; for all is vanity. All go to one place; all are from the dust, and all turn to dust again.

I would say the soul is the name of every living being and the spirit makes it happen. There is no difference between men and animals up to this point. But something had happened to man when Adam ate the fruit of good and evil. I am going to discuss about this in next chapter.

The spirit that activates the body and enables it to move around grows as the body grows and characterized responding to the body's movement like a baby grows to be characterized as good man or bad man.

Like the spirit activates the body to move around, man made batteries activate the cars too.

This means we men also do the job similar to what God does. The difference is God creates and we use what God created. God's creature does God's job and man's creature does man's job. The point is we can not do better than God ever. We are only copying and learning from God.

Since the spirit is life, it moves freely in God's given condition of body and grow to form a character while moving around. But man-made battery cannot grow to form a character because it does not have spirit, the life, to respond to the movement of the car.

So, when the spirit is imprisoned in a man, it grows to have the man character and when the spirit is imprisoned in an animal it grows to have the animal character.

Here I want to emphasize the imprisonment of spirit. It's like a wild horse. Training a wild horse is said to break the horse. You never be able to train the horse leaving the horse in the wild field. Likewise imprisoning the spirit in the body is a necessary process for the spirit to grow to have a certain character. The body looks like life itself because you can actually see the body moves, but the bible says:

John 6:63
It is the spirit that gives life, the flesh is of no avail; the words that I have spoken to you are spirit and life.

Raising the spiritual character is the reason God imprisoned the spirit in the body. We are going to discuss more detail about it in chapter "What is being a child of God?"

The body in which God imprisoned the spirit is the condition God gave. The spirit was set to move freely in that condition and grows to have own character. So, however you train an animal really good, you never can make it have man's character. It could be similar for the best but it can not have man's character.

This spirit remains life even after it left the body but it can not do anything because it does not have body. It stays like it is sleeping until the judgment and revives in a new body. The Holy Spirit to the holy body in peace and the evil spirit to the evil body in never quenching fire with pain. I'd like to think about this for a moment.

God breathes the spirit into body to raise it and then take away. When the harvest comes, the spirit resurrects in different body. The holy spirit in a holy body in heaven where the tree of life is, and an unholy spirit in an unholy body in hell where the tree of life is not. Which is the resurrection. That resurrected holy spirits in holy body lasts forever because it has the tree of life. However, the resurrected unholy spirit in unholy body can not last forever because it does not have the tree of life. I assume it would repeat birth and death of unholy life and suffer in pain and tear until it becomes holy. Apostle Paul said about that:

Corinthians I 15
But some one will ask, "How are the dead raised? With what kind of body do they come?" You foolish man! What you sow does not come to life unless it dies. And what you sow is not the body which is to be, but a bare kernel, perhaps of wheat or of some other grain. But God gives it a body as he has chosen, and to each kind of seed its own body. For not all flesh is alike, but there is one kind for men, another for animals, another for birds, and another for fish.

From this scripture I found the resurrection is pretty much like the transmigration of Buddhism in part.

Even if we eat good food and take care of our body well, everyone dies. And our body cell keeps expanding until the youth age and shrinks afterwards. This means the food we eat is not for the life but only for the body like the machine needs to be greased and taken care of regularly.

Even though our body is of dust, it is such a masterpiece made by the best knowledge and skill of omnipotent God. Like the man of primitive society would take a clock as alive by its ticking, our body is such a complicate and delicate piece as scientists approve.

But it's not life. Then why do we feel so painful when our body is damaged?

Because our spirit is imprisoned in the body so it grows responding to the body. Anyway, the judgment is upon the invisible spirit, the life.

Good and Evil

Genesis 2:15
The LORD God took the man and put him in the garden of Eden to till it and keep it. And the LORD God commanded the man, saying, "You may freely eat of every tree of the garden; but of the tree of the knowledge of good and evil you shall not eat, for in the day that you eat of it you shall die."

This causes such a controversy among most of the Christians who believes God is good.

Why good God put such a bad tree in the middle of the garden and commanded not to eat? Isn't it better not to make such a thing from the beginning than to put it in the middle of the garden with a warning not to eat? Before we get into "why", we are going to discuss about what is good and what is evil.

Genesis 2:18
Then the LORD God said, "It is not good that the man should be alone; I will make him a helper fit for him." So, the LORD God caused a deep sleep to fall upon the man, and while he slept took one of his ribs and closed up its place with flesh; and the rib which the LORD God had taken from the man he made into a woman and brought her to the man. Then the man said, "This at last is bone of my bones

and flesh of my flesh; she shall be called Woman, because she was taken out of Man."

From this time, man began to love his bone of bones and flesh of flesh more than God, the spirit.

Genesis 3:1
Now the serpent was more subtle than any other wild creature that the LORD God had made. He said to the woman, "Did God say, 'You shall not eat of any tree of the garden'?" And the woman said to the serpent, "We may eat of the fruit of the trees of the garden; but God said, 'You shall not eat of the fruit of the tree which is in the midst of the garden, neither shall you touch it, lest you die.'" But the serpent said to the woman, "You will not die. For God knows that when you eat of it your eyes will be opened, and you will be like God, knowing good and evil."

We should remember that God created not only meek sheep but also wicked serpent.
God created the medicinal herb and the poisonous herb too.
He does not only create. He destroys also as he said as following.

Isaiah 45:7
I form light and create darkness, I make weal and create woe, I am the LORD, who do all these things.

All these things associate each other to accomplish God's will and make the only one good. That good is truth and God is good.

Genesis 3:6
So when the woman saw that the tree was good for food, and that it was a delight to the eyes, and that

the tree was to be desired to make one wise, she took of its fruit and ate; and she also gave some to her husband, and he ate. Then the eyes of both were opened, and they knew that they were naked; and they sewed fig leaves together and made themselves aprons. And they heard the sound of the LORD God walking in the garden in the cool of the day, and the man and his wife hid themselves from the presence of the LORD God among the trees of the garden. But the LORD God called to the man, and said to him, "Where are you?" And he said, "I heard the sound of thee in the garden, and I was afraid, because I was naked; and I hid myself." He said, "Who told you that you were naked? Have you eaten of the tree of which I commanded you not to eat?"

When someone asked Jesus

Matthew 19:17
"Teacher, what good deed must I do, to have eternal life?"

Jesus said:

"Why do you ask me about what is good? One there is who is good.
If you would enter life, keep the commandments."

This means whatever God does is good and denying it is evil.
As we discussed, men have no big difference than any other animals except that God made men to subdue and have dominion over every living being that move upon the earth. But after man ate the fruit of the tree of good and evil, man happened to have one big different thing.

Genesis 3:7

Then the eyes of both were opened, and they knew
that they were naked; and they sewed fig leaves
together and made themselves aprons.

Men became to know what is good and what is bad to them. Not to God!

This means men became to have own standard of distinguishing good and evil based upon their own benefit.

In a word, the self-consciousness had been rooted in men. We call it "I" or "Ego".

This self-consciousness formed "I" in men and began to distinguish good and evil upon own standard. Which is profitable to "I" was good and which is unprofitable to "I" was evil. Before, when men's eyes were not open they did not know they were naked.

They could not and did not have any reason to distinguish it as good or bad.

Because there was no "I" in them.

But now, when "I" was rooted, their eyes were opened to realize they were naked and made apron with leaves and hid. Which was not evil before turned out to be evil now.

This very first action after men's eyes were opened explains well about men's self- centered good and evil concept. It's interesting to find none of other animals, insects or what so ever is not naked. Only men on earth are ashamed of being naked. If living naked is bad God wouldn't let any other animals live naked.

As we see, men's good and evil concept is not like God's.

One thing we have to remember is, once we had our eyes open, we cannot make it closed unless we deny ourselves. Since everything is subject to "I", the more we try to survive the more we judge God and get closer to death.

Because of this "I", men became responsible for their deed and had to stand at the judgment for their deed whether their deed was good or evil before God.

That's because "I" did.

When "I" was not in men there were no responsibility because there were no one to put the responsibility on. That's because God did and God wouldn't judge himself.

When "I" was not in men, men could not complain or proud of what happened to him.

But after "I" took place in men, men began to complain or proud of what happens to him.

The difference between animals without "I" and men with "I" is that animals do not complain or proud of oneself because they do not have "I". But men complain and proud of oneself because men have "I".

We can understand the difference easily if we watch a baby carefully.

Babies have the root of "I" but not yet grown up to show it. So, babies act instinctively just like animals. They just react on hunger, thirst, cold.... No complain or shame!

But as the babies grow, the "I" placed in the spirit also grows and becomes to know what is good and what is bad to "I" and begin to judge God, saying God's this work is good and God's that work is bad. While the other animals remain the same as they were born.

Since the main principal body that judges God is "I", that very "I" is going to be Holy or Satanic when grown in God or grown in one's own desire respectively.

I am not saying the "I" rooted in us is bad.

I am saying this "I" is going to be judged and classified as grain or mean tare.

When this "I" was cut off in the middle of it and grafted to God, it grows to be a Son of God and when this "I" grows pursuing what it likes, it grows to be a son of Satan God made this Fruit of Good and Evil as a mean to raise the spirits as Sons of God. Since men only have "I", I would say everything happening in this world is just a phenomenon to each one that shows how God works to each one to raise men's spiritual character to that of God's character. In other words, every happening in this world including oneself is for "I" to raise it to Son of God.

Subduing and having dominion over every moving thing is how God raises this spirit "I".

Sin, good, bad, shame, proud, save, heaven, hell...are not the words for the animals. Those words are only for men. Because animals do not have "I" to be proud of, to be shamed of and to go to heaven or hell. So, we do not say a dog, monkey, gorilla… goes to hell or heaven.

Likewise, the babies are not for heaven or hell also because their spirit is not yet grown up. They might be pretty much like other animals except it has the possibility to become Son of God. In that sense, abortion is against God's will. Jesus Christ said the heaven is for those who are like the babies. That does not mean every baby will be in heaven. If so, our life is meaningless. It means the heaven is for those who are so pure like the babies. Only those who are pure like a baby can see the heaven and grow to fit into it.

In that sense again, killing animals to control and eat is not against God's will. The reason why I am saying this is because I once felt some kind of guilt myself when eating meat. Because God said God gave every edible thing as food. I see some interesting thing that occurs frequently these days concerning this.

Recently it happened in California that a dog bit a man seriously and the man killed the dog to survive. It used to be quite normal up to this point. But next day the owner of the dog sued the man for the cruelty against animal and the animal lover's association backed it up. This is the result of misunderstanding the bible. Loving animals is quite a natural character of men but "animal first" is not God's will because God gave every moving being to men to control. God made this world for men and men are supposed to control animals. I do not mean it's OK to abuse animal.

That's another story.

That's why we need to wake up and understand God through the bible.

Without understanding, we do not know where we are going. We might be going far away from God not even knowing we are and say God loves us and we are saved.

Now, let's go back to main subject.

Thus, grown up spirits of "I" have own characters accordingly how they grew up, and show individual characters built upon own life.

Someone shows his character with the wealth one built. Someone with knowledge, someone with honor and someone with position….

We call this characteristic based upon self-centered man's standard as character. Animals also build animal character based upon God's standard.

We call God's character based upon truth and absolute standard as divine character.

As the first man Adam ate the fruit of good and evil, this self-centered standard took place in him and descended through his seed and every body has it now.

This fact would work differently according to each one's point of view.

When you look from the physical point of view, it means God wanted to kill everybody.

Because everybody dies. But remember the life is never dying spirit though.

When you look from spiritual point of view it means God wanted to raise man's character to that of God.

Because, by doing so, God could plant "I" in our spirit and could raise that "I".

You can not raise something if you do not plant it. You have to plant something first to raise it. That something is "I", the ego, and the seed is the fruit of good and evil.

So, everyone has both characteristics of good and evil. God wanted to raise the standard of this good and evil concept of men to that of God's standard.

Followings show what the result of our self-centered good and evil is.

Genesis 3:16
To the woman he said, "I will greatly multiply your pain in childbearing; in pain you shall bring forth children, yet your desire shall be for your husband, and he shall rule over you." And to Adam he said, "Because you have listened to the voice of your wife, and have eaten of the tree of which I commanded you, 'You shall not eat of it,' cursed is the ground because of you; in toil you shall eat of it all the days of your life;

It is very interesting again to find none of the animal work to get food from the ground.

Only men work to get food from ground as God said.

Since men's standard is self-centered, they had to win to be good. Every kinds of fighting followed anywhere men go. To be good, men had to compete and win. That is war and human history proves it with war after war since the existence and it's still continuing.

This generic character is shown not only in war. Every athletic game, vote, competition, acceptance test, qualification test... Whatever it is if it limits the number and grades the level shows the same problem.

Why don't we know there could be a winner because there is a loser?

Both did the same thing and both are precious. Yet the self-centered standard doesn't allow it and the winner take everything and they are called good while the loser loose everything and get disgrace despite they did the same thing.

Many would say "Competition creates better job, so what's bad about it?"

As we discussed in the chapter of "How God accomplishes", the "winner takes everything" is not God's will. God's will is "Let it be accomplished as much as it is done."

That is righteousness. So, "the winner takes everything" is just based upon men's self-centered standard.

Because of this self-centered mind, men try to get more while doing less, begin war to take for nothing, give and take bribe, murder and underestimate others...

Because of this self-centered mind, man became to think the winner is precious and blessed by God while the loser thinks his job is not precious and it's not God's job.

We know many of the NFL players or many other players in athletic games earn multimillion dollars a year. When we consider annual income of the average American workers is not more than thirty thousand dollars, I wonder how many American people would take their job as precious as those players. And how many would think God is fair?

All these are the result of the self-centered standard.

However, we can find out one thing common from all these.

All these are about physical things and all are due to the physical limit.

This problem can not be solved physical way because physical things have limit.

Besides, these things have nothing to do with the spirit, the life.

Genesis 3:22

Then the LORD God said, "Behold, the man has become like one of us, knowing good and evil; and now, lest he put forth his hand and take also of the tree of life, and eat, and live for ever" ------ therefore the LORD God sent him forth from the garden of Eden, to till the ground from which he was taken. He drove out the man; and at the east of the garden of Eden he placed the cherubim, and a flaming sword which turned every way, to guard the way to the tree of life.

God did not allow men live forever with men's own standard of good and evil. If allowed, that would mean there is no truth and there is another God.

Now, then how do we raise our spiritual character or build the character of "I" rooted in us? We know the food we eat is not for the spirit "I". It's for the body.

Jesus said:

John 4:34

Jesus said to them, "My food is to do the will of him who sent me, and to accomplish his work.

Our body grows by eating food and our spirit grows by doing God's will.

Our body eats food but our spirit eats "Doing God's will". By doing God's Will, our spirit grows. And God's will is the bible. Therefore, we do not know what is God's precious job and what is God's mean job unless we know the bible.

Because we can not discern which is God's will and which is not.

That is just like we discern which food is good for our body and which are poisonous.

So, knowing the bible is having the ability to discern spiritual food and doing the will of God is bearing fruit of belief and the accomplishment of God's will is the fruit of belief.

As Jesus said the belief without performance is dead belief, just understanding God's will does not help the spirit unless the bible knowledge accompanies the performance. It's like someone who keeps plenty of food in the storage and does not eat. This man is sure to die of hunger. I want to remind again that God talks to God's children spiritually through the bible.

Now I think we can understand what Jesus wanted to tell us with following.

> **Matthew 26:26**
> **Now as they were eating, Jesus took bread, and blessed, and broke it, and gave it to the disciples and said, "Take, eat; this is my body." And he took a cup, and when he had given thanks he gave it to them, saying, "Drink of it, all of you; for this is my blood of the covenant, which is poured out for many for the forgiveness of sins.**

Jesus said to his disciple, spirit to spirit, at the last dinner table.

As we understood "Eat my body" means to perform what Jesus taught and "Drink my blood" means to believe what Jesus taught.

Jesus explained it clearly.

> **John 6:33 For the bread of God is that which comes down from heaven, and gives life to the world." They said to him, "Lord, give us this bread always." Jesus said to them, "I am the bread of life; he who comes to me shall not hunger, and he who believes in me shall never thirst.**

As Jesus said "Those who eat my body has life in it and those who does not eat my body does not have life in it", those spirits who do not perform God's will cannot raise the spiritual character of "I" and the "I" looks like alive but it doesn't grow and stay as good as dead just like the animals which doesn't have "I".

From Adam to Jesus Christ

It is interesting to look into the lifetime of those who played the major role in the bible and how men spread over the earth.

When God drove Adam out from the Garden of Eden men's lifetime was not set yet.

If we look into the lifetime of their descendants:

The first man Adam lived 930 years. He got the 3rd son Seth in his own likeness after his image as the replacement of the 2nd son Abel who was killed by the 1st son Cain. He lived 912 years. Enosh, Seth's son, lived 905 years and his son Kenan lived 910 years.

Kenan's son Ma-hal'alel lived 895 years, his son Jared lived 962 years, his son Enoch lived 365 years and God took him and he was not in this world.

His son Methu'selah lived 969 years, his son Lamech lived 777 years, his son Noah lived 350 years after the great flood and died at the age of 950.

Adam got Seth at the age of 130. Seth got Enosh at the age of 105. Enosh got Kenan at 90. Kenan got Ma-hal'alel at 70. Ma-hal'alel got Jared at 65. Jared got Enoch at 162. Enoch got Methu'selah at 65. Methu'selah got Lamech at 180. Noah got Shem, Ham and Japheth after the age of 500.

It took 1049 years for 10 generations from Adam to Noah.

Considering the average lifetime God gave to these people was 912 years, we can see most of the people of this whole 10 generation had lived all together until the great flood swept them away.

Through the only survival Noah, men began to flourish on earth again and God said:

Genesis 6:1

When men began to multiply on the face of the ground, and daughters were born to them, the sons of God saw that the daughters of men were fair; and they took to wife such of them as they chose. Then the LORD said, "My spirit shall not abide in man for ever, for he is flesh, but his days shall be a hundred and twenty years."

From this time God did not strive with men and men had to live like animals without communication with God. The only difference was men had their own self-centered standard to judge good and evil. They could not understand God and therefore they could not know they were living to accomplish God's will.

They just lived instinctively to fill the physical desire. Spiritually dead!

Thereafter, men's lifetime had been reduced gradually to 120 years as God said. Noah had three sons of Shem, Ham and Jabeth.

The 1st son Shem got Arphaxad at the age of 100, Arphaxad got Salah at 35, Salah got Eber at 30, Eber got Peleg at 34, Peleg got Reu at 30, Reu got Serug at 32, Serug got Nahor at 30, Nahor got Terah at 29. Tera got Abram, Nahor and Haran at the age of 70. And it took 390 years of 10 generations.

Shem is the 1st son of Noah and God was to accomplish his plan through this family line.

Looking into the lifetime of these people after Noah:

Shem lived 600 years. His son Arphaxad lived 438 years, and Arphaxad's son Salah lived 433 years, his son Eber lived 464 years, and his son Peleg lived 239 years. At this time people built a sky-high tower at Babel to avoid being scattered all over.

God said about this:

Genesis 11:1

And the whole earth was of one language, and of one speech. And it came to pass, as they journeyed from the east, that they found a plain in the land of Shinar; and they dwelt there. And they said one to another, Go to, let us make brick, and burn them thoroughly. And they had brick for stone, and slime had they for mortar. And they said, Go to, let us build us a city and a tower, whose top may reach unto heaven; and let us make us a name, lest we be scattered abroad upon the face of the whole earth. And the LORD came down to see the city and the tower, which the children of men builded. And the LORD said, Behold, the people is one, and they have all one language; and this they begin to do: and now nothing will be restrained from them, which they have imagined to do. Go to, let us go down, and there confound their language, that they may not understand one another's speech. So, the LORD scattered them abroad from thence upon the face of all the earth: and they left off to build the city. Therefore is the name of it called Babel; because the LORD did there confound the language of all the earth: and from thence did the LORD scatter them abroad upon the face of all the earth.

Let's think about this a little before we continue.

As we discussed earlier, we know it is our hope to have a unified government to avoid war between countries and live in peace.

These people tried exactly the same thing as we are trying now.

*And what's wrong with this? It sounds good. Why did God scatter them? The above verse **11:6** explains it.*

When Adam ate the fruit and had own standard of Good and evil, God drove them out lest they eat the fruit of life and live forever, judging things upon their own standard, making God's truth deteriorated and making God is not the only good.

God did this just for the same reason.

God wanted to restrain men from men's own that is not truth and changing always. God wanted to hold on to God's will as God planned and accomplish it.

God explained why God needed to confound the language and scatter men all over:

Genesis 11:6
Nothing will be restrained from them, which they have imagined to do.

Now, let's go back to main subject.

Peleg's son Rue lived 239 years also, his son Serug lived 230 years, his son Nahor lived 148 years, his son Terah lived 205 years and his son Abram lived 175 years.

Abram was the man with whom God established the covenant for his righteousness of believing God.

God is to carry out his plan through this family line as promised as following.

Genesis 17:7
And I will establish my covenant between me and thee and thy seed after thee in their generations for an everlasting covenant, to be a God unto thee, and to thy seed after thee. And I will give unto thee, and to thy seed after thee, the land wherein thou art a stranger, all the land of Canaan, for an everlasting possession; and I will be their God. And God said unto Abraham, Thou shalt keep my covenant therefore, thou, and thy seed after thee in their generations.

God said this family the chosen people. Which means God chose this family to show God's being only God to everybody to make everybody respect and afraid of God.

As above scripture says, Israel people first moved into the land of Canaan at this time. God told Abram that his people will leave Canaan and be strangers in foreign land for four hundred years and will be delivered back to the land of Canaan which God gave to Abram. It is said as following.

Genesis 15:13
And he said unto Abram, Know of a surety that thy seed shall be a stranger in a land that is not theirs, and shall serve them; and they shall afflict them four hundred years; And also that nation, whom they shall serve, will I judge: and afterward shall they come out with great substance.

This God's plan begins to accomplish through Abram's great grandson Joseph. As we see, men's lifetime was getting reduced dramatically as time went. Abram's son Isac lived 180 years, his son Jacob lived 147 years, and his son Joseph lived 110 years.

As mentioned above God's pre-arranged plan on Israel people began to accomplish through this Joseph beginning Joseph's being sold to Egypt as a slave by his own brothers.

Later, this Joseph became a ruler of Egypt and brought all of his family from Canaan and saved from terrible famine. After hundreds of years, this Israel people out numbered the Egyptians and the Egyptians did not know about Joseph. They were afraid of the Israel's power getting bigger than theirs and began to persecute the Israel people.

After 400 years Moses was born in Levi branch, which is one of Jacob's twelve sons and he was to deliver the Israel people from Egyptian's persecution with the help of God's lot of miraculous works. He led the Israel people to their land of Canaan God gave to Abram before. But Moses could not enter the land of Canaan and see it. He lived 120 years.

Joshua entered into the land of Canaan and fought against the inhabitants to settle down. He lived 110 years.

When Israel was ruled by prophets, Israel did not have a king. God allowed Saul as the 1ˢᵗ king of Israel and let him rule and Samuel was the prophet at that time. When Saul became the king, his age was 40. He killed himself defeated at the battle. Since the 2ⁿᵈ king David became the king at the age of 30 we can presume the 1ˢᵗ king Saul died early in his fifties or sixties. David ruled Israel for 40 years and died at the age of 70. David was a shepherd and his father's name was Jesse. 1,000 years later, 27 generations after David, Jesus Christ came to this family line.

David's son Solomon also ruled Israel for 40 years. Considering he ascended the throne normally we can presume he lived around 70-80 years.

After the king Solomon died, the Israel was split into two countries of Israel and Judah in BC931.

19 kings ruled Judah for 345 years until the capital Jerusalem surrendered to Babylon in BC 586 and Israel was ruled by 18 kings for 209 years before the capital Samaria surrendered to Assyria 136 years earlier than Judah on BC 722. On the other hand, Thompson bible explains how men were spread over the earth after the great flood as following.

Noah had three sons of Shem, Ham and Jabeth after his age of 500 and entered the Ark at the age of 600 together with his wife, sons and their wives and could escape the great flood. Through these people men became to flourish again.

The third son Jabeth's families dwelt at western and northern part of Palestine and spread over the area of the Black Sea, Caspian Sea and Urasia to become the ancestors of Aryans and the Greeks.

Ham is the 2ⁿᵈ son who told his brothers of his father Noah's fallen asleep naked in the tent after drinking too much wine. Noah got angry about this and said:

Genesis 9:25
And he said, Cursed be Canaan; a servant of servants shall he be unto his brethren. ***(Canaan was the youngest son of Ham)***

Ham' families dwelt at Africa and spread along the Mediterranean Sea to the west and settled down at the upper stream of Nile River. Later they spread again out to Arabia, Babylon and India. They lived at Lybia, the North of Africa, North of Ethiopia, Jerusalem and the suburbs, both side of Jordan River and the mountainous area of Judah. One of Ham's sons, the Cush's(Etheopians) descendants are said to had black skin and strong body as written as:

Genesis 10:8
And Cush begat Nimrod: he began to be a mighty one in the earth.

Philistim was one of this tribe. And Nineveh, Asshur Babel and Shinar...were their land. The descendants of Canaan who was cursed by Noah were Sidon, Heth, Jebusite, Amorite, Girgasite, Hivite, Arkite, Sinite, Arvadite, Zemarite and Hamathite.

They lived at Sidon, Gerar, Gaza, Admah, Zeboim and Lasha.

Sodom and Gomorrah God destroyed with fire at the time of Abram were said to be their land too. They all were to be conquered and exterminated when Israel entered the land of Canaan after Moses delivered Israel from Egyptian by Joshua and Solomon.

The 1st son Shem is known as Hebrew and they dwelt at the northern part of Persian Gulf. God chose this branch and established covenant with Abram and kept the covenant as the Israel history shows. It is interesting that Noah prayed to God as following.

Genesis 9:26
And he said, Blessed be the LORD God of Shem; and Canaan shall be his servant. God shall enlarge Japheth, and he shall dwell in the tents of Shem; and Canaan shall be his servant.

(And that was the history of Israel.)
Since God's spirit did not strive the men anymore, even these chosen people could not understand God. They pursued own desire and God dealt with their deeds accordingly sometimes with blessing and sometimes with curse telling his being only God through the prophets.

However God's spirit which did not strive the men since the time of Noah descended upon Jesus Christ as written in the bible as:

Matthew 3:16
And Jesus, when he was baptized, went up straightway out of the water: and, lo, the heavens were opened unto him, and he saw the Spirit of God descending like a dove, and lighting upon him: And lo a voice from heaven, saying, This is my beloved Son, in whom I am well pleased.

And anyone who come to Jesus Christ could communicate with God again after Jesus Christ died on the cross as it is said:

Matthew 27:51
And, behold, the veil of the temple was rent in twain from the top to the bottom; and the earth did quake, and the rocks rent;

Because until that time nobody except the priests could enter the temple behind the veil to pray. From this time God allowed anyone who comes to Jesus Christ understand God. Let's find out what was hidden in the fruit of Good and Evil. Again, don't forget that only those who believe in God can understand what God says.

Secret Hidden in the Fruit of Good and Evil

Through the chapter Free Will, we discussed about our freedom and now we understand we are free only in God's will. That means we are bound in God's plan and we are free only in that plan.

Since I think this understanding holds the key to open the secret hidden in the fruit of the tree of good and evil, I am going to refresh the understanding with following words.

James 4:13
Come now, you who say, "Today or tomorrow we will go into such and such a town and spend a year there and trade and get gain"; whereas you do not know about tomorrow. What is your life?For you are a mist that appears for a little time and then vanishes. Instead you ought to say, "If the Lord wills, we shall live and we shall do this or that." As it is, you boast in your arrogance. All such boasting is evil.

———•—■●■—•——

Romans 9:10
when Rebecca had conceived children by one man, our forefather Isaac, though they were not yet born and had done nothing either good or bad, in order that God's purpose of election might continue, not because of works but because of his call, she was told, "The elder will serve the younger." As it is written, "Jacob I loved, but Esau I hated." What shall we say then? Is there injustice on God's part? By no means! For he says to Moses, "I will have mercy on whom I have mercy, and I will have compassion on whom I have compassion." So it depends not upon man's will or exertion, but upon God's mercy. For the scripture says to Pharaoh, "I have raised you up for the very purpose of showing my power in you, so that my name may be proclaimed in all the earth." So then he has mercy upon whomever he wills, and he hardens the heart of whomever he wills. You will say to me then, "Why does he still find fault? For who can resist his will?" But who are you, a man, to answer back to God? Will what is molded say to its molder, "Why have you made me thus?" Has the potter no

**right over the clay, to make out of the same lump
one vessel for beauty and another for menial use?**

*In a word, it means we are like dust or fog and just a creature that
are made as God make. Like Jesus Christ holds the key to understanding
God's word, I would dare to say understanding above word holds the key
to the secret of fruit of the tree of good and evil.*

*Now, God is good. Then why good God put such a bad tree in the
middle of the garden and commanded not to eat? Isn't it better not to make
such a thing from the beginning than to put it in the middle of the garden
with a warning not to eat?*

*Our common understanding is men had free will and disobeyed to
eat the fruit.*

However, bible teaches us we are free only in God.

*That means God made us disobey and eat the fruit like God makes
someone blind from the birth. As Jesus said that's because God wanted to
accomplish something the blind man does not know by making him blind.
Likewise, God wanted to accomplish something Adam did not know by
making him disobey and eat the fruit to die.*

Let's find out what is that something through the bible.

**Romans 8:20
for the creation was subjected to futility, not of its
own will but by the will of him who subjected it in
hope; because the creation itself will be set free from
its bondage to decay and obtain the glorious liberty
of the children of God.**

*That the creature Adam ate the fruit knowing that God commanded
not to eat is not his will but the will of God who subjected him to futility.*

**Romans 11:32
For God has consigned all men to disobedience, that
he may have mercy upon all.**

That God consigned Adam to disobedience and let him eat the fruit God commanded not to eat is because God wanted to have mercy on everybody.

Romans 5:12
Therefore as sin came into the world through one man and death through sin, and so death spread to all men because all men sinned--

Because Adam ate the fruit, his descendants are all destined to die. By eating the fruit, men became to have own standard to judge good and evil based upon own benefit.
Thereafter no one could be called as righteous to God.

Romans 3:19
Now we know that whatever the law says it speaks to those who are   under the law, so that every mouth may be stopped, and the whole world may be held accountable to God. For no human being will be justified in his sight by works of the law, since through the law comes knowledge of sin.

Like we judge somebody by the law whether he is guilty or not, same way God gave us law to judge all as not righteous and sentenced the death penalty. Everybody is the witness for that because everybody dies without exception. And the reason why God sentenced the most severe penalty of death is to have most compassionate mercy upon us.

Romans 5:17
If, because of one man's trespass, death reigned through that one man, much more will those who receive the abundance of grace and the free gift of righteousness reign in life through the one man Jesus Christ. Then as one man's trespass led to condemnation for all men, so one man's act of righteousness leads to acquittal and life for all

men. For as by one man's disobedience many were
made sinners, so by one man's obedience many will
be made righteous. Law came in, to increase the
trespass; but where sin increased, grace abounded
all the more, so that, as sin reigned in death, grace
also might reign through righteousness to eternal
life through Jesus Christ our Lord.

*We thought we become righteous by keeping the law. Yet, God says this
law is not to make us righteous but to make us know sin by making the
sin more sinful and added more sin to us. And God is doing that so Jesus
Christ could forgive more and have more mercy on us. Why?*

John 5:22
**The Father judges no one, but has given all judgment
to the Son, that all may honor the Son, even as they
honor the Father. He who does not honor the Son
does not honor the Father who sent him.**

*It is to let men honor God's son Jesus Christ even like men honor God.
Why God needed to make men honor Jesus Christ?*
*So Jesus Christ can lead and teach men to make Sons of God. That's
to save men!*

Romans 8:14
**For all who are led by the Spirit of God are sons of
God.**

*Jesus led and taught men how to live and made himself a good example
so men can follow. He did not have any reason to die but he died saying
that he is dying to show men are dying because of the sin. Until that time
people did not know why people die. When he does not need to die, he
volunteered to die for everybody' sin to show why everybody die. That's
what the bible says as Jesus died for everybody's sin. And he rose from the
dead as he said before. He said that he was killing himself to get another*

life. He got spiritual life and said to die about physical body to get spiritual life. He proved it by rising again.

Anybody who dies about the physical body following Jesus Christ will be forgiven of his sin and save his spirit. Only those who fight with his physical desire will save his life, the spirit.

> **For this reason the Father loves me, because I lay down my life, that I may take it again. No one takes it from me, but I lay it down of my own accord. I have power to lay it down, and I have power to take it again; this charge I have received from my Father."**

----•—••—•----

> **Romans 8:13**
> **for if you live according to the flesh you will die, but if by the Spirit you put to death the deeds of the body you will live.**

Since the deed is subject to the body, as far as the body is alive, we can not be completely free from sin. We can only pretend that we don't have body. So this world is not the real world for the spirit. It is only the practicing field to raise the spiritual character using our body.

----•—••—•----

> **Romans 8:28**
> **We know that in everything God works for good with those who love him, who are called according to his purpose. For those whom he foreknew he also predestined to be conformed to the image of his Son, in order that he might be the first-born among many brethren.**
> **And those whom he predestined he also called;**

and those whom he called he also justified; and those whom he justified he also glorified.

Everything collaborates each other to make one good for those who were called according to God's will. Thanks to the law that adds sin to us, we became thirsty of God's mercy and due to Jesus Christ's forgiveness we became to respect Jesus Christ and follow him to have his image and character to be called Sons of God.

God's will is this: making Jesus Christ the first born of God's Sons to be and let those sons follow Jesus Christ to resemble the first-born son Jesus Christ. And all these were to build God's nation stronger upon God's will and it was predestined upon God's plan.

Someone would say:

God is omnipotent and he can do whatever it is just by saying one word.

What would he be short and why would he need to build his nation for any reason and why would he need anything whatever it is? When he just say, "Be strong", it becomes strong and when he just say "Be there" then it exists. Why would he need sons any way?

I think I've answered about it with the chapter of "How God accomplishes".

Besides, however you are almighty, wouldn't you like to have a son like you?

The point that God gave sin and then forgave or took it back is a little difficult to understand. But it's something like a man who is refining gold stone. When someone crushes the gold stone and mix with some chemicals to let it pass through the furnace to get pure gold, you can not tell the man is not righteous.

Can anyone ever say: "I am not a creature"?

Thus, the secret of fruit of the tree of good and evil were brought into light I believe.

Romans 5:19
For as by one man's disobedience many were made
sinners, so by one man's obedience many will be
made righteous.

Sin is a kind of disease that is rooted in men and transmits through the generation.As the first man died of it, so everybody is dying of it. We are the offspring's of the seed of sin no matter what we say "I didn't do anything wrong". That means our natural character itself is only sinful. Jesus Christ is like the only doctor who knows how to cure the disease as he introduced himself as:

John 14:6
Jesus said to him, "I am the way, and the truth, and
the life; no one comes to the Father, but by me.

As a patient cures the illness by following doctor's instructions, those who follow Jesus Christ's instructions will cure the disease sin and save own spirit. So the healthy people do not need Jesus Christ.

It is interesting that more rich, happy and healthy people come to church saying they are blessed and want to be blessed more. On the other hand poor and spiritually sick people come to church less, saying they can not even see Jesus Christ because they sinned too much. Isn't it ironical if someone very sick says he is too sick to see the doctor?

Spiritual living and Killing oneself.

As we discussed before, the body and the spirit can not be independent. These two becomes related each other when the spirit was rooted in the body at the time of birth.

So, when the body was destroyed, which is the death of body, the spirit has to wear a certain form of body to work as life again even if itself is a never dying life.

Therefore, men have dual desire of spiritual one and physical one.

But since these two are related each other, it is hard to tell which is spiritual and which is physical.

With the same fact, it is spiritual when it was carried out with emphasis of spiritual thing and it is physical when it was carried out with emphasis of physical thing.

So, the best way to figure out which is which is trying to explain with some good examples.

Before we get into the example I want to clear the biblical meaning of followings first.

Luke 12:4

I tell you, my friends, do not fear those who kill the body, and after that have no more that they can do. But I will warn you whom to fear: fear him who, after he has killed, has power to cast into hell; yes, I tell you, fear him!

This word reminds us that we have eternal life, the spirit, in the body.

That someone has killed somebody means someone has destroyed the body and the body has no life or spirit. For it has left the body.

And to fear him who has the power to cast into hell means the spirit can not die even the body has been destroyed. It just leaves the body and then cast into hell or brought into the Kingdom of God.

The spirit cannot die and also cannot do anything without body.

While the death of body means the spirit left the body, the death of spirit is it has no body to work with.

So even in the perishable body, it is better to have it than without it.

What the spirit in the painful perishable body wants is wearing a never perishable holy body for painless peaceful eternal life.

Therefore, those who die without a promise of wearing a new holy body are hopeless.

Matthew 10:39

He who finds his life will lose it, and he who loses his life for my sake will find it.

Those who use his body until the body destroyed will have his life in a new holy body. That is the spiritual life.

Luke 14:26
If any one comes to me and does not hate his own father and mother and wife and children and brothers and sisters, yes, and even his own life, he cannot be my disciple.

This also means the same thing. Those who want to follow Jesus Christ and get a new holy body has to kill own physical desire and use the body for the spiritual life.

What is killing physical desire exactly? The dead person could explain it very clearly.

They do not know whether they are naked, honored, rich, poor…and they do not know whether it is gold, money, diamond, beautiful or ugly…

God wants us to use our own body so cruelly like this. That is killing physical desire.

Let's take an example.

Say your plane was crashed and fell down in the desert and you have only minimal gallon of water and emergency food.

One man tries to figure out what he had, which way to go, what he should do and carry out what he believes. This man would be very careful to eat and drink the minimum amount to survive longer and will be very decisive for the action to carry out. He is never afraid of anything but to carry out his plan to survive with all his heart. He tries not to drink, not to eat but only eat and drink to survive. That is killing oneself.

Hence, another man complained that the pilot made mistake. He did not try to figure out how to survive and just worried about what if the rescue team wouldn't come. He was not careful of eating and drinking and consumed all of the water and food. At last, he just sat and waited for nothing saying he could not make it.

He just did what his body likes and he did not know he was killing the spirit at the same time.

When you kill your bodily desire of thirsty and hunger and kept moving on even though your body does not like, you are saving your spirit.

That is what the training your spirit is about. I believe the discipline is that.

Jesus explained it as following.

John 12:24
Truly, truly, I say to you, unless a grain of wheat falls into the earth and dies, it remains alone; but if it dies, it bears much fruit. He who loves his life loses it, and he who hates his life in this world will keep it for eternal life.

So, anybody who would just give up his life will lose his spirit too. But those who love his spirit and kill bodily desire to control the body will save the body together with the spirit. Even the body dies, God will save him because he loved God, the spirit in him.

God showed us how to control the body and live everyday life with the commandment. But we have to remember that we are living to accomplish God's plan.

We can not accomplish anything just by keeping God's commandment. It's just the law we have to behave in it. We are supposed to keep the commandment. But God's plan on us is not just keeping the commandment. God's plan on us is to accomplish God's will.

And God's will is to make us God's Son. For that purpose, God put the spirit, the life, in the body to train it using the body that has limit.

Jesus said even to hate your life. That does not mean to hate one's never dying spirit.

Raising the spirit is not only practicing killing physical desire but also it should have direction to which way it has to be practiced. It has to be focused to God with the teaching of Jesus Christ.

Let's see another example

A man became blind accidentally.

There could be two responses from this man.

One could be just desperate and do nothing and another could struggle to survive. While that man does nothing, this man tries to figure out whatever he can do and try to learn anything needed to do it. That man loves his body and afraid of possible injury when he moves around while this man loves his spirit and do not afraid of being injured of his body and try to get the skill to move around safely responding to his physical movement.

That man is living a physical life trying not to be troubled from his blindness while this man is living a spiritual life trying to save his spirit and enjoy being free from body.

In that sense being blind is more blessed than being normal because normal persons do not have chances like this.

Like there could be two different responses from the blind man, every poor man can not be said blessed always. So, the man who encourages the blind man to live a spiritual life is also living a spiritual life.

Since the spirit is tight connected to the body, giving up body is giving up spirit too. So, anybody who give up struggling to survive is also killing spirit. The point is which way is he focusing. Is he focusing to save his body or is he focusing to save his spirit? Focusing to his body will be ended up into vanity. Everyone dies anyway. But God knows who was trying to save the spirit. God will save those spirits. For those are precious spirits.

Let's see one more example.

You have $20,000 and you want to buy a car.

If you buy $10,000 worth car and save $10,000 for future use, you are living spiritually.

If you buy $40,000 luxurious car and work harder to pay the monthly payment, you are living a physical life. Because the spirit pursues peace of mind and physical body pursues filling the physical desire.

That physical desire creates burdens on you and causes you heavily loaded and die. When you work for spiritual relief, then you are living spiritually. But when you work to fill your physical desire of having a nice car, luxurious house… then you are living physical life. When you practice the piano for spiritual purpose you are living spiritual life. But if you practice the piano to win a competition you are living physical life.

When the spirit grew up through one's life spiritually like this, with the direction focused onto Jesus Christ, God is going to save the spirit as God's son. Then until when does God want us live like this? God says:

John 12:24
Truly, truly, I say to you, unless a grain of wheat
falls into the earth and dies, it remains alone; but
if it dies, it bears much fruit.

The grain means body. This implies to use body for the spiritual growth until the body is destroyed.

John 12:25
He who loves his life loses it, and he who hates his
life in this world will keep it for eternal life.

God wants us to live like this until our body is destroyed, and then God wears our spirit with new holy body.
Jesus explained how hard it is going to be as following.

Matthew 24:22
And if those days had not been shortened, no human
being would be saved; but for the sake of the elect
those days will be shortened. By your endurance you
will gain your lives.

The Words of God is free, but your salvation is not free. You will have to pay for your salvation with all your possession including your physical life. The bible explains the life in the great tribulation as following.

Revelation 13:16
Also it causes all, both small and great, both rich
and poor, both free and slave, to be marked on the
right hand or the forehead, so that no one can buy
or sell unless he has the mark, that is, the name of
the beast or the number of its name. This calls for
wisdom: let him who has understanding reckon the
number of the beast, for it is a human number, its
number is six hundred and sixty-six.

We will not be able to buy or sell our own without some kind of mark. And the bible says all those marked on the right hand or forehead will not be saved. Imagine how hard it could be when one can not buy or sell. I think most of the Christians know this and I guess most of them even the non-Christians will try not to get the beast mark until they can endure and give up gradually. I'd like to discuss on this beast mark in separate chapter of Computer Civilization.

When Jesus sent out his disciples to preach, he said to them as following.

Matthew 10:7
And preach as you go, saying, 'The kingdom of heaven is at hand.'

Heal the sick, raise the dead, cleanse lepers, cast out demons. You received without paying, give without pay.

Mentioning above words, people say that the salvation is given free only if you believe in Jesus Christ. When one was healed of the sickness, do you think he was saved? Let's see the bible what it says.

Luke 17:12
And as he entered a village, he was met by ten lepers, who stood at a distance and lifted up their voices and said, "Jesus, Master, have mercy on us." When he saw them he said to them, "Go and show yourselves to the priests." And as they went they were cleansed. Then one of them, when he saw that he was healed, turned back, praising God with a loud voice; and he fell on his face at Jesus' feet, giving him thanks. Now he was a Samaritan. Then said Jesus, "Were not ten cleansed? Where are the nine? Was no one found to return and give praise to God except this foreigner?" And he said to him, "Rise and go your way; your faith has made you well."

Jesus said what he did was to prove God's being only God to the people and to let them know he is Son of God and that is to make them follow Jesus Christ to save own spiritual life. It has nothing to do with the salvation itself. Do you think these nine out of ten were saved of their spirit? Jesus says the power of God is given free so heal the sick people free. But again, the salvation is not free. It costs everything what we have including the time, possession, position and even our physical life. You need belief to invest all of yours. Jesus did miraculous things to make you believe that if you follow Jesus with all your possessions including your life, you shall rise again like Jesus rose from the death. That's why it requires the belief.

We know that the great tribulation is the test for the harvest.

We also know that only those who passed the test would go into the Kingdom of God and that is salvation. Jesus explained with many examples that the salvation is not free.

We are now going to examine what Jesus Christ explained about the Kingdom of Heaven.

It is not the place we can go doing nothing but only saying with our mouth that we believe in Jesus Christ. Believing in Jesus Christ causes us to follow Jesus Christ to resemble him and have the character of Jesus Christ. But how can we go where he is if we do not follow his footprint? It is the place that requires all of our possessions, time, money, heart and effort... like Jesus explained so many times about the heaven. Jesus did it and asks us to believe that he saved himself doing that way and also asking us to do the same for the salvation.

I know most people say how can we, just a creature, do what Jesus did as God. Doesn't the bible say Jesus is the first-born Son of God, the first fruit of man, and our faith stands only on being a Son of God?

Believe in Jesus Christ leads us to follow Jesus Christ's instruction.

———•—■—•—

As we read the bible we find the bible is God's plan what to accomplish and how. So far, we have discussed about the relationship between God and men and examined with the history of men to confirm. From next chapter, I'm going to explore the future God planned upon us.

God said:

Hebrews 11:3
By faith we understand that the world was created
by the word of God, so that what is seen was made
out of things which do not appear.

———•——•—•——•———

Corinthians II 4:18
because we look not to the things that are seen but
to the things that are unseen; for the things that are
seen are transient, but the things that are unseen
are eternal.

The future is acceptable only by faith because the future is not visible. And the faith is to believe what God said because God is Word.

God created Adam and kept in the bondage of death with pain to have them long for eternal peaceful life without pain. Jesus Christ came to let people know there is eternal peace in the kingdom of God. That was the Good News. And he made himself an example to have people follow and get there. He is coming again to open the gate this time.

Just before his coming, there will be a great distress in this world.

That is to classify the Sons of God from the mean tares. It is going to be like a furnace. Everybody is going to be put into test and only those who remain not burnt to the end will be saved as Sons of God and enter the kingdom. All others will suffer in the 2nd death. However, those already self-purified do not need to pass the furnace. For they are pure.

Jesus is talking to these people to stay awoke to be able to evade this distress. Those self-purified will be saved. These people will save themselves but after having real hard time in the furnace like others if they do not stay awoke. I'd like to talk about what is being burnt later. So, great tribulation is to classify the grain and tares. Let's set forth for the future to explore these things.

7. Judgment Days

Great Tribulation

Daniel 12:1
At that time shall arise Michael, the great prince who has charge of your people. And there shall be a time of trouble, such as never has been since there was a nation till that time; but at that time your people shall be delivered, every one whose name shall be found written in the book. And many of those who sleep in the dust of the earth shall awake, some to everlasting life, and some to shame and everlasting contempt. And those who are wise shall shine like the brightness of the firmament; and those who turn many to righteousness, like the stars for ever and ever. But you, Daniel, shut up the words, and seal the book, until the time of the end. Many shall run to and fro, and knowledge shall increase.

Daniel who wrote this was a prophet 600 years before Jesus Christ. God told him to shut up this word.
After Jesus Christ first came, God said through John as following. Pay attention that God said to open the word this time.

Revelation 22:10
And he said to me, "Do not seal up the words of the prophecy of this book, for the time is near.

And God continued to say:

22:11 Let the evildoer still do evil, and the filthy still be filthy, and the righteous still do right, and the holy still be holy."Behold, I am coming soon, bringing my recompense, to repay every one for what he has done. I am the Alpha and the Omega, the first and the last, the beginning and the end."

Together with this word, following words let us know the bible is not for everybody but only for the Sons of God.

Matthew 7:6
Do not give dogs what is holy; and do not throw your pearls before   swine, lest they trample them under foot and turn to attack you.

Genesis 9:15
I will remember my covenant which is between me and you and every living creature of all flesh; and the waters shall never again become a flood to destroy all flesh. When the bow is in the clouds, I will look upon it and remember the everlasting covenant between God and every living creature of all flesh that is upon the earth.

The coming judgment is not of water.

1Thessalonians 5-1
There is no need to write to you, brothers, about the times and occasions when these things will happen. For you yourselves know very well that the Day of the Lord will come like a thief comes at night. When people say, "Everything is quiet and safe," then suddenly destruction will hit them! They will not escape- it will be like the pains that come upon a woman who is about to give birth. But you, brothers,

are not in the darkness, and the Day should not take
you by surprise like a thief.

All of you are people who belong to the light, who
belong to the day. We are not of the night or of the
darkness. So then, we should not be sleeping, like
the others; we should be awake and sober.

*It looks like a little difficult to understand what is to sleep and what
is to be awake. What is Day and what is Night? What is belonging to Day
and what is belonging to night?*

Let's see what God said about this through John.

John 1:1
**In the beginning was the Word, and the Word was with
God, and the Word was God. He was in the beginning
with God; all things were made through him, and
without him was not anything made that was made.
In him was life, and the life was the light of men.**

It says God is word, word is light and the light is life. And God is spirit.

*So, belonging to Day is belonging to God and it is those who live by
God's word. Since God is spirit, those who do not live spiritually cannot
understand God and that is sleeping in the night. Those are belonging to
night. Therefore, the great tribulation can not come like a thief to those
who believe in God and live a spiritual life but it comes like a thief to those
who do not live spiritually.*

*Anyway, it comes to both. Known to the one and unknown to the other.
Following words explain more explicitly what is sleeping.*

Luke 21:34
**But take heed to yourselves lest your hearts be
weighed down with dissipation and drunkenness
and cares of this life, and that day come upon you
suddenly like a snare; for it will come upon all who
dwell upon the face of the whole earth.**

Following words tell us we can escape the great distress. It's also encouraging us to stay awoke and escape.

Luke 21:36
But watch at all times, praying that you may have strength to escape all these things that will take place, and to stand before the Son of man."

———•—•—•—•———

Peter II 3:3
First of all you must understand this, that scoffers will come in the last days with scoffing, following their own passions and saying, "Where is the promise of his coming? For ever since the fathers fell asleep, all things have continued as they were from the beginning of creation." But by the same word the heavens and earth that now exist have been stored up for fire, being kept until the day of judgment and destruction of ungodly men. But do not ignore this one fact, beloved, that with the Lord one day is as a thousand years, and a thousand years as one day. The Lord is not slow about his promise as some count slowness, but is forbearing toward you, not wishing that any should perish, but that all should reach repentance.

People would scoff those who talk about the great tribulation.

3:10
But the day of the Lord will come like a thief, and then the heavens will pass away with a loud noise, and the elements will be dissolved with fire, and the earth and the works that are upon it will be burned up.

In many places, bible shows the coming judgment will be of fire.

Isaiah 66:15
**For behold, the LORD will come in fire, and his
chariots like the stormwind, to render his anger in
fury, and his rebuke with flames of fire. For by fire
will the LORD execute judgment, and by his sword,
upon all flesh; and those slain by the LORD shall
be many. Those who sanctify and purify themselves
to go into the gardens, following one in the midst,
eating swine's flesh and the abomination and mice,
shall come to an end together, says the LORD.**

*Recollecting that eating Jesus Christ's body is learning and doing
what Jesus taught, we can presume that eating the swine's flesh and the
abomination and mice means being taught from the false prophet and
doing things what they teach.*

*Those false prophets, who teach false things, pretending to be holy, shall
come to an end all together.*

Matthew 7:15
**Beware of false prophets, who come to you in sheep's
clothing but inwardly are ravenous wolves. You will
know them by their fruits. Are grapes gathered from
thorns, or figs from thistles? So, every sound tree
bears good fruit, but the bad tree bears evil fruit. A
sound tree cannot bear evil fruit, nor can a bad tree
bear good fruit. Every tree that does not bear good
fruit is cut down and thrown into the fire. Thus you
will know them by their fruits. "Not everyone who
says to me, 'Lord, Lord,' shall enter the kingdom of
heaven, but he who does the will of my Father who
is in heaven.**

Matthew 24:23

Then if any one says to you, 'Lo, here is the Christ!'
or 'There he is!' do not believe it. For false Christs
and false prophets will arise and show great signs
and wonders, so as to lead astray, if possible, even
the elect. Lo, I have told you beforehand. So, if they
say to you, 'Lo, he is in the wilderness,' do not go
out; if they say, 'Lo, he is in the inner rooms,' do not
believe it. For as the lightning comes from the east
and shines as far as the west, so will be the coming
of the Son of man.

Many false prophets will arise and teach false things. So, do not believe blindly. You can figure out by the fruit one bears. Anyone who wants to discern and save oneself should wake up.

———•—•—•———

Matthew 24

Then two men will be in the field; one is taken and
one is left.

Two women will be grinding at the mill; one is
taken and one is left.

Watch therefore, for you do not know on what
day your Lord is coming.

But know this, that if the householder had known
in what part of the night the thief was coming, he
would have watched and would not have let his house
be broken into. Therefore, you also must be ready;
for the Son of man is coming at an hour you do not
expect. "Who then is the faithful and wise servant,
whom his master has set over his household, to give
them their food at the proper time?

Blessed is that servant whom his master when

he comes will find so doing. Truly, I say to you, he will set him over all his possessions.

But if that wicked servant says to himself, 'My master is delayed,' and begins to beat his fellow servants, and eats and drinks with the drunken, the master of that servant will come on a day when he does not expect him and at an hour he does not know, and will punish him, and put him with the hypocrites; there men will weep and gnash their teeth.

Luke 19:43

For the days shall come upon you, when your enemies will cast up a bank about you and surround you, and hem you in on every side, and dash you to the ground, you and your children within you, and they will not leave one stone upon another in you; because you did not know the time of your visitation."

That we take these things is because we do not know when.
Nowhere in the bible is it written unavoidable! Rather, God says to wake up to avoid these things and stand before Jesus Christ in perfect peace.

Peter II 3:14

Therefore, beloved, since you wait for these, be zealous to be found by him without spot or blemish, and at peace.

Luke 21:29

And he told them a parable: "Look at the fig tree, and all the trees; as soon as they come out in leaf,

you see for yourselves and know that the summer is already near. So also, when you see these things taking place, you know that the kingdom of God is near.

We do not know the exact time but God told us we should know what part of the time we are living by seeing what's happening around us.

Matthew 24:37
As were the days of Noah, so will be the coming of the Son of man. For as in those days before the flood they were eating and drinking, marrying and giving in marriage, until the day when Noah entered the ark, and they did not know until the flood came and swept them all away, so will be the coming of the Son of man.

The great tribulation would come like the time of Noah for those who do not wake up. When it began to rain people would have thought it's good to have rain on time. When the water comes up to the knee, people begin to scoop out the water complaining something else. When the water comes up to the belly, people begin to pack to move to higher place. When the water comes up to the neck, people throw away every possession and begin to swim to survive. Until the water swallowed them all, they still would not know it was the great flood written in the bible. But Noah knew it and escaped!

Imagine a man building an ark on the mountain for the great flood. Most of the people would have scoffed and ridiculed him.

Believe or not, I myself tried to discuss about this great tribulation with so many people and found myself being scoffed. It is quite distressing. I do not mean I am such a Noah.

I am saying believing in God is not such a gimmick. God also said it is so hard to be saved as following.

Mark 8:35
For whoever would save his life will lose it; and whoever loses his life for my sake and the gospel's will save it.

———•———•●•———•———

Mark 10:25
It is easier for a camel to go through the eye of a needle than for a rich man to enter the kingdom of God."

———•———•●•———•———

Matthew 13:45
Again, the kingdom of heaven is like a merchant in search of fine pearls, who, on finding one pearl of great value, went and sold all that had and bought it.

Following words show us that the great tribulation is to sort precious ones and not precious ones before Jesus Christ comes again to open the gate of kingdom of God.

Matthew 13:47
Again, the kingdom of heaven is like a net which was thrown into the sea and gathered fish of every kind; when it was full, men drew it ashore and sat down and sorted the good into vessels but threw away the bad. So, it will be at the close of the age. The angels will come out and separate the evil from the righteous, and throw them into the furnace of fire; there men will weep and gnash their teeth.

———•———•●•———•———

Let both grow together until the harvest; and at harvest time I will tell the reapers, Gather the weeds first and bind them in bundles to be burned, but gather the wheat into my barn.

———•——•—•——•———

God told us how people would behave as the time comes closer to it. I'd like to leave to readers to say what part of the time we are living actually.

Luke 12:49
I came to cast fire upon the earth; and would that it were already kindled! I have a baptism to be baptized with; and how I am constrained until it is accomplished! Do you think that I have come to give peace on earth? No, I tell you, but rather division; for henceforth in one house there will be five divided, three against two and two against three; they will be divided, father against son and son against father, mother against daughter and daughter against her mother, mother-in-law against her daughter-in-law and daughter-in-law against her mother-in-law.

———•——•—•——•———

Luke 23:29
For behold, the days are coming when they will say, 'Blessed are the barren, and the wombs that never bore, and the breasts that never gave suck!' Then they will begin to say to the mountains, 'Fall on us'; and to the hills, 'Cover us.'

———•——•—•——•———

Mark 13:12
And brother will deliver up brother to death, and
the father his child, and children will rise against
parents and have them put to death; and you will be
hated by all for my name's sake. But he who endures
to the end will be saved.

------◆━━◆●◆━━◆------

Matthew 24:44
Therefore you also must be ready; for the Son of man
is coming at an hour you do not expect. "Who then
is the faithful and wise servant, whom his master
has set over his household, to give them their food
at the proper time? Blessed is that servant whom his
master when he comes will find so doing.

I believe mission work is supposed to lead Sons of God to kingdom of God.

Since eating Jesus Christ's body is doing what he told, feeding Sons of God is teaching and leading God's children to do what Jesus Christ instructed like Moses instructed Israel people to do what God said.

When God says to open, then opening is good and Sons of God will be part of the opening. Likewise, when God says to close, then closing is good and Sons of God will be a part of that closure also. Just like God told Isiah to close the word of great tribulation and yet to open it to John.

So, God's word has the priority.

When God says to be ready for the great tribulation, teaching Sons of God to do so is giving them their food at the proper time. The shepherds do not only lead the sheep but also protect the sheep from the dangers. So the priests who would do the same will be the right shepherds.

Then, let's see what would it be look like when the great tribulation comes to its climax just before Jesus Christ comes.

(Matthew 24)

And Jesus answered them, "Take heed that no one leads you astray.

For many will come in my name, saying, 'I am the Christ,' and they will lead many astray.

(Do not believe anybody but only the bible.)

And you will hear of wars and rumors of wars; see that you are not alarmed; for this must take place, but the end is not yet. For nation will rise against nation, and kingdom against kingdom, and there will be famines and earthquakes in various places: all this is but the beginning of the birth-pangs. Then they will deliver you up to tribulation, and put you to death; and you will be hated by all nations for my name's sake.

And then many will fall away, and betray one another, and hate one another. *(Many people who used believe in Jesus Christ will fall apart as the distress gets serious.)* And many false prophets will arise and lead many astray. And because wickedness is multiplied, most men's love will grow cold. *(People would seek own pleasure rather than God's will. They will even deny God's existence)* But he who endures to the end will be saved. And this gospel of the kingdom will be preached throughout the whole world, as a testimony to all nations; and then the end will come.

One of the many reasons why some Christian organizations say the great tribulation is not ready to come yet is, because the bible is not translated into every language on earth yet and that means the gospel is not delivered to the whole earth. However, spreading the word about the kingdom of God does not need to translate the bible to every language on earth. Those who are interested in kingdom of God would know before the bible was translated into all languages on earth. Everybody on earth knows about Christmas, about heaven what it is and about Jesus Christ who he was.

Instead, we better watch what's happening around us to know about when as Jesus said:

> **So when you see the desolating sacrilege spoken of by the prophet Daniel, standing in the holy place (let the reader understand), then let those who are in Judea flee to the mountains; let him who is on the housetop not go down to take what is in his house; and let him who is in the field not turn back to take his mantle. And alas for those who are with child and for those who give suck in those days! Pray that your flight may not be in winter or on a sabbath.**

(It is likely to happen in winter and on Saturday. Because nobody prays for it. Nobody is even interested in it. Pay attention that it says run away. To where? It will show up to each one according to the amount of belief allowed to each one.)

> **For then there will be great tribulation, such as has not been from the beginning of the world until now, no, and never will be.**

(It is the one that was never before and will never be in the future. So, it is unbelievable.)

> **And if those days had not been shortened, no human being would be saved; but for the sake of the elect those days will be shortened.**

(There should be a survival like Noah. God says Noah was saved and he is in the kingdom of God now. However, I do not see anybody who wants to be a survival like Noah.)

Then if any one says to you, 'Lo, here is the Christ!'
or 'There he is!' do not believe it. For false Christs
and false prophets will arise and show great signs
and wonders, so as to lead astray, if possible, even
the elect. Lo, I have told you beforehand. So, if they
say to you, 'Lo, he is in the wilderness,' do not go
out; if they say, 'Lo, he is in the inner rooms,' do not
believe it. For as the lightning comes from the east
and shines as far as the west, so will be the coming
of the Son of man.

(Everybody will see the coming of Jesus with own eyes.)

Wherever the body is, there the eagles will be
gathered together.
Immediately after the tribulation of those days
the sun will be darkened, and the moon will not give
its light, and the stars will fall from heaven, and the
powers of the heavens will be shaken;

*(These all are the things that can happen after the massive atomic bomb
explosions. And God said it is going to be of fire)*

then will appear the sign of the Son of man in heaven,

(So, the atomic warfare will be the climax of the great distress.)

and then all the tribes of the earth will mourn, and
they will see the Son of man coming on the clouds
of heaven with power and great glory; and he will
send out his angels with a loud trumpet call, and
they will gather his elect from the four winds, from
one end of heaven to the other.

*(This word indicates Sons of God will disperse to everywhere on earth
to escape and be gathered again as Jesus Christ comes.)*

From the fig tree learn its lesson: as soon as its branch becomes tender and puts forth its leaves, you know that summer is near. So also, when you see all these things, you know that he is near, at the very gates.

(We do not know the exact time like the year, month, day and hour like we do not know when the thief would come into the house. But we know the thief comes when we are all asleep. It is going to happen when we are all spiritually asleep pursuing own pleasure not knowing God's will. So we know what part of the time we are living by the seriousness of that symptoms.)

Truly, I say to you, this generation will not pass away till all these things take place. Heaven and earth will pass away, but my words will not pass away. "But of that day and hour no one knows, not even the angels of heaven, nor the Son, but the Father only. As were the days of Noah, so will be the coming of the Son of man. For as in those days before the flood they were eating and drinking, marrying and giving in marriage, until the day when Noah entered the ark, and they did not know until the flood came and swept them all away, so will be the coming of the Son of man. Then two men will be in the field; one is taken and one is left. Two women will be grinding at the mill; one is taken and one is left. Watch therefore, for you do not know on what day your Lord is coming. But know this, that if the householder had known in what part of the night the thief was coming, he would have watched and would not have let his house be broken into.

(We do not know the exact time but we know around when.)

Therefore you also must be ready; for the Son of man is coming at an hour you do not expect. "Who then is the faithful and wise servant, whom his master has set over his household, to give them their food at the proper time?

Only those who are awoke and discern could let God's children know it and those are the faithful wise servants. Teaching to serve others, to obey God, to love each other…are teaching people to raise as Sons of God but leading God's children to right way and protecting them from danger is also another job the faithful wise servants are supposed to do.

Blessed is that servant whom his master when he comes will find so doing. But if that wicked servant says to himself, 'My master is delayed,' and begins to beat his fellow servants, and eats and drinks with the drunken, the master of that servant will come on a day when he does not expect him and at an hour he does not know, and will punish him, and put him with the hypocrites; there men will weep and gnash their teeth.

It is written in another book of Luke as following.

Luke 21
And they asked him, "Teacher, when will this be, and what will be the sign when this is about to take place?" And he said, "Take heed that you are not led astray; for many will come in my name, saying, 'I am he!' and, 'The time is at hand!' Do not go after them. And when you hear of wars and tumults, do not be terrified; for this must first take place, but the end will not be at once." Then he said to them, "Nation will rise against nation, and kingdom against kingdom; there will be great earthquakes,

and in various places famines and pestilences; and there will be terrors and great signs from heaven. But before all this they will lay their hands on you and persecute you, delivering you up to the synagogues and prisons, and you will be brought before kings and governors for my name's sake.

(As the natural disasters, famines, pestilence and wars get tougher, the unbelievers will begin to blame Christians of all these happenings and try to persecute them.)

This will be a time for you to bear testimony.

(God does this to test each one's belief.)

Settle it therefore in your minds, not to meditate beforehand how to answer; for I will give you a mouth and wisdom, which none of your adversaries will be able to withstand or contradict. You will be delivered up even by parents and brothers and kinsmen and friends, and some of you they will put to death; you will be hated by all for my name's sake. But not a hair of your head will perish. By your endurance you will gain your lives. "But when you see Jerusalem surrounded by armies, then know that its desolation has come near.

(Know the atomic warfare is near when the Jerusalem being surrounded by army.)

Then let those who are in Judea flee to the mountains, and let those who are inside the city depart, and let not those who are out in the country enter it; for these are days of vengeance, to fulfil all that is written. *(Then it is time to run away.)*

Alas for those who are with child and for those who give suck in those days! For great distress shall be upon the earth and wrath upon this people; they will fall by the edge of the sword, and be led captive among all nations; and Jerusalem will be trodden down by the Gentiles, until the times of the Gentiles are fulfilled.

(At last, the Jerusalem will fall into gentile's hand.)"**And there will be signs in sun and moon and stars, and upon the earth distress of nations in perplexity at the roaring of the sea and the waves, men fainting with fear and with foreboding of what is coming on the world; for the powers of the heavens will be shaken.**

(And there will be massive atomic bomb explosion.)

And then they will see the Son of man coming in a cloud with power and great glory. Now when these things begin to take place, look up and raise your heads, because your redemption is drawing near."**And he told them a parable: "Look at the fig tree, and all the trees; as soon as they come out in leaf, you see for yourselves and know that the summer is already near. So also, when you see these things taking place, you know that the kingdom of God is near.**

(Then Jesus Christ comes.)

Truly, I say to you, this generation will not pass away till all has taken place. Heaven and earth will pass away, but my words will not pass away. "But take heed to yourselves lest your hearts be weighed down with dissipation and drunkenness and cares of this

life, and that day come upon you suddenly like a snare; for it will come upon all who dwell upon the face of the whole earth.

(Those who are not awoken cannot discern this.)

But watch at all times, praying that you may have strength to escape all these things that will take place, and to stand before the Son of man."

This great tribulation would be such a humiliating and utterly exhausting thing. For an example, there was a time in Israel that the capital Samaria was surrounded by the enemy and the hunger prevailed among people. It is written in II Kings as following.

Kings II 6:28
And the king asked her, "What is your trouble?" She answered, "This woman said to me, 'Give your son, that we may eat him today, and we will eat my son tomorrow.' So we boiled my son, and ate him. And on the next day I said to her, 'Give your son, that we may eat him'; but she has hidden her son.

Since it is going to be the worst one ever in human history, it is going to be more terrible than this. Bible says stay awoke to discern so we can be ready and have strength to escape when the time comes. That's what god says to stay awoke and discern the time and be prepared. People describe the great tribulation as the end of the world and even express it like the extinction of human being. This wrong understanding makes people do not prepare and give oneself in despair. The great distress would change the whole life style of human being and is going to be such a big event that was not in the past and will not ever happen again in the future in human history. But it is not to cut off human beings from existence. It is harvest time of human beings.

As we discussed before, salvation is being free from this limited physically evil world. So, we are not going to be saved actually until the physical death. Then, even we survive the great tribulation, that does not mean we are saved, are we? That's right. It's just the survival like we struggle to survive now. It is just before the salvation. The actual salvation is going to happen after Jesus Christ come. Because we are all fell in the swamp of sin. However hard we try to clean ourselves, we are only adding more dirt on us with our dirty hands. Nobody can save oneself. Only Jesus Christ can save, seeing the fruit we bear like we know the tree in the swamp is a grape tree when we see it bears grape even in the dirt. Then why do we try to survive? Isn't it better to die before the great tribulation? Personally, I thought so as a normal person of modern days. But we are not made for our well being. We are made to accomplish God's will. We are living for the hope of living in the Kingdom of God, being freed from the bondage of this world.

What can we do if God take our limbs away? As a normal man, it looks better to die than to live without limbs. Let's recollect that God made some person blind from his birth to show God's will through him. The same way we are just dust or fog that have no choice other than take what God gives. And we are living in that condition struggling to survive. That's how God accomplishes and that's the life God gave us in this end time. When we know a car is rushing into us, we never stand still. If someone knows it and stand still, then he is committing suicide.

The same theory applies to this end time preparation. I found one thing very interesting and common to most of the people I talked to. When I talked to anybody to discuss about the great distress, the general responses were:

Do you think you can escape what God planned upon us?

God said only those who prepared can escape. **How?** *Like Noah prepared. Noah prepared very scientifically. That's written in the bible.*

So, you know every scientific thing to escape from, like atomic bomb and famine…?

No. I do not know. But God will lead me as to the progress. All we need is only belief to carry out what God says to each one. Because without belief, nobody would follow what God says. You are not going to give all of your possessions without belief that you are going to get another life, are you?

What's good about living alone in a desolate world?

It's not because I like but because God said so.

It's like God made someone blind from the birth to live like that.

Who knows it's better and God says we are living for that.

Everyone die. Then why are you alone so afraid of death?

It's not because of my physical death. It's because of my eternal spiritual death.

Wouldn't it be because you are not saved?

That's right. I want to save my spirit, my life.

Jesus says to prepare just like Noah prepared.

Following is another word that let us know the great tribulation is not inescapable.

Matthew 25

Then the kingdom of heaven shall be compared to ten maidens who took their lamps and went to meet the bridegroom. Five of them were foolish, and five were wise. For when the foolish took their lamps, they took no oil with them; but the wise took flasks of oil with their lamps. As the bridegroom was delayed, they all slumbered and slept. But at midnight there was a cry, 'Behold, the bridegroom! Come out to meet him.'

Then all those maidens rose and trimmed their lamps. And the foolish said to the wise, 'Give us some of your oil, for our lamps are going out.' But the wise replied, 'Perhaps there will not be enough for us and for you; go rather to the dealers and buy for yourselves.' And while they went to buy, the bridegroom came, and those who were ready went in with him to the marriage feast; and the door was shut. Afterward the other maidens came also, saying, 'Lord, lord, open to us.' But he replied, 'Truly, I say to you, I do not know you.' Watch therefore, for you know neither the day nor the hour.

To help understanding, I'd like to discuss about the preparation we can think of at this time.

The first thing *needed is the belief that there is Kingdom of God, prepared for the children of God. The more you believe the more you will prepare for it.*

The next thing *needed is the belief of God to stay awoke to discern. Otherwise we might be preparing at the wrong time, on the wrong place and miss the chance to run away.*

The third thing *needed is the belief to carry out the plan with patience. For the belief is the cause of action.*

Remember every prophet before our time including Jesus Christ were betrayed and ridiculed by friends, families and handed over to the authorities to be executed.

So, those who love families, friends, neighbors and even oneself more than God can not carry out God's instruction. They will carry out God's instruction as to each one's belief to a certain point up to their own belief.

Bible explains the tribulation would be famine, pestilence, war, earthquake, flood, betrayal, rising false prophets....

These things would proceed like a thief. The distress this time will be greater than ever before and that is the great tribulation.

After this period, finally Jesus Christ will come at the peak of the massive destruction.

What can we prepare for is this former part of the tribulation?

I think many would laugh when I say followings.

But remember what and how Noah did.

Maybe we need food for the tribulation, medicine for the pestilence, arms for the war, first aid products for the natural disaster, bible knowledge to discern false prophets, every possible information of each God's children who is who and who has what to maximize the effectiveness.

We will be also needed to find the right place and channel to get the right information about what's happening in this world.

But, most of all, we need to try not to lose love among us. As the people loose love they will begin to betray and hand over own brothers, sisters, father, mother, sons, daughters, friends and neighbors to killing place.

Only the love will get people together and make stronger.

People will seek own pleasure and kill anybody who is against their purpose. To protect from it, we need to get together.

That cannot be made without love.

Because the resources will be limited, we need to make two families into one, three families into two and make the family larger. However, I do not see it would be possible in this environment of lack of love. How can we get together when we separate due to lack of love?

Only those who have love to God can believe and do this.

Specially, God told through the prophet Amos about the rising false prophets as following.

Amos 8

"And on that day," says the Lord GOD, "I will make the sun go down at noon, and darken the earth in broad daylight. I will turn your feasts into mourning, and all your songs into lamentation; I will bring sackcloth upon all loins, and baldness on every head; I will make it like the mourning for an only son, and the end of it like a bitter day.

(This word also indicates there will be massive atomic bomb explosions.)

"Behold, the days are coming," says the Lord GOD, when I will send a famine on the land; not a famine of bread, nor a thirst for water, but of hearing the words of the LORD. They shall wander from sea to sea, and from north to east; they shall run to and fro, to seek the word of the LORD, but they shall not find it. "In that day the fair virgins and the young men shall faint for thirst.

When the time comes, it is going to be really hard to hear God's voice.

People would want to hear the voice and look for it, but they wouldn't be able to find it. So, we will have to try to find when we can.

Many, not many but most people say the great tribulation is about saving our spirit and it has to be explained in spiritual manner. I think it's one another problem caused by misunderstanding the bible. It is to test each one whether one loves the spirit of life or the body. Since these two are connected each other if you destroy one, the other one also looses.

God wanted to see which one you belong to. You are going to stay alive until God takes your life away for another use. Until then, you are going to struggle. If you prepare, you are not going to have hard time and if you do not prepare you are going to have trouble.

So, the great tribulation comes to everyone regardless one likes it or not. And God says to his children to prepare and escape.

However, many people say the salvation is not for the body but for the spirit and it wouldn't be able to get by preparing physically.

That's right. But we are not there yet. I am talking about the distress our body would have before the salvation and God is telling us to escape. We have to remember when our body is destroyed our spirit also looses the place to stand too. And God is going to save those who followed God's instruction.

As a creature we know we are being made as God wants and planned.

We do not know who is going to be saved and who is not. As God allowed each individual different faith and different benefit as God needed, it is quite natural that each one reads the same bible scripture and interprets differently. So, each one should keep each one's faith firm and follow it. I do not mean I will be saved. I just want to give what I found directly from God's word to those who are interested in God and help them to see God right. So, whoever thinks himself found the right way, I encourage him to go that way standing on firm belief. But I can tell for sure that we shouldn't follow anyone blindly. Each one should follow own interpretation and I hope my understanding is wrong. When my understanding is right, most of the people would have real hard time. The ones who wouldn't prepare will have hard time because they are not prepared and the ones who would prepare will have hard time also because they are going to be scoffed and ridiculed real hard from their friends, families and neighbors.

Those prepared will save their spirit. But who in the world wouldn't say it's ridiculous when somebody prepares the worst things when everything looks safe and peaceful. Bible says it's going to happen when everything looks safe and peaceful.

Anyway, the great tribulation is for everyone regardless each one has faith or not. But the same great tribulation is hope for the sons of God and despair to others.

Salvation: It is earned, not given free

Salvation is the ultimate goal and the reason why we live in this painful limited world. The real freedom of living in perfect peace and joy without limit, pain, tear and worry is not possible in this world.

It is only possible in the Kingdom of God. Most Christians say they got peace in mind after they accepted Jesus Christ as their personal savior. The salvation is that kind of spiritual thing. But according to the bible, the actual salvation happens after Jesus Christ's 2nd coming. So, that kind of peace in mind is just a kind taste one can have when one came to believe in Jesus Christ. It can not last forever and every Christians prove it. We are going to live in this satanic world in pain and tear until actual salvation.

God let Sons of God knows what and when to do to avoid the big trouble that men would confront with in the near future.

So, going into the Kingdom of God is the salvation. Jesus explained how we could go into the Kingdom of God with following examples.

> **Matthew 13:44**
> **The kingdom of heaven is like treasure hidden in a field, which a man found and covered up; then in his joy he goes and sells all that he has and buys that field.**

This man invested all of his possessions to buy the treasure. And the other people who did not know about the treasure could not understand why this man sold all of his possession to buy the field.

235

Matthew 13:45

Again, the kingdom of heaven is like a merchant in search of fine pearls, who, on finding one pearl of great value, went and sold all that he had and bought it.

This merchant also invested all of his possession to buy the fine pearl. Only those who are interested in Kingdom of God can find it and only those who believe Kingdom of God exist would invest all of his possessions to get it.

Matthew 7:21

"Not every one who says to me, 'Lord, Lord,' shall enter the kingdom of heaven, but he who does the will of my Father who is in heaven.

Not every believers but only those who does what God says will enter the Kingdom of Heaven.

(Luke 13:23)

And some one said to him, "Lord, will those who are saved be few?" And he said to them, "Strive to enter by the narrow door; for many, I tell you, will seek to enter and will not be able."

When once the householder has risen up and shut the door, you will begin to stand outside and to knock at the door, saying, 'Lord, open to us.' He will answer you, 'I do not know where you come from.' Then you will begin to say, 'We ate and drank in your presence, and you taught in our streets.'

(This is what Jesus talking to the believers like us.)

But he will say, 'I tell you, I do not know where you come from; depart from me, all you workers of iniquity!'

Going into Kingdom of Heaven is never going to be easy. Like a race, many would run but only a few wins. It is such a valuable one as would cost one's every possession including the physical life.

———•—•—•———

James 2:14
What does it profit, my brethren, if a man says he has faith but has not works? Can his faith save him? But some one will say, "You have faith and I have works." Show me your faith apart from your works, and I by my works will show you my faith. You believe that God is one; you do well. Even the demons believe-- and shudder. Do you want to be shown, you shallow man, that faith apart from works is barren? You see that faith was active along with his works, and faith was completed by works, You see that a man is justified by works and not by faith alone.

Kingdom of Heaven is earned. It is not given free. We have to work and complete what we believe to get it.

———•—•—•———

Matthew 13:47
Again, the kingdom of heaven is like a net which was thrown into the sea and gathered fish of every kind;

Every kind of good and bad people live together in this world.

13:48

when it was full, men drew it ashore and sat down and sorted the good into vessels but threw away the bad.

When this world is full of men, God sorts out good and bad accordingly.

13:49

So it will be at the close of the age. The angels will come out and separate the evil from the righteous,

So, it is the closing of one age like the time of Noah. There should be another age to come.

13:50

and throw them into the furnace of fire; there men will weep and gnash their teeth.

13:52

And he said to them, "Therefore every scribe who has been trained for the kingdom of heaven is like a householder who brings out of his treasure what is new and what is old."

Children of God are those who are trained so they can live in the Kingdom of Heaven. They know well about the Kingdom of Heaven.

Matthew 20

For the kingdom of heaven is like a householder who went out early in the morning to hire laborers for his vineyard. After agreeing with the laborers for a denarius a day, he sent them into his vineyard. And going out about the third hour he saw others standing idle in the market place; and to them he

said, 'You go into the vineyard too, and whatever is right I will give you.' So they went. Going out again about the sixth hour and the ninth hour, he did the same. And about the eleventh hour he went out and found others standing; and he said to them, 'Why do you stand here idle all day?'

They said to him, 'Because no one has hired us.' He said to them, 'You go into the vineyard too.' And when evening came, the owner of the vineyard said to his steward, 'Call the laborers and pay them their wages, beginning with the last, up to the first.' And when those hired about the eleventh hour came, each of them received a denarius. Now when the first came, they thought they would receive more; but each of them also received a denarius. And on receiving it they grumbled at the householder, saying, 'These last worked only one hour, and you have made them equal to us who have borne the burden of the day and the scorching heat.' But he replied to one of them, 'Friend, I am doing you no wrong; did you not agree with me for a denarius? Take what belongs to you, and go; I choose to give to this last as I give to you. Am I not allowed to do what I choose with what belongs to me?

Or do you begrudge my generosity?'

So the last will be first, and the first last.

The Kingdom of Heaven is not limited only to those who found it earlier in his life. Regardless one was born again early or late everyone would be allowed to see it. The ones who were born again late would be forgiven more and love God more. These people would appreciate more than the ones who were born again earlier. On the other hand, the people who were born again earlier would proud of their being born again earlier and wouldn't appreciate what they get. Because they would think they deserve more and neglect to raise own character.

So, the first would be the last and the last would be the first.

Matthew 22

The kingdom of heaven may be compared to a king who gave a marriage feast for his son, and sent his servants to call those who were invited to the marriage feast; but they would not come. Again he sent other servants, saying, 'Tell those who are invited, Behold, I have made ready my dinner, my oxen and my fat calves are killed, and everything is ready; come to the marriage feast.' But they made light of it and went off, one to his farm, another to his business, while the rest seized his servants, treated them shamefully, and killed them. The king was angry, and he sent his troops and destroyed those murderers and burned their city. Then he said to his servants, 'The wedding is ready, but those invited were not worthy. Go therefore to the thoroughfares, and invite to the marriage feast as many as you find.' And those servants went out into the streets and gathered all whom they found, both bad and good; so, the wedding hall was filled with guests. "But when the king came in to look at the guests, he saw there a man who had no wedding garment; and he said to him, 'Friend, how did you get in here without a wedding garment?' And he was speechless. Then the king said to the attendants, 'Bind him hand and foot, and cast him into the outer darkness; there men will weep and gnash their teeth.' For many are called, but few are chosen.

Many people were invited to the Kingdom of God. But most of them were not interested in it. Because they did not see and couldn't believe that God prepared everything needed for the people who comes to the Kingdom of God. People would take it as just a regular feast, not of the creator God, and wouldn't value it. So, even those who come to the feast wouldn't prepare to fit for the feast. When the feast is about to begin God would sort those who don't fit for the feast and kick them out. We take it as quite natural when someone is not accepted at a party because he is not dressed for that party. I do not understand how could one think one would be accepted at the feast of God who created us even though one is not ready.

Corinthians I 10:12
Therefore let any one who thinks that he stands take heed lest he fall. No temptation has overtaken you that is not common to man. God is faithful, and he will not let you be tempted beyond your strength, but with the temptation will also provide the way of escape, that you may be able to endure it.

I do not know how to prepare exactly as I confessed before. But Jesus let me know that God will provide us the way as to the progress so we can endure. And the confession I made is what I believe we should do now.

Now, then what is going to happen after the great tribulation?

Bible says there is going to be the resurrection of every human being that has ever lived on earth to stand before Jesus Christ for the judgment.

Let's go to next chapter for it.

The Resurrection and The Salvation

When the great test is over, those who passed the test will enter the Kingdom of God as the children of God and that is the salvation.

Then what about the people who died already? There will be resurrection of those.

From this time the perfect spiritual life begins.

The bible shows those who are going to be saved clearly.

Let's read followings very carefully.

Revelation 20:1

Then I saw an angel coming down from heaven, holding in his hand the key of the bottomless pit and a great chain. And he seized the dragon, that ancient serpent, who is the Devil and Satan, and bound him for a thousand years, and threw him into the pit, and shut it and sealed it over him, that he should deceive the nations no more, till the thousand years were ended. After that he must be loosed for a little while.

Then I saw thrones, and seated on them were those to whom judgment was committed. Also I saw the souls of those who had been beheaded for their testimony to Jesus and for the word of God, and who had not worshiped the beast or its image and had not received its mark on their foreheads or their hands. They came to life, and reigned with Christ a thousand years. The rest of the dead did not come to life until the thousand years were ended.

This is the first resurrection.

(There will be two resurrections occurring. The first one for the salvation and the second one for the Judgment)

Blessed and holy is he who shares in the first resurrection! Over such the second death has no power, but they shall be priests of God and of Christ, and they shall reign with him a thousand years.

(Those who were saved by the first resurrection have nothing to do with the second resurrection for the Judgment. For they were moved into heaven before the Judgment. Those are blessed and that's what we pursue living in this world.)

And when the thousand years are ended, Satan will be loosed from his prison and will come out to

deceive the nations which are at the four corners of the earth, that is, Gog and Magog, to gather them for battle; their number is like the sand of the sea.

(After the tribulation, men will flourish again like the time of Noah for one thousand years.)

And they marched up over the broad earth and surrounded the camp of the saints and the beloved city; but fire came down from heaven and consumed them, and the devil who had deceived them was thrown into the lake of fire and sulphur where the beast and the false prophet were, and they will be tormented day and night for ever and ever.

Then I saw a great white throne and him who sat upon it; from his presence earth and sky fled away, and no place was found for them.

And I saw the dead, great and small, standing before the throne, and books were opened. Also another book was opened, which is the book of life. And the dead were judged by what was written in the books, by what they had done. And the sea gave up the dead in it, Death and Hades gave up the dead in them, and all were judged by what they had done.

(Anybody who has ever lived on earth will be resurrected to stand before the Judgment. This is the second resurrection)

Then Death and Hades were thrown into the lake of fire. *This is the second death*, the lake of fire; and if any one's name was not found written in the book of life, he was thrown into the lake of fire.

Revelation 21:1

Then I saw a new heaven and a new earth; for the first heaven and the first earth had passed away, and the sea was no more.

And I saw the holy city, new Jerusalem, coming down out of heaven from God, prepared as a bride adorned for her husband; and I heard a loud voice from the throne saying, "Behold, the dwelling of God is with men. He will dwell with them, and they shall be his people, and God himself will be with them;

he will wipe away every tear from their eyes, and death shall be no more, neither shall there be mourning nor crying nor pain any more, for the former things have passed away."

And he who sat upon the throne said, "Behold, I make all things new." Also he said, "Write this, for these words are trustworthy and true."

And he said to me, "It is done! I am the Alpha and the Omega, the beginning and the end. To the thirsty I will give from the fountain of the water of life without payment.

Let me summarize this for better understanding.

There will be two resurrections occurring. The first resurrection is for the salvation of Sons of God and the second resurrection is for the judgment of those who were not saved by the first resurrection. Those who did not have the mark of beast and those who were killed for the words of God would take part in the first resurrection. And these first resurrection participants have nothing to do with the judgment any more. We are now living right at the time just before the first resurrection and that means we could have a chance to be saved without tasting death.

The Satan would be caught when Jesus Christ came and put in the prison of hell while Jesus Christ rule men with Sons of God for 1,000 years.

After 1,000 years, the Satan will be released again and gather men who were flourished again after the great tribulation and fight with the saints and be defeated.

This Satan and the devils that deceived the whole world are to be thrown into the lake of fire forever.

At that time, everyone who has ever lived on earth will be resurrected for the judgment according to each one's deed. This is the second resurrection.

So, regardless whether one is righteous or not, everyone except those saved at the first resurrection are going to stand before the judge.

Since everyone sinned, no one is going to be saved.

That's why the first resurrection participants are blessed.

Because those are going to be moved before the second resurrection of the judgment and their sin has nothing to do with the judgment.

Remember we cannot be free as far as we live in this Satanic limited world.

So, anyone who was not saved at the first resurrection will be thrown into the lake of fire and sulfur where the Satan and the devil superintends and be torment day and night forever.

This is the second death.

I'd like to make one thing very clear here.

What we normally have in mind about the death is being destroyed completely and know nothing any more. But bible says the 2nd death is being thrown into the fire and being tormented. This also shows the bible is about the everlasting life, the spirit.

If being thrown into the lake of fire would be the 2nd death then what should be the 1st death? I would dare to say being thrown into this world of pain, tear... from the paradise, the Garden of Eden, should be the first death.

If the second death is being in the hell where the Satan manages, then this world where the Satan manages also is another hell too.

Because Jesus said God gave this world to Satan.

If the Garden of Eden where Adam first lived and managed by God was the heaven then this world where Adam was kicked out to live and managed by Satan should be the hell.

Therefore, salvation means being saved from this world of death, the hell.

Now I believe the great tribulation does not mean the end of the world as normal people would have in mind.

Let's come back to the main subject.

After that, Sons of God are to live together in peace with God in Holy new city of Jerusalem without pain or tear. This is what the actual life is supposed to live. That is another heaven like the Garden of Eden.

After all these, God said:

"It is done! I am the Alpha and the Omega, the beginning and the end."

(Revelation 22-13)

Nobody knows what God would plan afterwards, however this is what God planned to accomplish upon men up to this point written in the Bible.

8. At the End of an Age

Denial mentality

Matthew 13:49
So it will be at the close of the age. The angels will come out and separate the evil from the righteous,

People think the great tribulation is the end of human being. But bible says it is the closing of one age like the time of Noah. And this one is going to be the most epochal theme than the time of Sodom and Gomorra or the great flood. As the bible says so many unfamiliar things that men have never experienced in human history would happen as following during the tribulation and that's why it looks hard for people to believe that.

Peter II 3:10
the heavens will pass away with a loud noise, and the elements will be dissolved with fire, and the earth and the works that are upon it will be burned up

Matthew 24:29
Immediately after the tribulation of those days the sun will be darkened, and the moon will not give its light, and the stars will fall from heaven, and the powers of the heavens will be shaken; then will appear the sign of the Son of man in heaven, and then all the tribes of the earth will mourn, and they will see the Son of man coming on the clouds of heaven with power and great glory;

Isaiah 26:19
Thy dead shall live, their bodies shall rise.

John 5:28
**Do not marvel at this; for the hour is coming when
all who are in the tombs will hear his voice**

*But who in the world even just a hundred years ago had ever believed
that a man would step on the moon and hop, a bomb as small as a suit
case can destroy more than one whole city, men would fly, the German
Nazis would kill six million Jews in holocaust …? Can you believe a big
bang bigger than all these was prearranged as the closing of an age? Only
those who believe this could and would prepare for it. Isaiah the prophet
witnessed it as following.*

Isaiah 26:19
**Thy dead shall live, their bodies shall rise. O dwellers
in the dust, awake and sing for joy! For thy dew is a
dew of light, and on the land of the shades thou wilt
let it fall. Come, my people, enter your chambers,
and shut your doors behind you; hide yourselves for
a little while until the wrath is past. For behold, the
LORD is coming forth out of his place to punish
the inhabitants of the earth for their iniquity, and
the earth will disclose the blood shed upon her, and
will no more cover her slain.**

*Then, what happens to the Sons of God physically after the great
tribulation?*

Corinthians I 15
**But some one will ask, "How are the dead raised?
With what kind of body do they come? You foolish
man! What you sow does not come to life unless it
dies. And what you sow is not the body which is to**

be, but a bare kernel, perhaps of wheat or of some other grain. But God gives it a body as he has chosen, and to each kind of seed its own body.

For not all flesh is alike, but there is one kind for men, another for animals, another for birds, and another for fish.

This word shows us human's life is no different than any other animals. The only difference is the character of the life. So, raising our character is the only way to be different from other animals and that is how we get closer to Sons of God. And that's what Jesus teaches us.

There are celestial bodies and there are terrestrial bodies; but the glory of the celestial is one, and the glory of the terrestrial is another.

There is one glory of the sun, and another glory of the moon, and another glory of the stars; for star differs from star in glory.

So is it with the resurrection of the dead. What is sown is perishable, what is raised is imperishable.

It is sown in dishonor, it is raised in glory. It is sown in weakness, it is raised in power. It is sown a physical body, it is raised a spiritual body. If there is a physical body, there is also a spiritual body.

Thus it is written, "The first man Adam became a living being"; the last Adam became a life-giving spirit. But it is not the spiritual which is first but the physical, and then the spiritual. The first man was from the earth, a man of dust; the second man is from heaven. As was the man of dust, so are those who are of the dust; and as is the man of heaven, so are those who are of heaven. Just as we have borne the image of the man of dust, we shall also bear the image of the man of heaven. I tell you this, brethren: flesh and blood cannot inherit the kingdom of God, nor does the perishable inherit the imperishable. Lo! I tell you a mystery. We shall not all sleep, but we shall all be changed, in a moment, in the twinkling of an eye, at the last trumpet. For the trumpet will sound, and the dead will be raised imperishable, and we shall be changed. For this perishable nature must put on the imperishable, and this mortal nature must put on immortality. When the perishable puts on the imperishable, and the mortal puts on immortality, then shall come to pass the saying that is written: "Death is swallowed up in victory."

John I 3:2
Beloved, we are God's children now; it does not yet appear what we shall be, but we know that when he appears we shall be like him, for we shall see him as he is.

As written in the bible as following, people's denial mentality has rooted in men so deeply. It is hard to see a man who even thinks about it. When it is hard to find a man who thinks about it, finding those who would prepare for it is not going to be just hard but almost impossible like a camel pass through the hole of a needle. It is interesting to find most people agree that we are living the end time.

Agree, but do not think about it? Especially when God says to discern to escape? That doesn't make sense.

Brethren! Let's think and go out to shout to everywhere. God's lost sheep will hear and come out from somewhere. Let's make noise to wake them up!

Peter II 3:3
First of all you must understand this, that scoffers will come in the last days with scoffing, following their own passions and saying, "Where is the promise

of his coming? For ever since the fathers fell asleep, all things have continued as they were from the beginning of creation."

From next chapter I am going to try to figure out what part of the time we are really passing by looking around what's happening around us with the eye of Jesus Christ.

Luke 21:29 And he told them a parable: "Look at the fig tree, and all the trees; as soon as they come out in leaf, you see for yourselves and know that the summer is already near. So also, when you see these things taking place, you know that the kingdom of God is near.

Computer Civilization and the Mark of Beast

Anybody who has ever studied about the computer science would know that the basic concept of computer is 0 or 1. The most simple and stupid theory but most effective invention it is in human history. Now human beings rely on that totally.

Revelation 13:15
and it was allowed to give breath to the image of the beast so that the image of the beast should even speak, and to cause those who would not worship the image of the beast to be slain. Also it causes all, both small and great, both rich and poor, both free and slave, to be marked on the right hand or the forehead, so that no one can buy or sell unless he has the mark, that is, the name of the beast or the number of its name. This calls for wisdom: let him who has understanding reckon the number of the

beast, for it is a human number, its number is six hundred and sixty-six.

Revelation 14:9

And another angel, a third, followed them, saying with a loud voice, "If any one worships the beast and its image, and receives a mark on his forehead or on his hand, he also shall drink the wine of God's wrath, poured unmixed into the cup of his anger, and he shall be tormented with fire and sulphur in the presence of the holy angels and in the presence of the Lamb. And the smoke of their torment goes up for ever and ever; and they have no rest, day or night, these worshipers of the beast and its image, and whoever receives the mark of its name." Here is a call for the endurance of the saints, those who keep the commandments of God and the faith of Jesus.

Let's explain with actual examples happening around us all the time. I do not mean the computer is a bad thing but those things written in the bible could happen because of the convenience and the effectiveness. Computer is such a weapon of civilization for modern life. It helps our life in every way. But if we do not awake, that same effective and convenient weapon can be used to destroy ourselves effective enough to make that happen in a second and convenient enough that we wouldn't even realize it is destroying us. As the bible says, it comes to everyone on earth. So, if those things happen only in America it is not the one the bible says.

ABC-abc-1234

In 1995 there was a news in Los Angeles that we can inject some kind of material into the neck of pet or animals so we can find the owner easily when it was lost and it costs around $15. This material is a little advanced one that can replace the barcode printed on the paper, which looks like above picture. We can find the printed barcode easily from any product in any store and everywhere in the world. Actually, the material injected into the neck of the pets or animals works the same thing the bar code does. It is some kind of material that a scanner can detect and read by way of magnetic wave, laser ray or some other technique.

After one year in 1996, I heard the same news that it can be done in Washington.

This bar code began to come into our society since early 80's and rooted deeply for 20 years.

As we give names to each individual to identify easily, combining several different sizes of thick or thin bars we can create limitless different codes and thus we can identify so many merchandises easily.

If you go to a prison you can see every prisoner carry their own number on the chest and the officers call the numbers instead of their names for easy identification.

When you have something to talk about a prisoner you name the number and the officer will look for the file of that number. The file is made when the prisoner comes to the prison to keep every information about the prisoner of that number like his name, age, birth, blood type, address, family, scars, hair and hobby....

If the faces were sorted into the file you will have to look through all of the files to find out. But the numbers of each prisoner were sorted and the only thing you have to do is just pick the right number. Then it comes out right away.

You can identify by the names, numbers, faces, fingerprints and something else.

However, the number is the most convenient and effective way.

The bar code is one way to write the number like we write two as "2" or "II".

This idea was introduced into business to manage a store effectively by controlling the merchandise stock easily. It was convenient, but still needed to find out the file to work with. As the computer techniques developed men began to apply computer to this idea.

And there happened an unimaginable change.

Before, you had to write the information on the paper and it took a lot of time and space to keep. If we think about the printing process of newspaper, we can easily understand what kind of difference this made.

The printing companies had to keep every type faces of letters by the size, by the shape, by the quantity and by the language. It would take the whole office easily.

Now, it is stored in one disk of paper-thin CD as small as our palm and that with much more information.

That big difference did not happen only in storing space but also in speed.

Before, you had to go to the file storage and wrestle to find a couple of pages of information.

Now, just a few strokes on the keyboard will do it with a book of information.

Let's make this example a little bit more practical.

When we buy something at the super market we wait in line before the cashier.

The cashiers take the merchandises one by one and pass it through on the glass top table.

The computer beeps overtime the merchandizes passes the glass top tables.

The computer was reading the bar code. Every time it beeped it found the file of the merchandize.

When we complain something, the cashier gets the file out on the monitor screen and check the necessary information like the price, the manufacturer, quantity, place where kept and the maker…as much as the information was stored.

Exactly the same things are happening to human beings.

When we violate the traffic regulations the police ask the driver's license.

Showing our driver's license is we are passing over the glass top table to be read of the bar code given to each of us. The driver's license number works like the bar code does.

The police can draw out our file instantly and check every detail information like a cashier of a store check every detail information about the merchandizes. Our personal information like the birth place, blood type, hair color, who is the father, who is the mother, medical history, criminal record, current address, annual income, tax report, traffic violation record, finger print, any unpaid penalty, whether wanted by the police....

So, once a criminal is arrested for a certain reason his previous criminal deeds are going to be checked out at the same time when he shows his driver's license.

Our personal records are kept in the computer classified by our driver's license numbers or social security numbers. And it is mandatory to present this number to get the passport to go abroad, to start a new business, to report annual income tax return or to vote.... However, it is restricted to these certain fields of social activities now.

We cooperate to show our number to get what we want.

But what if it is not restricted to these certain fields?

What would happen if we could not buy or sell unless we show this number?

That means we will have to record ourselves what we buy or sell in our personal files in the computer overtime we buy or sell. It is just like writing every detail report about what we bought or sold every time in somebody else's diary.

Let's take more practical example for the better picture.

A bad person woke up at 11o'clock and went to McDonald to fill the empty stomach with a cup of coffee and a hamburger. He found the gas tank was almost empty and filled $15 worth of unleaded gas at a Texaco gas station in Vienna at 12 o'clock. He bought the day's news paper at a Seven Eleven store right after and went to a National Zoo in Washington D.C and spent one hour reading the paper. After that he went to a bank and saw nobody was inside and the bank was about to close. He entered and robbed the bank and ran away. He went to Front Royal that is about 100 miles away from his home and hide himself into a theater at 4 o'clock and watched the movie Titanic. After being relieved a little at the multiplex cinema theatre he went to Pizza Hut for dinner at 7 o'clock. He checked in at a Holiday Inn at 8 o'clock and checked out at 10 o'clock next morning to go home and arrested as soon as he arrived at his house by the police who was awaiting him there.

What this man did was recording in his personal file in another man's computer that he bought what, when, where and how much.

Anywhere he showed his individual number like as driver's license or the social security number, he was recording with his own hand to his personal file in another man's computer about what, when, where and how much he bought. And this information was being transferred through the telephone line to the main computer where his file was stored.

That is, this man bought a cup of coffee and a hamburger from a McDonald at 11 o'clock and filled $15 worth of gas at Texaco in Vienna at 12 0'clock and bought news paper at a Seven Eleven store right after. And then parked at the National Zoo in Washington D.C. at 1 o'clock in the afternoon. He saw the movie Titanic at 4 o'clock in a multiplex cinema theatre and ate pizza at Pizza Hut at 7 o'clock and checked in at a Holiday Inn at 8 o'clock and checked out next morning at 10 o'clock. Exactly the same thing was being recorded in his file in the computer except one thing that he robbed the bank where he did not show his personal number.

These things are prohibited by the law and are not happening now at this time with the good intention of protecting private life. Simply, the time has not come yet. But we have absolutely no difficulties doing so technically and financially.

If each computer is isolated and can not be linked each other these things can not happen. These things are only possible through the computer network.

Under the personal life protection law, the information can not be transferred to higher level of computers now. If those main computers were to be connected to the highest level of one main computer, the one who manage the super main computer would know who did what, where and when not even leaving his desk like he reads his palm.

Actually, the store managers know which cashier sold what, when, how much, to whom and if it was paid by credit card.

Since the main computers are not connected to the super main computers the manager of the super main computers does not know about what we buy or sell but the managers of the lower level main computers know partially about what, when, where we bought and paid how much. That means we already stepped in the beginning situation of the supervision of the computer. I had following experience myself.

I had to place an order for merchandise by the telephone. Since it was my first order, they asked me to pay in advance. Even if I send the check right away it would take a couple of days for them to clear the check and I couldn't get it on time as necessary.

They suggested paying by credit card then they can ship it right away. So, I gave them necessary information about my credit card like the card number, the expiration date and the name. About 2 hours later after I hung up the phone, there was a call from my credit card company asking if I ever had bought such merchandise. They said they thought something was different from my normal purchasing pattern and they are checking if I had ever lost my credit card so somebody else might be using it. I told them I bought that merchandize actually and hung up with appreciation for checking.

It was after I hung up the phone that I realized it was exactly what I am saying now and shocked.

The credit card companies manage each customer with their own main computer.

When someone buys something with the credit card at a store, the cashier passes the credit card through a slot then the machine reads the credit card number by the magnet stripe on the back side of the credit card. And the detail information about the purchase like what, when, where and how much...are transferred to the computer of the credit card company and the credit card company pay the money to the merchants and then collect the debit from the card holder with interest.

257

So, purchasing with credit card means asking supervision by the credit card company because that makes the credit card company know what you are buying, when, where and how much. That exact thing had happened to me as I said above.

Therefore, we know we are already in it and we are only waiting until some man appears to connect all the main computers to the super main computer.

Once the man got connections of all these main computers to the super main computer and regulate that everyone who wants to buy or sell has to show own individual number or special mark, he is going to be able to control all the human beings.

The special marks could be the bar codes or the special material like the one injected into the body of an animal or the magnetic stripes of the credit card....

We have thought purchasing is buying a merchandize only.

But we have to understand the voice mail service of a telephone company is also a purchase. When we purchase a merchandise, we are recording our purchasing at the same time. The same way when we buy a voice mail service, we are recording our voice to the computer. Through our purchasing deed we are recording what we are doing ourselves. Through investing to the stocks, through purchasing the insurance, through purchasing air ticket, through financing our house...we are recording our daily life with our hand into the individual file stored in the super main computer in detail.

We can show our own individual number with the driver's license or credit cards. But these things have the risks of being stolen or missing and some other people can use it.

In that case the controller of the super main computer can not have correct information and cause confusion. So, the credit cards or the driver's license we are using now will be replaced with something else that can not be erased and invisible like the material injected into the neck of pets or animals to prevent this problem.

I think soon after all the computers are connected to the super main computer, we are going to be forced to carry these marks on our forehead *or on the right hand to make it easiest to show or read. This will be the mark of beast*

Again, it is more than ready technically and financially as we see it from the example of the injection to the animal body. We are just awaiting the person who is going to do the job.

Let's go back to the bible to see what the bible says about this.

I want to write it again as following to refresh our idea about it.

Revelation 13:15

and it was allowed to give breath to the image of the beast so that the image of the beast should even speak, and to cause those who would not worship the image of the beast to be slain.

We know the computer even speaks. Those who wouldn't want to carry the personal ID will be killed because that means they did not want to worship the computer.

13:16

Also it causes all, both small and great, both rich and poor, both free and slave, to be marked on the right hand or the forehead,

13:17

so that no one can buy or sell unless he has the mark, that is, the name of the beast or the number of its name.

Because we fell so deeply into the computer civilization, we can not live without computer and that cause us to carry the beast mark.

Everyone is going to be given own personal ID number and that is becoming the beast mark. Those who have the mark have no choice other than following the instruction of the computer. That's because the computer knows what they do.

The number each one has is the name of the beast given by the computer.

And the number can be made as barcode, magnetic stripe or some material that can be injected into body.

We should know we already have it but not only marked on our body. The number we have now does not cover the whole world and we do not carry it on our forehead or right hand yet.

13:18
This calls for wisdom: let him who has understanding reckon the number of the beast, for it is a human number, its number is six hundred and sixty-six.

We know so many people have the same name. It is impossible to give every people different name with current name system. It is inevitable to replace the name with numbers to make as many different names as the number of human beings to identify.

As many as human population!

In modern society, we count by three digits worldwide. I mean we put ",", every three digits like 6,660,000,000. I recall that I used to count by four digits in Korea like 66,6000,0000. They use ",", every four digits in oriental countries until not so long time ago but only 40 years. I presume there must be some counting unit that makes the number 6,660,000,000 writes as 666,0000000 having the comma right after 666 like we express 2,000 as 2k. Or they did not have such unit that can count with more than 10 million. And the bible says it's the human numbers. The human number on earth now is 6 billion, that is 666 x 10 million.

I believe we human beings will be forced to carry the beast mark on the forehead or on the right hand as soon as the human population reaches the number of 6,660,000,000.

Revelation 14:9
And another angel, a third, followed them, saying with a loud voice, "If any one worships the beast and its image, and receives a mark on his forehead or on

**his hand, will himself drink God's wine, the wine
of his anger, which he has poured at full strength
into the cup of his wrath!**

*Who can ever survive if one can not buy or sell? Most people who believe
in Jesus Christ will try not to receive this mark. They understand they can't
go to the doctor and they can't even buy the medicine. As the time goes by,
they will find themselves dying of sickness or hunger even if they know they
can buy food or go to doctor if they just receive the beast mark. All of the
Christians will be put to test whether to receive it to buy or not to receive and
suffer. Those who choose to receive will live physically and loose his spiritual
life and those who choose not to receive will die physically but save his spiritual
life. That's why I call it exchanging our mortal life with the immortal life.*

So, it's a matter of choosing this world or Kingdom of God.

*Since the Kingdom of God is not seen, only those who believe there is
Kingdom of God will be able to refuse to get the mark and die for another life.
Only, those who believe the existence of Kingdom of God would choose not
to receive the mark and would willingly suffer to enter it because they know
it is worth to do so. That's the way our belief towards Jesus Christ saves us.*

God said:

Matthew 24:22
**And if those days had not been shortened, no human
being would be saved; but for the sake of the elect
those days will be shortened. By your endurance you
will gain your lives.**

*We will have to prepare so we can endure until the time God allowed
to shorten for the believers.*

Let's go back to revelation again.

Revelation 14:10
**he also shall drink the wine of God's wrath, poured
unmixed into the cup of his anger, and he shall be**

tormented with fire and sulphur in the presence of the holy angels and in the presence of the And the smoke of their torment goes up for ever and ever; and they have no rest, day or night, these worshipers of the beast and its image, and whoever receives the mark of its name."

Here is a call for the endurance of the saints, those who keep the commandments of God and the faith of Jesus.

As we discussed before, those who received the mark will be supervised and managed by the controller of the super main computer and couldn't be free from the computer. They have no choice other than following computer's instruction. Why is it bad?

God made man to make Sons of God. Yet, these people can't follow God's instruction because they cannot be free from computer. Those are sons of beast.

They can't have the spirit of God and it's worthless like material things. The computer will make them work, work and work until it satisfies. There will be no rest for them and the smoke of their torment goes up for ever and ever. The bible says that is the second death.

Let's discuss more about why these people couldn't be free from computer and what the life in that world would be?

Everybody should have the experience of borrowing a tape from the Erols Video Store.

When we rent a tape, we pass through some kind of gate first and the cashier hands over the tape to us through the outside of the gate. This is to protect from the shoplift.

Some kind of magnetic material is attached to the tapes and when it passes through the gate the scanner installed in the gate is to respond to it and sounds.

It's the same kind of things like the barcodes of merchandises. When it passes the glass top table, the scanner reads the bar code and respond to make the computer work.

The bar code human is to receive soon on his forehead or on the right hand is this kind of thing. Where ever they go, they will be detected by every kind of scanners like the gate in Erols Video store, the glass top table or some kind of cameras....

And if they were not complying with the computer's instruction, the computer will intervene and try to correct that. Sometimes, by sending a police officer, sometimes by charging penalty and sometimes by giving some pain like we install something on a dog's neck to give some pain so it would not cross the invisible electronic fence, which is already being in use to dogs.

Actually, the invisible electronic fence is being used for human also to make it easier to keep the criminals in certain boundary and watch them.

The cameras installed in several places to watch traffic violators are also the kinds.

I do not mean these things are bad. I just mean we are living the age that we need that kind of things and since the bible says about it, we are discussing about it as a Christian.

As we know the bar code helps people and the cameras also help human. Same way, the electronic fence helps man too. But the bible says men gets wicked and corrupted and these things are going to be used onto human beings just like it is used to the animals and things.

Once everyone receives the marks of beast the crime can not find its place because the moment the crime was committed, the super main computer knows it and send the police to get the criminal. As far as the criminal has the mark on his forehead or on his right hand, the criminals can hardly run away and hide. He can not avoid exposing to the scanners installed everywhere like the gas station, motel, parking lot, Seven Eleven Store.... That's because he has to show his individual mark to buy gas, to park, to sleep.... Even if he doesn't show it like we show our credit cards today, so many things like the electronic gates in Erol's video store can scan the mark on his forehead or on his right hand.

All these things are actually happening today but not connected to the super main computer yet.

Then when would these things happen?

Nobody knows the time but we can forecast when it would be like we know it would rain soon when the sky gets cloudier and darker.

It was just about 20 years ago that the computerized cash registers were introduced to individual small stores as dry cleaners or a family owned grocery store.

Now you can see cash registers anywhere you go.

Remember the cash register is the computer and the tax reports are made based upon the record of this cash register. All of these computers are operated separately by the business. But once the regulations were changed to connect all the computers to super main computer, it wouldn't take time to connect or cost much just like it does not cost a lot to connect telephone line today. For they are already there. We cannot over describe how fast the computer technique develops these days.

The new technique today becomes old one next day and the $3,000 computer becomes $2,000 computer next year. It's moving so fast that even the government have headaches in imposing the property tax. Because of the high depreciation rate of computers, regular tax rate can not be applied.

Many would ask:

"How could we store so much information of as many as 6 billion people?"

Looks like people just give oneself to the convenience and the speed not thinking what it means.

Some homes used to keep one set of Encyclopedia Dictionary in their bookshelf for the children's education or for the future reference. It would take almost one full bookshelf. This much information is stored in one paper thin palm size CD to be sold at the store.

Looking for an information from a book takes time and need to flip over page after page.

However, when you look for the information through the computer screen, all you need is just a couple of strokes on the keyboard. Further, when it is bar coded, you don't have to type in the code. Just pass the bar code through the scanner then the scanner will do it instantly.

Looking for someone's information does not take time and storing someone's detail information including the voice neither takes lot of space like this.

In technical terms, the storage size of this one CD is 600 megabytes.

This was first introduced to the public about 12 years ago. The most publicly used storage at that time was about the same size of soft diskette, which has 1.2 megabytes. It is 500 times different compared to the CD that is most commonly used nowadays.

If we compare nonmovable storage of hard disk capacity, the most popular sizable hard disk was 20 megabytes 12 years ago. The most sizable hard disk now is 15 gigabytes, which is 13,000 megabytes. 750 times bigger now! I heard 20 gigabytes hard disk is now available at the store, which is 1,000 times bigger. This was happening only for the last 12 years!

Now let's compare the speed of computers.

The speed of normal computers was 12 MHz 10 years ago, 33MHz 7 years ago and now it is 300 MHz. I heard 450 MHz is available at the store now. Almost 40 time faster now.

So, if someone is carrying a notebook computer of 300 MHz speed and 6 gigabytes storage, that means he has much better computer than the one that a medium size company used to carry 15 years ago investing a lot of money to it. And that means he is carrying the whole computer room of 15 years ago in his hand. Imagine what it would be if it is the super main computer. How fast would it be? How big memory space would it have?

Everybody is sick and tired of the Monica Rewinsky scandal. I saw a paper carrying the dialogue made between the President and Monica Rewinsky. Probably it had been recorded in the computer and remained there until it was opened to public.

Recording daily life of 6 billion people all over the world is not a problem at all with current computer techniques.

These things wouldn't happen peacefully. When the society is in total chaos due to war, famine, flood, riot, stock market collapse, earthquake, the atomic bomb explosion or massive economic failure, some one will arise and do this with good excuses of repressive measure.

However, it is going to be a worldwide international problem that would cause to seek the international solution. I don't think one incident could cause this kind of problem.

I would rather say every kind of things like above will happen to surface gradually and pull us into the total chaos like a thief breaks into our house and put a knife onto our neck. Many people told me if ever I threatening them even while I write this book.

I do not and can not threaten anybody because I am such a powerless person.

But if it is ever threatening, that means the environments we are facing now make us feel it could really happen. It's not me. It's God, because I'm talking about what the bible says.

Many should have heard about cash-less banking system.

Our current society is on the half way to the cash-less banking system. Many companies use their computer banking net work to pay their employees. They just transfer the amount of paycheck to each employee's bank account and give the copy of the paycheck as receipt. You find the money was directly deposited to your account later even though you didn't see it. When you buy groceries, you pay with your credit cards instead of paying with the actual paper money or coin. When the bills come from the credit card companies, you just transfer the amount of money you owe to the credit card companies through the banking network. You do not need to carry the money. In that society, nobody would hurt anyone for money because nobody carries money. Crime like bank robbery would disappear. At the same time, you will be completely exposed to the computer and controlled by the computer. As we know, we are already in that society half way. When the computer networking was completed, the complete cash-less society would take place at the same time also. That will be when all of the computers were connected to one main super computer.

Moral Collapse and the Homosexuality

2,000 years ago, the homosexuality in Rome was not a problem at all like now. People were so corrupted and as the result Rome was ruined also. I am going to see why this happens through the bible and compare with the time of Sodom and Gomorra to see what age we are passing now.

The bible explains why men become immoral and homosexual as following.

Romans 1:20

Ever since the creation of the world his invisible nature, namely, his eternal power and deity, has been clearly perceived in the things that have been made. So they are without excuse; for although they knew God they did not honor him as God or give thanks to him, but they became futile in their thinking and their senseless minds were darkened. Claiming to be wise, they became fools, and exchanged the glory of the immortal God for images resembling mortal man or birds or animals or reptiles. Therefore God gave them up in the lusts of their hearts to impurity, to the dishonoring of their bodies among themselves, because they exchanged the truth about God for a lie and worshiped and served the creature rather than the Creator, who is blessed for ever! Amen.

For this reason God gave them up to dishonorable passions. Their women exchanged natural relations for unnatural, and the men likewise gave up natural relations with women and were consumed with passion for one another, men committing shameless acts with men and receiving in their own persons the due penalty for their error. And since they did not see fit to acknowledge God, God gave them up to a base mind and to improper conduct. They were filled with all manner of wickedness, evil, covetousness, malice. Full of envy, murder, strife, deceit, malignity, they are gossips, slanderers, haters of God, insolent, haughty, boastful, inventors of evil, disobedient to parents, foolish, faithless, heartless, ruthless. Though they know God's decree that those who do such things deserve to die, they not only do them but approve those who practice them.

Bible says it's because people do not honor God even though they know

God. The homosexual people commonly say they did not know they were homosexual until the day it surfaced to them suddenly.

It is just like sugar, drug or cigarette smoking.

Everybody knows sugar is sweet and every child likes sugar.

However, those who know sugar would destroy the body and teeth do not eat sugar much. Nobody knows the sugar is sweet before tasting it like the homosexuals say they did not know they were homosexual before they experienced it.

I would say there is no such a homosexual thing.

Like anybody who does not know about sugar would eat too much sugar making own body diabetic and destroy teeth, anybody who does not understand God's will can not protect oneself from making own body homosexual. When we think about the drug the same way, we can understand it more clearly.

There will be none that does not respond to the drug. There should be some difference in responding, person to person, like an egg hatches a little bit earlier while another egg hatches a little late. If an egg doesn't hatch, it must be a different kind of eggs.

Those who know the drug is addictive and destructive would fear doing the drug and wouldn't do it. And those who do not know about the drug or do not care about its destructive nature do not care about doing it and become addictive and destroy themselves.

Since God made the drug addictive and destructive, it is God's will. If one understands God and fear of God, he wouldn't do the drug. Likewise, if someone does not understand God and does not fear God, he would do the drug.

The bible says:

Proverbs 1:7
The fear of the LORD is the beginning of knowledge;
fools despise wisdom and instruction.

At the time of Sodom and Gomorra, God sent angels to destroy the Sodom and Gomorra because they were so corrupted and the homosexuality was prevailed.

Let's see what they did just before God destroyed those two cities.

Genesis 19

The two angels came to Sodom in the evening; and Lot was sitting in the gate of Sodom. When Lot saw them, he rose to meet them, and bowed himself with his face to the earth, and said, "My lords, turn aside, I pray you, to your servant's house and spend the night, and wash your feet; then you may rise up early and go on your way." They said, "No; we will spend the night in the street." But he urged them strongly; so they turned aside to him and entered his house; and he made them a feast, and baked unleavened bread, and they ate. But before they lay down, the men of the city, the men of Sodom, both young and old, all the people to the last man, surrounded the house; and they called to Lot, "Where are the men who came to you tonight? Bring them out to us, that we may know them." Lot went out of the door to the men, shut the door after him, and said, "I beg you, my brothers, do not act so wickedly. Behold, I have two daughters who have not known man; let me bring them out to you, and do to them as you please; only do nothing to these men, for they have come under the shelter of my roof."

But they said, "Stand back!" And they said, "This fellow came to sojourn, and he would play the judge! Now we will deal worse with you than with them." Then they pressed hard against the man Lot, and drew near to break the door. But the men put forth their hands and brought Lot into the house to them, and shut the door. And they struck with blindness the men who were at the door of the house, both small and great, so that they wearied themselves groping for the door.

Then the men said to Lot, "Have you any one else here? Sons-in-law, sons, daughters, or any one you have in the city, bring them out of the place; for we are about to destroy this place, because the outcry against its people has become great before the LORD, and the LORD has sent us to destroy it." So Lot went out and said to his sons-in-law, who were to marry his daughters, "Up, get out of this place; for the LORD is about to destroy the city." But he seemed to his sons-in-law to be jesting. When morning dawned, the angels urged Lot, saying, "Arise, take your wife and your two daughters who are here, lest you be consumed in the punishment of the city." But he lingered; so the men seized him and his wife and his two daughters by the hand, the LORD being merciful to him, and they brought him forth and set him outside the city. And when they had brought them forth, they said,"Flee for your life; do not look back or stop anywhere in the valley; flee to the hills, lest you be consumed." And Lot said to them, "Oh, no, my lords; behold, your servant has found favor in your sight, and you have shown me great kindness in saving my life; but I cannot flee to the hills, lest the disaster overtake me, and I die. Behold, yonder city is near enough to flee to, and it is a little one. Let me escape there--is it not a little one? --and my life will be saved!" He said to him, "Behold, I grant you this favor also, that I will not overthrow the city of which you have spoken. Make haste, escape there; for I can do nothing till you arrive there." Therefore the name of the city was called Zo'ar. The sun had risen on the earth when Lot came to Zo'ar. Then the LORD rained on Sodom and Gomor'rah brimstone and fire from the LORD out of heaven; and he overthrew those cities, and all

**the valley, and all the inhabitants of the cities, and
what grew on the ground. But Lot's wife behind him
looked back, and she became a pillar of salt. And
Abraham went early in the morning to the place
where he had stood before the LORD; and he looked
down toward Sodom and Gomor'rah and toward all
the land of the valley, and beheld, and lo, the smoke
of the land went up like the smoke of a furnace.**

*It was only 20 years ago that the person in charge would warn not
to walk along with hand in hand between man and man or woman and
woman in America before issuing the passport. Because, they said it is going
to be mistaken as homosexual and have hard time. That was American
culture at that time. Now let's see what's happening around us.*

I heard the same sex marriage right was put to vote in Hawaii.

*Thousands of thousand gay and lesbian people march in Washington
DC asking no discrimination. They can not have a baby so they ask to
allow they can adopt a baby.*

*It became a policy to teach children at school that homosexuality is
normal like everybody has different personality.*

*It was only 15 or so years ago that homosexuals could not even go to
church due to their own sense of guilt.*

*Now, some ministers are said to teach homosexuality is a privilege not
given to everybody so should the homosexuals appreciate it and come to the
church to pray and thank God.*

*God designed man first and then made woman to help man. Since
woman was made to help man, woman should follow man and it is only
possible by obedience.*

*And since woman was taken out of man, woman is bone of bone and
flesh of flesh of man as Adam said.*

So, man should love woman more than own body. Let's look what God said.

**Genesis 2:18
Then the LORD God said, "It is not good that the
man should be alone; I will make him a helper fit**

for him." So the LORD God caused a deep sleep to fall upon the man, and while he slept took one of his ribs and closed up its place with flesh; and the rib which the LORD God had taken from the man he made into a woman and brought her to the man. Then the man said, "This at last is bone of my bones and flesh of my flesh; she shall be called Woman, because she was taken out of Man." Therefore a man leaves his father and his mother and cleaves to his wife, and they become one flesh.

So, we men and women are supposed to live together loving, helping, leading and following. Hence, our present society doesn't look like that.

One out of two couples are experiencing divorce. It is going to be much more than that if we consider so many people do not marry and live together in fear of possible divorce and then separate. Besides, many people experience the 2ⁿᵈ and 3ʳᵈ marriage. It looks more serious than we imagine.

Bible says God gave man and woman a different role.

However, people want be equal.

Man wants to be like woman and woman wants to be like man.

Man is supposed to love woman more than own body and woman is supposed to follow man than own will. Because man abuse woman, woman does not follow man and insists own will. And because woman does not follow man, man does not love woman more than oneself. Men want to do what women do and women want to do what men do.

It's hard to find a manlike man and womanlike woman. There is no man and there is no woman. There is only human. So, what's the problem with we human beings remain as human? The problem is man and woman are different. Two different man and woman make one human being. So now what we call human is not human. Needs new proper word for that.

Not to mention about the teenagers, I do not think young people of 20's have the sense to discern which is good and which is evil about what's happening nowadays based upon God's words. Because all these things are happening only for the last 20 years and they do not know what it is living in different environment not like this. The middle aged like above 40's would know it because they have experienced both environments.

So, it is going to be really difficult to discuss about this end time things with young people.

Not only the moral things but also all the things that happening in every area. Just like those who lived only a fast running society would not know that the society has been changed suddenly and think it is normal. It is hard to expect a young person among these people appear to educate about the end time things.

Let's move on to next topic about increasing knowledge that is written in the bible as one of the signs of the end time to see what time we are passing.

Increasing Knowledge and the Civilization

Daniel 12:1
At that time shall arise Michael, the great prince who has charge of your people. And there shall be a time of trouble, such as never has been since there was a nation till that time; but at that time your people shall be delivered, every one whose name shall be found written in the book. And many of those who sleep in the dust of the earth shall awake, some to everlasting life, and some to shame and everlasting contempt. And those who are wise shall shine like the brightness of the firmament; and those who turn many to righteousness, like the stars for ever and ever. But you, Daniel, shut up the words, and seal the book, until the time of the end. Many shall run to and fro, and knowledge shall increase.

It was not so long time ago but only 40 years that people used ship to travel abroad. If it's not for pleasure like the cruise I guess nobody would travel by sea these days. I heard even some people come to America from the other side of earth to play golf. I do not mean to blame them but to point that people are moving so fast to make the small world smaller. Only 20 years ago people used write letters to communicate. I remember that I used to write business letters to other country. It took 10 days at the fastest to hear from the receiver. Now it takes only 1 minute by fax. If you use e-mail, it is instantaneous. It was only about 70 years ago that people used horse to deliver mail.

Now, you can see what's happening anywhere around the world by computer Internet right away.

As the above bible scripture says as **"Many shall run to and fro, and knowledge shall increase"** all these things are the signs of the end time. An incident happened somewhere can spread worldwide in very short period of time. Before, one problem that happened in this country took a month to reach to the other country so, while that thing travels to reach to the other country it was corrected in this country and could stop spreading.

Now, it reaches to the other side of earth instantly and has no time to correct. For an example, it took 10 days or more to send money to the other side of earth before.

Now, it is instantaneous.

Before, it took months or years for some kind of pestilence to be spread to other country.

Now, we have experienced the mad cow disease spreader so fast and so far.

It would take a year to destroy a city like New York before and now it will take a couple of minutes with one atomic bomb. I wonder if men could ever destroy the whole earth until as late as 1960 even after the atomic bomb was developed.

I guess many would say we could have it at the time of Cuba crisis.

What I don't understand is how come people do not care now about the end time things when it is much more evident to fit to it than the time of Cuba crisis or when the first atomic bomb was dropped at Hiroshima Japan.

Many people say, as the risks were increased dramatically so did the protection measurements strengthened.

Why can't people understand?

You do not make accident when you move slowly and even though the accident occurs the damage would be mild. As the speed goes up you have more chance to involve in an accident and once the accident occurs it is serious like no one survives the airplane crash.

Increasing knowledge is common to every field of communication, transportation, biology, medicine, economy, machine, printing, arms and etc.....

And the computer technology made it happen becoming the basic foundation of all these. Especially the medical and biological progress is remarkable.

The test tube baby, organ transplantation, animal cloning, choosing the sex of embryo...are those.

Looks like men's ability is almost limitless and many people say:

"Look! Men can copy even human. Men landed on the moon already and they can manipulate human body as they need. Don't you see they can replace even the heart? They even make material. Nylon, artificial diamond, plastic, artificial blood, artificial skin..."

But we have to know that our creation of all these are just using God's creation and we have never made what was not existed. We just find the secret of God's creation and use.

Therefore, the remarkable progress similar to that of God means God taught men as much as needed. In other words, it is to get ready for another world.

We know there is lot of controversy about human cloning.

I would say human cloning itself couldn't be controversial. Like it is up to the person whether one uses a knife constructive way or destructive way, it's the matter of man who use the human cloning technique.

One thing I know is men's wicked mind will allow using this technique for own satisfaction like we used atomic bomb.

Let's see what the controversy is about human cloning.

Everybody knows that man can copy an animal of its special characteristics and give it to another animal to have another animal of same shape and characteristics.

It was done to several animals successfully and those animals are already living on earth. Theoretically it is said to be possible to human also, but due to the morality is concerned, actual experiment was not made so far.

At this juncture, a doctor in Chicago announced that he will try this and caused trouble because there was no law about this to restrain. The congress is said to prepare to legalize this issue either yes or no to have control on this problem in the future.

Two parties are said to have different opinions. The affirmative party says it makes possible to get organs as needed to transplant to patients who are dying of unavailable organs and also it makes it possible to study on incurable diseases like Cancer or AIDS.

The negative party says it's a blasphemy and a challenge to the divine nature of God. The Christian and anti abortionist group are said to support this party.

I recollect that we are living this world to raise our spiritual character to that of Holy Spirit and passing through the furnace is God's way for it. Many would say if human cloning also copies human character, it is better to do so instead of passing the furnace. The problem is men's wicked mind will choose to copy what they like not what God like and what men like are evil because men have own standard of Good and Evil since the first man Adam ate the fruit of Good and Evil and that is sin. So human cloning will bring full of evil spirit in this world and that is my one personal reason why I believe it is harvest time.

Everyone knows that the test tube baby is living and growing naturally with normal babies. When the test tube baby is also a human, the baby born by human cloning would be a human for sure. Imagine what kind of life this human would have when doctors carry out experiments on them to find out how to cure Cancer or AIDS and take the organ out from them to transplant it to other patient who is dying of unavailable organs.

Since the first man Adam, men developed tools to make living easier but more for the war. The development shows steady, gradual progress until late 19th century.

However, the development was exploding as the century turning into 20th.

It is said the whole knowledge up until the year 1,900 since Adam would be much less than the knowledge human got for the last 100 years.

The conveniences of modern civilization began to show in the year of early 1,900 starting the telephone, electricity, automobile, airplane and etc....

These things added convenience to people's living but men's greedy mind caused the 1st world war.

Mobilized by every kind of early modernization convenience, this war brought as much damage as the knowledge increase. Mostly European countries were involved in this war and the total casualties due to the war during the period of 4 years (1914~1918) were 17 million people including civilians. When counted only military pestles, 8 million casualties, 20 million wounded, 6 million were missing and total 34 million people were seriously affected from this war.

We can imagine the seriousness when we consider the world population at that time as 2.2 billion and it was mostly limited to European countries.

After the war, the knowledge added more rapidly and radios, TV's, wireless telegram's and... etc. were invented in 1940's. These modern conveniences should have made life more peaceful and comfortable. But men caused another world war again only 25 years after the 1st world war to fill their greedy mind. All the knowledge and every modern convenience were introduced to this war to destroy each other and the damages were as big as the knowledge.

This war was the 2nd world war that continued for 6 years (1939~1945) all over the world. Compared to 8 million casualties of the 1st world war, 17 million casualties of military personnel during this war is beyond our imagination. This world war gave more damage to the civilians than the 1st world war gave damage to the civilian. Considering 8 million military personnel casualties and 9 million civilian casualties during the 1st world war, the civilian casualties of the 2nd world war would easily be over 20 million.

Add 6 million Jewish holocausts to this number.

It is said the exact number was not known but when totaled, 17 million military casualties, 20 million civilian casualties and 6 million Jewish holocaust casualties, the total casualties would be 43 million. Which means one out of every 60 persons was killed by the war when the world population was around 2.5 billion at that time. At least one family out of 10 families had experienced the death caused by the war.

Missile, submarine and atomic bomb were introduced and every kind of knowledge was used during this war making the war more terrible.

Knowledge had increased dramatically afterwards and men landed on the moon, succeeded in heart transplantation and gave birth to a test tube baby.

The computer accelerated the knowledge increase after 1980.

Now we can have son or daughter as our choice, we can copy a man and make the same person limitlessly.

We can send a robot to other planet and let it send every necessary information and let it move around to do the job needed to explore the planet. All these things mean we are imitating God and I think God would be very proud of it like we are proud of our children when they do something we didn't expect.

However, God says to know when these things happen it is the harvest time and there will be great distress and judgment of fire. It could be volcano, earthquake or collision with some other planet. However, when we look back our history of destroying ourselves with what we made using our knowledge, the atomic warfare is most persuasive.

People say everybody know it is going to kill not only the enemy but also everyone on earth and who would do that kind of stupid thing knowing that it would kill oneself. It's not the matter that we know or we do not know.

As God said, our desire conceives sin and the sin grows to death. Our desire for the modern convenience grows to destruction and since the knowledge is near to that of God, the destruction also is going to be the total destruction.

So, we know where we are by measuring the civilization because God said the knowledge would increase when the time comes.

Good and evil is like the compass that shows north or south. When the good things prevail, we know we are headed to life and when the evil things prevail, we know we are headed to death. But those who are away from God can not read the compass because they do not know what is good and what is evil. It is not need to mention that the modern civilization we built will be used for the destruction. The bible says there will be a great tribulation before the massive destruction and we are talking about how to escape the great tribulation as god said to discern and evade. God said the great tribulation period would be shortened for the sake of believers, otherwise nobody would be saved.

Increasing Knowledge and Culture

As the increasing knowledge causes technical development to feed the modern conveniences, it also affects human's culture greatly.

TV's, Videos and Movies are the major components that affects our culture representing our culture.

The main stream of the movies and videos are about violence, alien, science fiction, psychic, mystery and most of the TV shows are comedy.

Most common stories are about aliens invading the earth to occupy, a ghost going into someone's body to live like somebody else. A devil transforms into a robot or sometimes to an animal, a scientist travels through the time to the past and future, a spaceman having a date with a realistic man in fantasy, a man disappears from this place and appears in another place instantly. The computer makes something as to the order of a man right away....

We will talk about the ghost things later, but we discussed already about the other unrealistic things under the title of "how God accomplishes". These are not the way God accomplishes. Because God accomplishes actual things not like the magicians perform magic to cheat people. So, I would say these kinds of things could, would and should never happen in this world. God clearly showed us what God will accomplish as following.

> **Isaiah 9:6**
> **For to us a child is born, to us a son is given; and the government will be upon his shoulder, and his name will be called "Wonderful Counselor, Mighty God, Everlasting Father, Prince of Peace."**
> **Of the increase of his government and of peace**

there will be no end, upon the throne of David, and over his kingdom, to establish it, and to uphold it with justice and with righteousness from this time forth and for evermore. The zeal of the LORD of hosts will do this.

God will accomplish justice and the righteousness, and that is "You get as much as you do." These unrealistic things are completely against God's will.

These things are evil as Jesus showed us when he was tested by the devil as following. It shows us what is following demon things.

Matthew 4

Then Jesus was led up by the Spirit into the wilderness to be tempted by the devil. And he fasted forty days and forty nights, and afterward he was hungry. And the tempter came and said to him, "If you are the Son of God, command these stones to become loaves of bread." But he answered, "It is written, 'Man shall not live by bread alone, but by every word that proceeds from the mouth of God.' "Then the devil took him to the holy city, and set him on the pinnacle of the temple, and said to him, "If you are the Son of God, throw yourself down; for it is written, 'He will give his angels charge of you,' and 'On their hands they will bear you up, lest you strike your foot against a stone.'"

Jesus said to him, "Again it is written, 'You shall not tempt the Lord your God.'" Again, the devil took him to a very high mountain, and showed him all the kingdoms of the world and the glory of them; and he said to him, "All these I will give you, if you will fall down and worship me." Then Jesus said to him, "Begone, Satan! for it is written, 'You shall worship the Lord your God and him only shall you

serve.'" Then the devil left him, and behold, angels came and ministered to him.

Appearing and disappearing all of a sudden is not physical world and those two characters cannot be combined together in this physical world like our body cannot act like ghost unless our body actually dies.

So that a visible person goes into another body and actually acts like somebody else or jumping into 4th dimension to go back to the past is false.

Much false things are exercising with great influence and that is our present culture.

These invisible things are not of this world. As Jesus said only Holy Spirit can kick out these ghost things, we human beings can not do this kind of things. We shouldn't be afraid or expect or confused by these things. Because of these false things, many youngsters neglect to raise their spiritual character and wish unreasonable things like getting somebody else's good memory, money making dream machine, jumping around past and future....

We had little chance to contact these things before. But now, our children are living in that swamp to be confused to believe as it is real or it is going to become real in the future and wish false things that they didn't do. When it doesn't come true, they use the violence what they learned from the movies.

This is how the devil holds the youngsters in this world of death and this is what the bible says through following words.

Amos 8:11
"Behold, the days are coming," says the Lord GOD, "when I will send a famine on the land; not a famine of bread, nor a thirst for water, but of hearing the words of the LORD. They shall wander from sea to sea, and from north to east; they shall run to and fro, to seek the word of the LORD, but they shall not find it.

Youngsters cannot understand God and that makes youngsters wander around looking for the right direction or just give up in despair.

I'd like to talk to youngsters.

Live in practical world to train the spirit with practical things because every character of God is shown in practical things and you do not know what you cannot see. But do not pursue the practical things. For it disappears. Use it to train yourself.

And when something you can not solve happens, then ask God. God will solve it different way you don't understand. That is God's way and that is what you are going to do spiritually. But you have to grow spiritually to do spiritual things.

You need to raise your spiritual character to that of Holy Spirit. Otherwise that power doesn't come to you. So always stay in Jesus Christ and learn from Jesus Christ. He has the Holy Spirit.

As for the ghost or the demon, there is ghost or demon in this world as Jesus showed it by casting out so many demons as following.

> **Matthew 9:32**
> **As they were going away, behold, a dumb demoniac was brought to him. And when the demon had been cast out, the dumb man spoke; and the crowds marveled, saying, "Never was anything like this seen in Israel."**

> **Matthew 10:1**
> **And he called to him his twelve disciples and gave them authority over unclean spirits, to cast them out, and to heal every disease and every infirmity.**

But we can not win the devil or ghost without Holy Spirit in us because they are invisible. It is not strange at all that those devil or ghost goes to unbelievers or blind believers. Because only true believers know it and can discern which is which.

I want to mention that much of the movies are made by computer manipulation and we are actually living the world surrounded by false things.

The next popular program in TV show is comedy.

It is easy to find that most well known public channels filled the evening golden hours with comedy programs.

First of all, the bible teaches us this is not what Sons of God should pursue.

Many would say:

What's bad about laughing and joking? It helps you resolve the stress. Don't you know the stress make you sick?

It's up to the amount of faith God allowed to each one. Anyway, God said as following.

Philippians 4:8
Finally, brethren, whatever is true, whatever is honorable, whatever is just, whatever is pure, whatever is lovely, whatever is gracious, if there is any excellence, if there is anything worthy of praise, think about these things. What you have learned and received and heard and seen in me, do; and the God of peace will be with you.

And God said to this generation the psychic is so prevailed.

Isaiah 8:19
And when they say to you, "Consult the mediums and the wizards who chirp and mutter," should not a people consult their God? Should they consult the dead on behalf of the living? To the teaching and to the testimony! Surely for this word which they speak there is no dawn. They will pass through the land, greatly distressed and hungry; and when they are hungry, they will be enraged and will curse their

king and their God, and turn their faces upward; and they will look to the earth, but behold, distress and darkness, the gloom of anguish; and they will be thrust into thick darkness.

Financial crisis

It was just couple of years that the world began to suffer from money problem. Looks like the whole world envy America of its prosperity.

What happened to other countries like Japan, Germany, Indonesia, Hong Kong, Russia, Brazil, Mexico, Korea, Philippines, Thailand, and Australia, Pakistan...?

Including the Asian four dragons of Taiwan, Korea, Singapore and Malaysia, so many countries are said expecting financial aid from IMF.

The problem these countries are facing is called commonly the bubble economy.

Let's say somebody bought a house at $100,000 and sold it at $150,000 after one year. The person who bought the house did the same thing and sold it at $200,000 next year.

Many other people saw it and did the same thing for ten years. The house price soared and the $100,000 house became $500,000 house.

The first person bought the house with own money. So, he thought he made $50,000 profit and used that money for his child's college. He bought another house at $150,000 with the loan of $50,000. After seven years the interest rate went down considerably.

He found his house price tripled to $500,000. Since so many people were buying the house with only 10% down payment, he refinanced the same way borrowing $450,000 and invested to buy another house because it looked like most profitable.

Most companies and banks did the same thing rather than investing to own business. Because it brought more profit than their own business.

Farmers, blue collars, white collars and everybody did like that.

Banks lend money up to the limit of the house value and that's the source for extra spending. But, unfortunately, most American pay only 10% for the down payment.

So, when things go worse it's going to proceed rapidly.

When a customer makes a deposit in the bank, the bank does not keep it all in the safe to be ready for the withdrawal of the customer. They keep only the minimal to get ready for the daily customers and invest it to somewhere upon their policy and the Federal Deposit Insurance Cooperation guarantees to pay for the deposit. So, when a customer deposit $1,000 in the bank, the bank keeps minimal amount like $200 and invest the rest.

Since the money is not gold standard the government could print as much as needed to lend to the people.

Unfortunately, the house price couldn't go up forever and for some reason the economic situation became not so good like there are sunny days and rainy days.

Some companies were not doing well, so they had to lay off some of the employees.

As the economic slow down continued those people could not pay the monthly payment and tried to sell the house at lower price. Since most people made only 10 % down payment, it was better to give up than to sell the house and as the house price began to decline people did not buy the house. They could not even sell at significantly low price.

The banks had to foreclose the house and there were so many houses like that.

The banks had lots of houses but could not pay the money customer deposited.

As the deposit were insured by the FDIC, the government had to pay it and those banks were closed or merged to another bank.

The house value dropped to the level of 10 years ago and people who had owned the house lost not only the house but also the money because they had consumed all the money they had as a form of house 10 years ago. Those who bought two houses lost the money and became to owe more money. The result was the bankruptcy after consuming all the money piled in their property 10 years ago. They just played with the number not with the real things.

Exactly the same thing happened in those trouble countries to the real estate and the stock market.

Not to the Wall Street yet though.

That's what the bubble economy is.

It's not real value. It is blown up to a bubble and over valued.

That could not happen in gold standard money system.

For the government can not print money as much as the government need and therefore people can not borrow and invest or spend as much as they want. That's because the government needed to have that worth of actual gold to print that amount of money.

Anyway, one sure thing is people poured that much money to make that big bubbles.

Even though people had spent to make bubble, spent is spent. They do not have money or the house where their money was once piled. That is the problem. Then where to all the money have gone?

Actually, the government does not print the money. The money is written on the book as number like we do book keeping and it should remain in somebody's book as number.

So, it is just the number game. It's not the money that is growing. It is the number that grows.

While the number grows people spend as much as the number grows and as soon as the number shrinks, they find they spent all the money they had.

That is, as soon as the bubble explodes, they find they spent all the money they had.

Even though the house price goes up and down, the house is always the same house. We are playing with false things. I would call it as false economy. These things do not happen under the gold standard money system. Anyway, somebody is going to keep the houses or stocks for the money in the book with blown up over price. Who is that somebody? Those are the banks or the lenders and when they can not make their own payment to their investment, the government takes that place. As far as people spend money, there shouldn't be any problem and only thing the banks had to do was just write the number in the book to show the money was lent. The problem is the economy has to grow nonstop so people can pay the money back with interest and the economy can not grow forever with the same pace as the bubble grows.

Therefore, when it come to the limit they could pay, they can not spend any more and stop or slow down spending. Which causes the economy slow down and the price goes down also. As it rocketed to go up, it explodes when it goes down. That is the problem.

It happens between countries and countries too. Specially, between U.S. and other countries. For most of the money circulated in the world is U.S. dollar and only U.S. government can print U.S. dollar.

The above house example will happen in U.S. stock market also. For it is number game and false economy. Pay attention to what the graph about the derivatives of next page means. The properties or stock prices go up as people continue to buy and sell to make profit until its down turn. It is normal phenomenon of market and that's why market is there. But the problem is because the money was not backed up with some real things like gold, it has no limit and could go up sky-high and explodes like the bubble explodes when it touches something sharp. That is the current financial crisis in many countries. They just make money as numbers in the book, not in real things. It is number game and false economy. We don't see the sky rocketing house price in America, do we? I agree. As far as the house price is concerned it has less bubble than other countries. But we made bubble in stocks instead. We know we Americans do not save. We also know that probably 80% of Americans buy houses with 10% down payment while the people in other countries buy houses with own money or much more down payment. They have savings and they can draw some money from their house. But Americans do not save and do not have pile of money in the house. So once the bubble explodes the financial crisis is going to proceed much faster and severe than it was in other countries.

Do you know the U.S. national debt is 5.5 trillion U.S. dollars? The world largest debt nation is America. America is said to pay 260 billion dollars for interest only every year. Even the budget deficit was turned to surplus this year we have to pay what we owe. When the economy slows down, the budget surplus will submerge also.

Then why don't we print money and pay like the government print money and lend the money to American? The problem is, it is not only us *that made the bubble. The other countries bought lot of money from us with merchandise and made bubbles themselves. So, they have lot of U.S. dollar in their book and if we print dollar to pay our debt, they will dump the dollar they have because the dollar price will collapse. Remember they have 5.5 trillion dollars. I believe that was the reason why current bubble economy has happened in other countries first. How much was it ballooned? I would say it is more than American national debt of 5.5 trillion dollar at least.*

Then what is the world 2nd largest economy Japan's problem? They don't owe money.

Don't' they lend lots of money to other countries instead?

That's right. They did what American banks did to American people to the other countries with U.S. dollar. So, they have lots of dollar in their book but it is not collectible like our bank wouldn't be possible to collect money from American people when the economy slows down.

If the money system is gold standard, you are sure to have as much gold as the amount of money. But when the system is not backed with any standard, what you have is just the number on the paper that the value of it could vary on its own way. That is exchange rate between the currencies. When we look other countries' current collapse, we can understand what the false economy means.

You might remember the dollar exchange rate almost went to crisis in 1995. In just a couple of weeks the dollar value against Japanese Yen dropped from 100:1 to 80:1.

The same thing is happening now. Ever decreasing Yen value hit 145:1 as of mid Oct.1998. That was just a couple of weeks ago and now after only 2-3 weeks, the Yen exchange rate against US dollar is 115:1.

More serious things are happening all over the world.

Sometimes the currency value drops 50% over night.

Malaysia, Korea, Russia, Brazil, Mexico, Thailand... all over the world.

Then what is the problem with Germany?

They did to Russia like Japan did to Asian countries.

So, the whole economic crisis come from one problem like above.

Men fell into the trap men made.

Still do not understand why America alone enjoy prosperity despite the world largest debt?

That's because America only can print U.S. dollar and American people like spending. That's why Mr. Allen Greenspan, the chairman of federal reserve, is lowering the interest rates to make people have more room to spend.

However, it can not continue forever. Because people can spend only until they can make payment. So, the lower interest rate earns time but it doesn't solve the problem.

Nobody knows the exact time until when people can spend just like we do not know until when my almost bankrupt father could bring money for us so we can spend.

But the wise children know that their father is in trouble.

I guess it won't be long. Because delinquent rates of every kind payment are going up.

To explain about American national debt for better understanding:
It is almost 3 times of annual American government budget.

If the American national debt of 5.5 trillion dollars were used for IMF aid for the economic crisis, almost 300 countries can benefit when given 20 billion dollars each.

That means all the debt combined all the countries excluding America in the world is less than the American national debt.

The 260 billion dollars of annual interest is about the amount of American national defense budget.

The national debt of almost bankrupt Korea with population of 40 million is 120 billion dollars. We are paying as much as more than twice of Korean national debt every year for interest alone.

When we look what happened in Argentine in late 1980's we can see how seriously and how rapidly it proceeded.

Someone who knew the hyperinflation visited there and one of his friends came to meet him at the airport. Knowing the visitor was going to take the bus, the friend recommended taking taxi and explained. You are paying the bus fare in advance while you pay the taxi fare after you arrive. Since you don't know how much inflation would there be before you arrive it is better to take taxi.

It is interesting to look what was happening by the graph.

Let's look into some parts with graphs for the next couple of pages for the better picture.

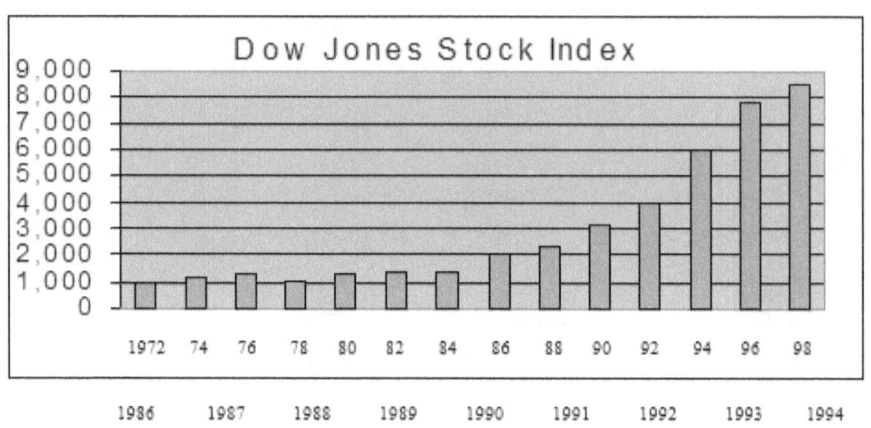

Source: Bank for International Settlement, Federal Deposit Insurance Corp. U.S. Federal Reserve Survey, Historical Statistics of U.S., The New Federalist

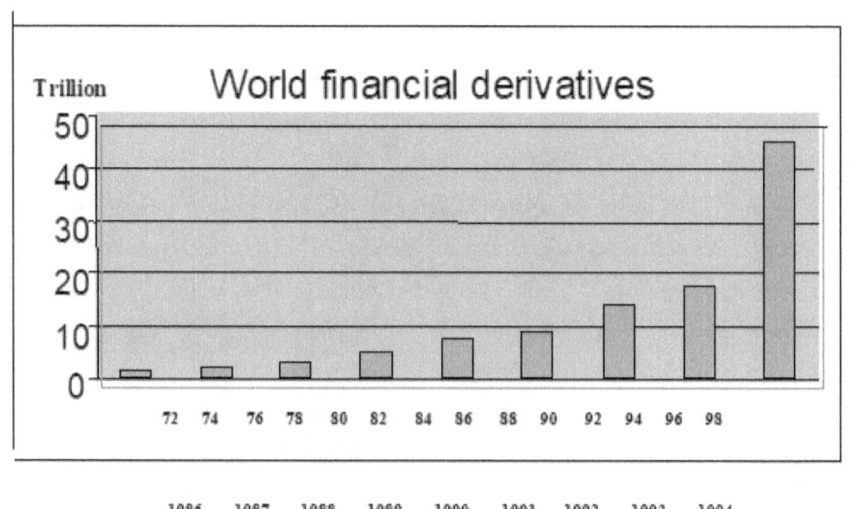

How could the government make the budget surplus?

Simple!

Just let the people spend more. The bubble gets bigger and people pay more tax for it.

The bubble grows until people can't spend any more and as soon as the bubble touches the limit it explodes like we see from so many other countries on earth now.

Computer Millennium Bug - Y2K problem

As we discussed in previous chapter, the computer development was beyond our imagination. That unimaginable development is just about to cause big trouble soon.

Since the computer required large space and the memory space was limited, people just tried to reduce the size in every way and it caused this problem. They did not expect the computer would be developed so fast and would extend to the future to control our life and made the systems leave off the first two digits of the year and programmed to work only on two digits. So the computer can read only the last two digits of "00" and confuse the year 2000 with 1900.

Why would this simple problem cause big troubles?

First, nothing can be done without computer these days.

This makes even the very simple computer problem cause big troubles. Look around us what we can do without computer. Shopping, mortgage financing, depositing, withdrawing, paying every kind of bills, printing, air ticketing, designing, billing….

From 411 telephone service to war, nothing can be done without computer.

Second, our life is time related.

We are living a life of 3 dimensional. We can live only in the frame of time.

So, time related every action like above examples are going to be affected. The air traffic control, expiration date control, train scheduling, electric billing, manufacturing plan, mortgage plan, attendance record, social security control, hotel reservation....

We can not get away from time.

If it is simple problem why don't we fix it? We still have more than a year.

We are fixing it now. However, it is wide spread too much and cost too much.

When you see a programmer programming, they write long lines of commands to have the computers carry out those commands. And it takes often time a year.

The computer is the most stupid invention men made because the basic foundation is only the combination of "yes" or "no". There is no in between. To speak in technical term, it is the combination of many "0's" and "1's". The bar code explains it well.

Therefore, if the program has one single error the computer can not carry out the program right. Since the computer is so stupid men had to code the commands so that the computer can understand. That is computer language. As we have many languages there are lots of computer languages and as the computer develops the computer languages were also developed. Like it is not easy to find a person who speaks many languages so is it hard to find a person who understands the computer languages and that makes it very costly. That's why it is hard to fix the problem.

Of course, most of the companies and the government authorities know this problem and are trying to fix it. But you will understand it is not likely to be fixed when you see the periodic discussions between the government authorities and the related peoples concerning this problem from the TV.

As we discussed in the previous chapter, the world is connected with computer network and the computers work together. Therefore, this is not a matter of company basis.

The whole computer network connected to each other to exchange information has to be fixed completely without one error.

Let's say a company in America opened a letter of credit to import some merchandize from a company in other country. Even all of the computers in America were fixed, if the computers in other countries do not work right, we may not be able to send money to import or receive money from other countries that are not ready for the Y2K. Naturally, the economy will be affected. We might be able to send or receive money in different way.

But still it is sure that the economy will be deteriorated. The problem is not only sending or receiving money but also in every way it could affect our life. Because we human beings came to the point that we can not do anything without computer. All of the computers in the world should be fixed as normal like now to get back to normal life as we used to live till now.

The world economic crisis makes it more difficult to fix this technical problem.

When economically most prosperous America wouldn't be ready for it, how could many other major countries that are already undergoing economic disaster fix the problem.

The computer giant Microsoft says it is too big and overwhelming even to Microsoft.

Some countries are already performing exercise to prepare against the possible situation when most of the computers wouldn't work properly. They say it is too much costly to fix and they are just waiting to see and pray for good luck.

I'd like to finish this chapter with what the Commissioner of the Internal Revenue Service told The Wall Street Journal (April 22, 1998) about Y2K quoted by Dr. Jerry Falwell.

"There's no point in sugarcoating the problem. If we don't fix the century-date problem, we will have a situation scarier than the average disaster movie you might see on a Sunday night. Twenty-one months from now, there could be 90 million taxpayers who won't get their refunds, and 95% of the revenue stream of the United States could be jeopardized."

Natural Disaster

Matthew 24:7
For nation will rise against nation, and kingdom against kingdom, and there will be famines and

earthquakes in various places: all this is but the beginning of the birth-pangs. "Then they will deliver you up to tribulation, and put you to death; and you will be hated by all nations for my name's sake.

The bible says the tribulation begins by rising nations and famines and natural disasters.

The whole world was divided by two and controlled by two blocs of Communists and Democrats and the two blocs were fighting so called a cold war until the Soviet Union was collapsed. There is no country controlling the whole world and every country is rising against the other country. Many people say America is the only super power but nobody believes America is controlling the whole world as the superpower now.

When we see the history until the Soviet Union was collapsed, there were some countries that controlled the whole earth or most of the part like the England, France, China and Roman Empire. Not any more though.

Bible says this is the beginning of great distress. And also, it says, at that time, there will be famines and natural disasters in various places.

Most of the people think the great tribulation as the end of the world and it happens all of a sudden destroying everything so men have no choice but to die.

That they agree it's the end of the world and do nothing about it means they are just waiting to die.

But the bible says these things are the beginning of great tribulation and it comes like a thief. It is not the end of the world. It is the end of one age like the time of Noah.

Following graph was taken from the Washington Post in July 1997 and it shows the sharp environmental change of the world after 1989.

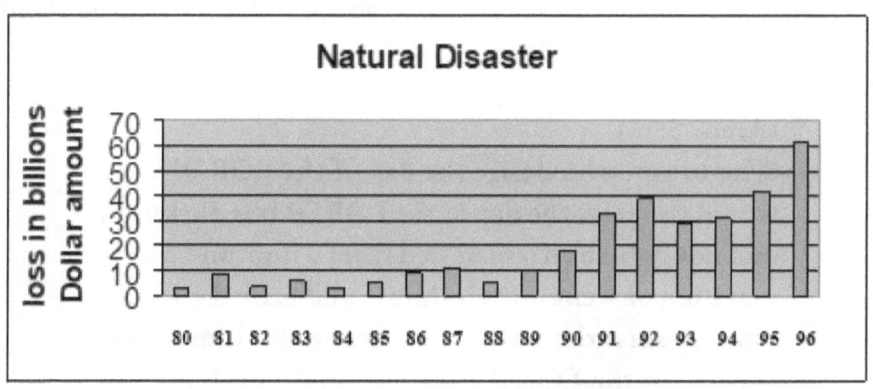

The situation looks getting even worse much rapidly as the year changes when we see the weather change all over the world caused by El Ninyo phenomenon. It is said the coming La Ninya phenomenon would be more serious.

As Jesus says we know it is going to rain when we see the cloud rise.

So far, we have tried to see what time of God's plan we are living by watching that are happening around us based upon the words Jesus told us.

What time are we living indeed?

I'd dare to say that as everybody has different vision, each one would see differently as to the amount of each one's belief.

One thing we can say for sure is every graph shows the world is rushing into one point.

Each one should prepare as each one would see, but God says as following.

(Peter II 3:3)
First of all you must understand this, that scoffers will come in the last days with scoffing, following their own passions and saying, "Where is the promise of his coming? For ever since the fathers fell asleep, all things have continued as they were from the beginning of creation."

People are immune to the end time words and don't want to think about it.

> **(Amos 5:18)**
> **Woe to you who desire the day of the LORD! Why would you have the day of the LORD? It is darkness, and not light: as if a man fled from a lion, and a bear met him; or went into the house and leaned with his hand against the wall, and a serpent bit him. Is not the day of the LORD darkness, and not light, and gloom with no brightness in it?**

Many people say the world is so evil. They say they accepted Jesus Christ as their personal savior with their mouth so they are moved from judgment to eternal life. They pray Jesus Christ to come quickly. But the bible says when the harvest comes Jesus Christ will come to judge everybody. Those who do not prepare for this judgment will be put into very serious situation. So we will have to prepare as Noah had prepared, then Jesus Christ will know who obeyed to follow his instruction and save those.

I don't think Jesus Christ would save those who commit suicide and those committing suicide are the ones that agree we are living the end time and do not prepare just like the one who does nothing even knowing the thief is coming into the house.

The concept of salvation that most people have in mind is spiritual and it has nothing to do with body. I agree about it because regardless our spirit be saved or not, the body is going to be destroyed and corrupted.

But let's think this way.

When a coach commanded a team not to go into a certain area to exercise even it looks good because somebody laid a mine in that area, one player didn't care and went in and got injured. The other player stayed outside and practiced carefully. Which one is obedient do you think? God will save the obedient people and Jesus described it as following.

Matthew 25

Then the kingdom of heaven shall be compared to ten maidens who took their lamps and went to meet the bridegroom. Five of them were foolish, and five were wise. For when the foolish took their lamps, they took no oil with them; but the wise took flasks of oil with their lamps.

As the bridegroom was delayed, they all slumbered and slept.

But at midnight there was a cry, 'Behold, the bridegroom! Come out to meet him.' Then all those maidens rose and trimmed their lamps. And the foolish said to the wise, 'Give us some of your oil, for our lamps are going out.' But the wise replied, 'Perhaps there will not be enough for us and for you; go rather to the dealers and buy for yourselves.'

And while they went to buy, the bridegroom came, and those who were ready went in with him to the marriage feast; and the door was shut.

Afterward the other maidens came also, saying, 'Lord, lord, open to us.'

But he replied, 'Truly, I say to you, I do not know you.'

Watch therefore, for you know neither the day nor the hour."

Everybody knows that we are living the end time like these maidens knew the bridegroom's coming and waited. But only those who prepared entered.

None of any spiritual things are involved in these words.

Together with this word, following words tell us that we have to prepare material things so we can endure until Jesus comes to this world because there will be great distress before Jesus Christ's coming.

Matthew 24:13
But he who endures to the end will be saved.

Who can ever survive until Jesus Christ's coming when one can not sell or buy? Jesus said nobody without beast mark on his forehead or right hand will be allowed to buy or sell. So, we will have to prepare to survive and endure until Jesus Christ's coming. And Jesus will save those who do not have the beast mark and those who died due to his words. Preparation is the only way to remain survived without beast mark. When to prepare? God will allow as much accurate vision to each one as to the faith each one has toward Jesus Christ.

Again, only those who believed what Jesus said and prepared things like Noah prepared could survive. Those who try to prepare will be scoffed from men because it looks stupid but will be saved by God for his obedience. It's the proof that shows one's belief toward Jesus Christ and his being Son of God.

Whether God would save one or not is absolutely in the hand of God. Only thing we can do is to obey what God told us to do for the hope of salvation. When we live the time other than the end time, we will have to obey the command for that time. Likewise, when we live the end time, we will have to obey the commands for the end time. The commands the soldiers should follow in the battlefield are different corresponding to each situation evolving. It's not pursuing material. It is obeying God.

God is going to judge us by seeing what and how we did with the material.

The Great tribulation, can we prepare for it anyway?

Amos 3:7
Surely the Lord GOD does nothing, without revealing his secret to his servants the prophets.

As prophet Amos wrote as above, if we examine the Israel history, we come to realize that God never does anything without revealing to God's children in advance.

God told to the first man Adam not to eat the fruit of the tree of good and evil or he will die. God said to Noah to prepare for the great flood and God said to Abraham to know that his people will be strangers in foreign country and serve for 400 years as slaves before the deliverance.

God said to Lot to leave Sodom and Gomorra before the complete destruction, to Joseph 7 years of abundance and 7 years of famine. God said to Solomon that God will tear Israel into two pieces, to Jeremiah the returning of Israel people to Samaria after 70 years captivity, to many prophets the Jesus Christ's coming, crucifixion, resurrection, great tribulation, salvation and judgment.

As we studied about God, God is the truth because God keeps what God said forever.

God is the only omnipotent God that created this world.

So, something looks unreasonable could happen and becomes the truth.

And the faith is to believe what God said.

Therefore, when we follow what God said, we are behaving wisely because that means we saw what would happen in advance and take action upon that happening.

Let's see what God instructed to Noah to prepare for the great flood.

Genesis 6:13
And God said to Noah, "I have determined to make an end of all flesh; for the earth is filled with violence through them; behold, I will destroy them with the earth. Make yourself an ark of gopher wood; make rooms in the ark, and cover it inside and out with pitch. This is how you are to make it: the length of the ark three hundred cubits, its breadth fifty cubits, and its height thirty cubits. Make a roof for the ark, and finish it to a cubit above; and set the door of the ark in its side; make it with lower, second, and third decks.

For behold, I will bring a flood of waters upon the earth, to destroy all flesh in which is the breath

of life from under heaven; everything that is on the earth shall die. But I will establish my covenant with you; and you shall come into the ark, you, your sons, your wife, and your sons' wives with you. And of every living thing of all flesh, you shall bring two of every sort into the ark, to keep them alive with you; they shall be male and female. Of the birds according to their kinds, and of the animals according to their kinds, of every creeping thing of the ground according to its kind, two of every sort shall come in to you, to keep them alive. Also take with you every sort of food that is eaten, and store it up; and it shall serve as food for you and for them." Noah did this; he did all that God commanded him. Then the LORD said to Noah, "Go into the ark, you and all your household, for I have seen that you are righteous before me in this generation. Take with you seven pairs of all clean animals, the male and his mate; and a pair of the animals that are not clean, the male and his mate; and seven pairs of the birds of the air also, male and female, to keep their kind alive upon the face of all the earth. For in seven days I will send rain upon the earth forty days and forty nights; and every living thing that I have made I will blot out from the face of the ground." And Noah did all that the LORD had commanded him.

As we see from the above, God instructed all the details. It should be very detail for the end time also. But as God said "Can I see even one righteous person at the end time", it looks like no one heard God's voice.

I hear so many people saying the end is near so wake up and do not sin, repent, love each other, try to get together, deliver the good news to the world, help the poor, do not lie, do not kill…

I'd like to say if we admit it is end time, we have to do all these things for the end time.

Love each other to prepare the end time and repent that we did not prepare for the end time. Get together to study what to prepare and deliver the good news to the world to make people know it is end time, help the poor to encourage the new world is near, do not lie that it's not end time, do not kill because the judgment is near….

If one admits it is end time, the attitude about one's life should be like that also.

But I've never seen a man who prepares upon God's word. While we have studied God's word, we've got the answer already about what to prepare, when to prepare and where to prepare and what to do. If someone understand God a little, he would know what to prepare, when to prepare and where to prepare a little. If someone understand God's words a lot, he would understand a lot about the preparation. But understanding the bible and the faith towards God are different story. Because Jesus said faith without deed is dead faith and surely that dead faith couldn't save oneself. Naturally, as the faith adds we could understand about what, when, where to prepare more clearly. I hope more people come out to discuss about this.

But the environment now is not like that. When someone does it, people just scoff saying "let's see what he does and what would he do when he survived alone in this world".

The believers do it more because they think the salvation has nothing to do with physical body and when Jesus Christ comes, they will be pulled up to heaven to be saved and welcome Jesus Christ in heaven.

What I am talking right now is that we should prepare for Jesus Christ's coming.

I myself too believe Sons of God will wear holy body and pulled up to heaven to be saved because Jesus said so. But it is after the great tribulation. Jesus also said the great tribulation comes to everybody on earth. So, I know we have to prepare the great tribulation. As I said in the preface, looks like the devil is keeping us so busy that we can not think about these things.

Anyway, I found we are living the very critical time of God's plan.

Let's see one more example about what God said to Jeremiah just before the Israel people went captivity.

(Jeremiah 16:1)

The word of the LORD came to me:

"You shall not take a wife, nor shall you have sons or daughters in this place. For thus says the LORD concerning the sons and daughters who are born in this place, and concerning the mothers who bore them and the fathers who begot them in this land: They shall die of deadly diseases. They shall not be lamented, nor shall they be buried; they shall be as dung on the surface of the ground. They shall perish by the sword and by famine, and their dead bodies shall be food for the birds of the air and for the beasts of the earth.

"For thus says the LORD: Do not enter the house of mourning, or go to lament, or bemoan them; for I have taken away my peace from this people, says the LORD, my steadfast love and mercy.

Both great and small shall die in this land; they shall not be buried, and no one shall lament for them or cut himself or make himself bald for them. No one shall break bread for the mourner, to comfort him for the dead; nor shall any one give him the cup of consolation to drink for his father or his mother. You shall not go into the house of feasting to sit with them, to eat and drink. For thus says the LORD of hosts, the God of Israel: Behold, I will make to cease from this place, before your eyes and in your days, the voice of mirth and the voice of gladness, the voice of the bridegroom and the voice of the bride.

Pay attention that God even said not to marry, not to have children because they shall perish by the sword, famine, diseases and their dead bodies shall be the food for the birds and beasts.

Knowing this, Jesus Christ told the people who were following and weeping for his being crucified:

Luke 23:27
And there followed him a great company of people,
and of women, which also bewailed and lamented
him. But Jesus turning unto them said, Daughters of
Jerusalem, weep not for me, but weep for yourselves,
and for your children. For, behold, the days are
coming, in the which they shall say, Blessed are the
barren, and the wombs that never bare, and the paps
which never gave suck.

Those who do not believe in God would never do this and if someone talk like this, they would take him as a member of cult group. Anyhow, who in the world would like to have a baby when one saw the Jewish holocaust and know own baby would be killed like that.

Anyway, people's wicked mind wants the way be as they want and it never changes.

Let's see what the people did to the prophets who said what God told.

Isaiah 30:8
For they are a rebellious people, lying sons, sons
who will not hear the instruction of the LORD;
who say to the seers, "See not"; and to the prophets,
"Prophesy not to us what is right; speak to us smooth
things, prophesy illusions, leave the way, turn aside
from the path, let us hear no more of the Holy One
of Israel."

Not only the people told the prophets like this but also, they treated the prophet Jeremiah as following and he described it as following.

Jeremiah 20
O LORD, thou hast deceived me, and I was deceived;
thou art stronger than I, and thou hast prevailed. I
have become a laughingstock all the day; every one

mocks me. For whenever I speak, I cry out, I shout, "Violence and destruction!" For the word of the LORD has become for me a reproach and derision all day long. If I say, "I will not mention him, or speak any more in his name," there is in my heart as it were a burning fire shut up in my bones, and I am weary with holding it in, and I cannot. For I hear many whispering. Terror is on every side! "Denounce him! Let us denounce him!" say all my familiar friends, watching for my fall. "Perhaps he will be deceived, then we can overcome him, and take our revenge on him." But the LORD is with me as a dread warrior; therefore my persecutors will stumble, they will not overcome me. They will be greatly shamed, for they will not succeed. Their eternal dishonor will never be forgotten. O LORD of hosts, who triest the righteous, who seest the heart and the mind, let me see thy vengeance upon them, for to thee have I committed my cause.

Sing to the LORD; praise the LORD! For he has delivered the life of the needy from the hand of evildoers. Cursed be the day on which I was born! The day when my mother bore me, let it not be blessed! Cursed be the man who brought the news to my father, "A son is born to you," making him very glad. Let that man be like the cities which the LORD overthrew without pity; let him hear a cry in the morning and an alarm at noon, because he did not kill me in the womb; so my mother would have been my grave, and her womb for ever great. Why did I come forth from the womb to see toil and sorrow, and spend my days in shame?

God said to Isiah when people scoffed and mocked at him as following.

Isaiah 41:10
fear not, for I am with you, be not dismayed, for I
am your God; I will strengthen you, I will help you,
I will uphold you with my victorious right hand.

Apostle Paul had the same problem and was to be executed at last.
He explained the difference between the spiritual beings and the physical
beings as following.

Corinthians I 2:9
But, as it is written, "What no eye has seen, nor ear
heard, nor the heart of man conceived, what God has
prepared for those who love him," God has revealed
to us through the Spirit. For the Spirit searches
everything, even the depths of God. For what person
knows a man's thoughts except the spirit of the man
which is in him? So also no one comprehends the
thoughts of God except the Spirit of God. Now we
have received not the spirit of the world, but the
Spirit which is from God, that we might understand
the gifts bestowed on us by God. And we impart this
in words not taught by human wisdom but taught
by the Spirit, interpreting spiritual truths to those
who possess the Spirit.

The unspiritual man does not receive the gifts
of the Spirit of God, for they are folly to him, and
he is not able to understand them because they are
spiritually discerned. The spiritual man judges all
things, but is himself to be judged by no one. "For
who has known the mind of the Lord so as to instruct
him?" But we have the mind of Christ.

———•——•——•———

Apostle John showed the way of end time missionary work as following.

Revelation 22:10

And he said to me, "Do not seal up the words of the prophecy of this book, for the time is near. Let the evildoer still do evil, and the filthy still be filthy, and the righteous still do right, and the holy still be holy." "Behold, I am coming soon, bringing my recompense, to repay every one for what he has done. I am the Alpha and the Omega, the first and the last, the beginning and the end." Blessed are those who wash their robes, that they may have the right to the tree of life and that they may enter the city by the gates. Outside are the dogs and sorcerers and fornicators and murderers and idolaters, and every one who loves and practices falsehood.

So far, we have traveled the long journey finding the treasure hidden in the bible leaving behind every idea generally prevailed all over the world about faith.

Even before coming to this point, I hope everybody found own way to the treasure as bold as the amount of faith God allowed to each one. That is because I recollect Apostle Paul's following message.

Romans 12:2

Do not be conformed to this world but be transformed by the renewal of your mind, that you may prove what is the will of God, what is good and acceptable and perfect. For by the grace given to me I bid every one among you not to think of himself more highly than he ought to think, but to think with sober judgment, each according to the measure of faith which God has assigned him. For as in one body we have many members, and all the members do not have the same function, so we, though many,

are one body in Christ, and individually members one of another.

That is my prayer to God that each one sees the light glittering over the faith and find the way reaching to the end of faith and get the treasure of spiritual relief.

For those who are still remaining to find the same treasure I found, I spared the last chapter to share what is being Sons of God and finish my journey.

9. Being Sons of God

Bible says Sons of God is spiritual beings and their life is like that of angel's. Let's see what bible says.

John 6:63
<u>It is the spirit that gives life,</u> the flesh is of no avail; the words that I have spoken to you are spirit and life.

Romans 8:13
for if you live according to the flesh you will die, but if by the Spirit you put to death the deeds of the body you will live. <u>For all who are led by the Spirit of God are sons of God.</u>

Romans 14:17
<u>For the kingdom of God is not food and drink but righteousness and peace and joy in the Holy Spirit;</u>

John 1:12
But to all who received him, who believed in his name, he gave power to become children of God; who were born, not of blood nor of the will of the flesh nor of the will of man, but of God.

Luke 20:34
And Jesus said to them, "The sons of this age marry and are given in marriage; but those who are accounted worthy to attain to that age and to the resurrection from the dead neither marry nor are given in marriage, for <u>they cannot die any more, because they are equal to angels and are sons of God, being sons of the resurrection.</u>

When Adam was kicked out from the paradise the spirit became to belong to corruptible physical body of this world. Now, becoming Son of God means this spirit is going to be free from the corruptible physical body of this world and wear a never corrupting new holy body of heaven.

Apostle Paul explained it as following.

Corinthians I 15

But some one will ask, "How are the dead raised? With what kind of body do they come?" You foolish man! What you sow does not come to life unless it dies. And what you sow is not the body which is to be, but a bare kernel, perhaps of wheat or of some other grain. But God gives it a body as he has chosen, and to each kind of seed its own body.

For not all flesh is alike, but there is one kind for men, another for animals, another for birds, and another for fish. There are celestial bodies and there are terrestrial bodies; but the glory of the celestial is one, and the glory of the terrestrial is another.

There is one glory of the sun, and another glory of the moon, and another glory of the stars; for star differs from star in glory. So is it with the resurrection of the dead. What is sown is perishable, what is raised is imperishable. It is sown in dishonor, it is raised in glory. It is sown in weakness, it is raised in power. It is sown a physical body, it is raised a spiritual body.

<u>If there is a physical body, there is also a spiritual body.</u>

Thus it is written, "The first man Adam became a living being"; the last Adam became a life-giving spirit. But it is not the spiritual which is first but the physical, and then the spiritual. The first man was from the earth, a man of dust; the second man is from heaven. As was the man of dust, so are those who are of the dust; and as is the man of heaven, so are those who are of heaven.

Just as we have borne the image of the man of dust, we shall also bear the image of the man of heaven.

I tell you this, brethren: flesh and blood cannot inherit the kingdom of God, nor does the perishable inherit the imperishable. Lo! I tell you a mystery. We shall not all sleep, but we shall all be changed, in a moment, in the twinkling of an eye, at the last trumpet. For the trumpet will sound, and the dead will be raised imperishable, and we shall be changed. For this perishable nature must put on the imperishable, and this mortal nature must put on immortality. When the perishable puts on the imperishable, and the mortal puts on immortality, then shall come to pass the saying that is written: "Death is swallowed up in victory."

Romans 9:6

For not all who are descended from Israel belong to Israel, and not all are children of Abraham because they are his descendants; but "Through Isaac shall your descendants be named." This means that it is not the children of the flesh who are the children of God, but the children of the promise are reckoned as descendants.

Those who believe God would accomplish the words God wrote in the bible are the Sons of God. However, everyone believes the promise when they feel good about God and doubt when they feel uncomfortable about God. That's why we need to practice to be perfect. Apostle Paul said to practice and try to be found in perfect.

So, I call this world a practicing field. Practice after practice. God will raise those qualified for the Kingdom of God.

We do not know who will be raised. We are only trying to believe the promise of salvation and when our belief becomes the belief without any doubt, then the belief will save us.

Matthew 12:50
For <u>whoever does the will of my Father in heaven is</u> <u>my brother, and   sister, and mother</u>."

Anybody who believes oneself is a Son of God would live complying with God's will.

John 6:40
For <u>this is the will of my Father, that every one who</u> <u>sees the Son and believes in him should have eternal</u> <u>life</u>; and I will raise him up at the last day."

God's will is to raise those spirits who believe in Jesus Christ in eternal holy bodies. To believe in Jesus Christ is to believe what he said because Jesus Christ is the word of God. However, the belief without deed is useless dead belief. Therefore, only those spirits that do what they heard from Jesus Christ will be raised in eternal holy bodies.

Philippians 3:20
But our commonwealth is in heaven, and from it we await a Savior, the Lord Jesus Christ, <u>who will</u> <u>change our lowly body to be like his glorious body,</u> <u>by the power which enables him even to subject all</u> <u>things to himself.</u>

John I 3:2
Beloved, we are God's children now; it does not yet appear what we shall be, but we know that <u>when he</u> <u>appears we shall be like him, for we shall see him</u> <u>as he is.</u>

John I 3:3
And every one who thus hopes in him purifies himself as he is pure.

Romans 8:29
For those whom he foreknew he also predestined to be conformed to the image of his Son, <u>in order that he might be the first-born among many brethren.</u> And those whom he predestined he also called; and those whom he called he also justified; and those whom he justified he also glorified.

There will be many Sons of God and Jesus Christ will be the first-born Son of God.

John 10:32
Jesus answered them, "I have shown you many good works from the Father; for which of these do you stone me?" The Jews answered him, "It is not for a good work that we stone you but for blasphemy; because you, being a man, make yourself God." Jesus answered them, <u>"Is it not written in your law, 'I said, you are gods'? If he called them gods to whom the word of God came</u> (and scripture cannot be broken), do you say of him whom the Father consecrated and sent into the world, 'You are blaspheming,' because I said, 'I am the Son of God'? If I am not doing the works of my Father, then do not believe me; but if I do them, even though you do not believe me, believe the works, that you may know and understand that the Father is in me and I am in the Father."

Psalms 82:6
<u>I say, "You are gods, sons of the Most High, all of</u>
<u>you;</u> nevertheless, you shall die like men, and fall
like any prince."

Those who have God's words are the Sons of God.

When the Israel were about to be ruined, these Sons of God were so corrupted as to take the possessions of the weak and poor people and persecuted the prophets who were telling the truth. They told the prophets not to prophesy the ominous things. God was talking to these people through David.

John 14:11
Believe me that I am in the Father and the Father in me; or else believe me for the sake of the works themselves. "Truly, truly, I say to you, <u>he who believes in me will also do the works that I do</u>; and greater works than these will he do, because I go to the Father.

When we believe in Jesus Christ, God listens to our prayer and does in our stead. That means we are having the power of God and we can do whatever we want in Jesus Christ. We have hundred times more people living in this world and thousand times more believers than ever before. Then why is it so hard to see a miracle these days?

That's because it is hard to see one righteous man as God said.

It is hard to see one righteous man in the end time!

If one righteous man Noah and his family were saved from the Great Flood and there wouldn't be no single one righteous man in this end time as God said, no man will be saved from the coming great tribulation. Becoming a Son of God is not easy. But God will do it as God wanted and planned at the time of creation and accomplish.

Philippians 4:4
Rejoice in the Lord always; again I will say, Rejoice.

Let all men know your forbearance. The Lord is at hand.

Have no anxiety about anything, but in everything by prayer and supplication with thanksgiving let your requests be made known to God. And the peace of God, which passes all understanding, will keep your hearts and your minds in Christ Jesus. Finally, brethren, whatever is true, whatever is honorable, whatever is just, whatever is pure, whatever is lovely, whatever is gracious, if there is any excellence, if there is anything worthy of praise, think about these things.

1Thessalonians 5:16
Be joyful always, pray at al times, thankful in all circumstances. This is what God wants of you , in your life in Christ Jesus.

Corinthians I 3:16
Do you not know that you are God's temple and that God's Spirit dwells in you? If any one destroys God's temple, God will destroy him. For God's temple is holy, and that temple you are.

Matthew 5:43
You have heard that it was said, 'You shall love your neighbor and hate your enemy.' But I say to you, Love your enemies and pray for those who persecute you so that you may be sons of your Father who is in heaven; for he makes his sun rise on the evil and on the good, and sends rain on the just and on the unjust. For if you love those who love you, what reward have you? Do not even the tax collectors

do the same? And if you salute only your brethren, what more are you doing than others? Do not even the Gentiles do the same?

<u>You, therefore, must be perfect, as your heavenly Father is perfect.</u>

Peter II 1:3

His divine power has granted to us all things that pertain to life and godliness, through the knowledge of him who called us to his own glory and excellence, by which he has granted to us his precious and very great promises, that through these you may escape from the corruption that is in the world because of passion, and <u>become partakers of the divine nature</u>. For this very reason make every effort to supplement your faith with virtue, and virtue with knowledge, and knowledge with self-control, and self-control with steadfastness, and steadfastness with godliness, and godliness with brotherly affection, and brotherly affection with love. For if these things are yours and abound, they keep you from being ineffective or unfruitful in the knowledge of our Lord Jesus Christ. For whoever lacks these things is blind and shortsighted and has forgotten that he was cleansed from his old sins. Therefore, brethren, be the more zealous to confirm your call and election, for if you do this you will never fall; so there will be richly provided for you an entrance into the eternal kingdom of our Lord and Savior Jesus Christ.

Peter I 4:7

The end of all things is at hand; therefore keep sane and sober for your prayers. Above all hold unfailing your love for one another, since love covers a multitude of sins. Practice hospitality ungrudgingly to one another. As each has received a gift, employ it for one another, as good stewards of God's varied grace: whoever speaks, as one who utters oracles of God; whoever renders service, as one who renders it by the strength which God supplies; in order that in everything God may be glorified through Jesus Christ. To him belong glory and dominion for ever and ever. Amen.

Beloved, do not be surprised at the fiery ordeal which comes upon you to prove you, as though something strange were happening to you. But rejoice in so far as you share Christ's sufferings, that you may also rejoice and be glad when his glory is revealed. If you are reproached for the name of Christ, you are blessed, because the spirit of glory and of God rests upon you. But let none of you suffer as a murderer, or a thief, or a wrongdoer, or a mischief-maker; yet if one suffers as a Christian, let him not be ashamed, but under that name let him glorify God.

For the time has come for judgment to begin with the household of God and if it begins with us, what will be the end of those who do not obey the gospel of God?

Peter II 3:11
Since all these things are thus to be dissolved, what sort of persons ought you to be in lives of holiness and godliness, waiting for and hastening the coming of the day of God, because of which the heavens will be kindled and dissolved, and the elements will melt with fire! But according to his promise we wait for new heavens and a new earth in which righteousness dwells. Therefore, beloved, since you

wait for these, <u>be zealous to be found by him without</u> <u>spot or blemish, and at peace.</u>

And count the forbearance of our Lord as salvation. So also our beloved brother Paul wrote to you according to the wisdom given him, speaking of this as he does in all his letters. There are some things in them hard to understand, which the ignorant and unstable twist to their own destruction, as they do the other scriptures.

Now we have tried to figure out what is being Son of God through the bible.
As we read from the bible, God says;

- They cannot die any more, because they are equal to angels and are Sons of God, being sons of the resurrection.
- If there is a physical body, there is also a spiritual body.
- Just as we have borne the image of the man of dust, we shall also bear the image of the man of heaven.
- For those whom he foreknew he also predestined to be conformed to the image of his Son, in order that he might be the first-born among many brethren.
- He who believes in me will also do the works that I do;
- Be perfect, as your heavenly Father is perfect.
- Become partakers of the divine nature.
- Whoever speaks, as one who utters oracles of God; whoever renders service, as one who renders it by the strength which God supplies; in order that in everything God may be glorified through Jesus Christ.
- Do you not know that you are God's temple and that God's Spirit dwells in you?
- When he appears we shall be like him,
- Whatever is true, whatever is honorable, whatever is just, whatever is pure, whatever is lovely, whatever is

gracious, if there is any excellence, if there is anything worthy of praise, think about these things.

Pay attention to understand what it is living forever, with power of God in perfect peace, in an incorruptible holy body, speaking like God speaks, partaking the divine nature of God, thinking whatever is lovely or gracious and living as a Son of God.

Most people say the arrogance of human's mind wanted to compete with God and tried to build sky high Tower of Babel to reach where God is, and the same way, the haughtily minded human beings want to put oneself higher place than where God is.

But God says as above.

I want to leave the meaning of these words to readers. Each one would interpret it as to each one's amount of faith. However, I can tell that is the reason why we are living, for what we are living, to where we are going and how should we live. That is God's plan set upon men at the time of creation.

We can have it self-answered when we think God is the God that never diminishes but expands forever endlessly. The universe is said to be expanding faster than the speed of light every moment and the end can not be measured. If the expanding universe is the expansion of God, more Sons of God also means another expansion of God.

God is spirit. Therefore, anyone who has the conviction of being Son of God should stand on the conviction to behave and think on behalf of the spiritual beings. Because, even the one who has the conviction of being Son of God will be corrupted to disappear as the body corrupts and disappears if he builds for the physical well beings on that conviction.

Therefore, the physical death means disability to the people who did not believe spiritual beings and built on the physical beings. Because they would have nothing to do with spirit after the bodies were destroyed. But the physical death means the real freedom and limitless ability to the people who built on the spiritual beings, because they do not have the limit of corruptible body. They are going to wear incorruptible holy body for eternal life. Those who believe we are living the time that our body could transformed to eternal holy body are blessed. For, those have a chance not to taste the death forever. Now, I'm going to finish my journey to exploring the bible by sailing into the harbor of Apostle Paul to anchor safely in Jesus Christ as following.

(Philippians 3:7)
But whatever gain I had, I counted as loss for the sake of Christ.

Indeed I count everything as loss because of the surpassing worth of knowing Christ Jesus my Lord. For his sake I have suffered the loss of all things, and count them as refuse, in order that I may gain Christ and be found in him, not having a righteousness of my own, based on law, but that which is through faith in Christ, the righteousness from God that depends on faith; that I may know him and the power of his resurrection, and may share his sufferings, becoming like him in his death, that if possible I may attain the resurrection from the dead. Not that I have already obtained this or am already perfect; but I press on to make it my own, because Christ Jesus has made me his own.

Brethren, I do not consider that I have made it my own; but one thing I do, forgetting what lies behind and straining forward to what lies ahead.

This was my exploration to the bible.

What I found from the journey was that the faith is not the thing that can be taught by someone who knows well about the bible. It rather grows by itself through faith towards God.

Since each one's faiths are different, each one's bible understandings are also different.

So, we cannot find own way given to each one if we follow somebody else. Each one has to grow in each one's faith.

As an imperfect creature, we can not understand perfect God. But we can understand with the help of Holy Spirit. We should not follow men's teaching. We should learn only from Jesus Christ directly. When we see there are so many different branches of church and each church tries to draw more people into it, we can understand why Jesus Christ said to enter into the narrow gate. When we recollect Jesus Christ said to be a lamp lightening the world brightly, we shouldn't be left alone either. Those who do not lighten the world can be compared to those who found the treasure but did not get it. These people are also going to be gathered as mean tare and burnt.

Like Jesus Christ said on the cross **"It is finished"** before he breathed his last, the sons of God also would follow his footprint, until breathing the last one, to say the same **"It is finished"** as God planned upon us.

I understand that means God accomplished what God planned on me whatever it is.

And I also understand that is the faith toward God.

I'd like to finish this book with the confession of Apostle Paul to make it mine as following.

> **"Not that I have already obtained this or am already perfect; but I press on to make it my own, because Christ Jesus has made me his own.**
>
> **Brethren, I do not consider that I have made it my own; but one thing I do, forgetting what lies behind and straining forward to what lies ahead,**
>
> **I press on toward the goal for the prize of the upward call of God in Christ Jesus."**
>
> **(Philippians 3:12)**

www.ingramcontent.com/pod-product-compliance
Lightning Source LLC
Chambersburg PA
CBHW021609120626
46545CB00001B/144